Wolves

Ryders in the Whirlwind

All stories are about wolves.

All worth repeating, that is.

Anything else is sentimental drivel.

Margaret Atwood, *The Blind Assassin*

Wolves
Ryders in the Whirlwind

by
Gordon Harrison

Published by Prometheus Publications
Peterborough, Ontario
Canada

Includes bibliographical references.
Issued in print and electronic formats.

Trade paperback ISBN 978-1-9992259-0-2
Electronic version ISBN 978-0-9879596-9-0

Cover design by the author
Picture of the author by Larry Keeley, photographer
First printing 2019

To Jennifer and Evelyn
the most important people in my life.

CONTENTS

Anything in *italics* in the next seven pages takes place
when Big Red is sleeping.

Waking up under the stars
Big Red continues his Homeric quest

What my dog taught me
Death in the woods
A road-killed deer
Big Red battles a black bear
They share the deer
   Hibernating bears
   Big Red's father attacks a sleeping bear
   A rite of passage
   The casting out of bear cubs
   Feeding bears
   A wolf & bear friendship
A run of suckers
Bear going fishing

Three wild boars
Enter Spitfire, Big Red's new mate
And then there were two
Incest avoidance
Golden Rule
Wolf Play
Prosocial or antisocial behavior
   Feral children raised by wolves
   Yawning
   Tripod, a wolf with three legs
   The morality of wolves
Spitfire is gone in the morning
Brings breakfast

Bears eating leaks (ramps)
Encounter with a sow & her two cubs
A mother's care
   A mystery animal
   Enter Mother Courage
   A paraplegic bear

PREFACE

We can only be said to be alive in those moments
when our hearts are conscious of our treasures.
Thornton Wilder, *The Woman of Andros*

I was blessed—I was born with wolves! If not in our house, then wandering about our orchards and our barns and through our few fields. We had a home in the wilderness of Central Ontario: no electricity, no running water, no indoor toilet. We did have running wolves and ambling bears year-round. And I loved that place. On late summer evenings and fortunate winter nights, silver forms would sing from the hills and valleys. On these occasions, somewhere in our rambling old house with two staircases, under warm blankets, a child would lie transfixed in mystery and enchantment. Here was another nation, a different civilization, who needed nothing from us, distrusted us, even hated us. And rightly so.

To all the adults I knew, nature was the enemy, something to be subdued. They had little interest or knowledge of the world outside. Rarely did they speak about it—hardly a bird's name or a flower's location. Infrequently, an aunt would express some fear or other, especially about poisonous snakes—we never found one—or skinks that might run up inside your pant leg to do considerable damage. Our evenings around the flickering lanterns were filled with tall tales about the big, bad wolf. It was all fear and fearmongering. I believed none of it.

Those years shaped all the ones that followed. Much of my adult life has been spent photographing the creatures I saw on the farm as a boy. And I have liberally sprinkled these throughout the book. As a young man, I bought the back 40 acres (16.2 hectares) from my uncle, built a home, and lived there for decades (*see* map page 273). It is here I learned about the Algonquin wolves. These animals were not, are not, and will not be in zoos, compounds, or enclosures. They are just out there!

My parents and my aunt and uncle left the farm because of the physical hardships: no central heating and outhouses without toilet paper—just a ragged Eaton's catalog. But we children were unmindful of this adversity for the adults never complained, never!

They dealt with each problem and moved on. Years later, my cousin sold the old house (with its five bedrooms and two staircases) for its logs. The happy rooms where he and I ran and played on rainy days were now valued only as a means of income—that the buyer never paid.

Nothing remains. No colossal wreck. Just weeds and wire bush. The barns were sold as well, and where horses and cows once held sway, fields of wild raspberry canes now hold court. And when the berries ripen, bears roam where the horses' stalls once stood. No one would know humans had ever lived here.

As well as all the buildings and barns that have disappeared, many of the attitudes and fears of those times are gone as well. In August, a strange pilgrimage occurs in Algonquin Park. In the late evening, hundreds of cars line the Park's only highway. The people get out of their vehicles and huddle close to a few Park rangers who howl into the darkening wilderness. On rare occasions, wolves answer. Their electrifying songs fill the fresh night air only to let us know who owns this place and you best not forget it. Wolves do not perform on demand, nor do they negotiate, and you do not get your money back. Yet, when they do sing your spine tingles to the sound of their transfixing arias, and for an instant, you can touch that ancient time when we roamed the forest with them.

The Nation of the Wolf is not at war with man. Whether we can learn to live near these incredible creatures is an open question. If the past is prologue for the future, the answer is grim.

This book is the story of a wolf who was never at a loss during his journey home across Algonquin Park. I call him Big Red. He travels during the day to avoid the wolves on whose land he is trespassing. His future will not be like his past. Tomorrow will not be like today. Every day is different. Big Red knows he must catch the apple when it falls and, sweet or sour, bite it hard!

When he sleeps, he dreams of all things wolfen: warrahs, dingoes, coyotes, gray wolves, painted wolves, and so on. His mother gave birth to him in an ancient den at the base of the plateau on which my home stands. In decades past, one of his ancestors sang for me on winter evenings as I snuggled under warm blankets. This book was born on those nights. This enchantment with the land and the wolves is still fresh in my memory. This happiness is still felt in my heart.

ACKNOWLEDGMENTS

The genesis for this book has been a lifetime. I have always considered myself to be fortunate. In writing this book, I have also been fortunate in having many friends who offered suggestions that have improved the text. My daughter, Jennifer, has listened to me rave about my photographs and has always been encouraging. My long-time friend, Evelyn, has been an essential sounding board and a source of ideas and unending support. And a special thanks to Larry Keeley for suggesting I write this book about wolves and his endless enthusiasm for this undertaking. Thanks to Christine W. and First Editing for polishing my words to their finished form. I am most grateful to everyone. An old proverb affirms, "Luck never gives; she only loans." But in the writing of this book, I have been Lady Luck's primary beneficiary, and these gifts she can never take away.

Although they will never know, I have a profound appreciation to all the Algonquin wolves who, at one time or another, made a home on my "farm." I am most grateful to have known Big Red, and for the many times he allowed me to photograph him. On this small planet, in a minor solar system, in an ordinary galaxy, at the edge of the universe, I have known this magnificent creature while scientists grub for microbes on Mars. Run! Run on Big Guy through the evergreen forests.

Most of the photographs in this book are the author's. Every reasonable effort has been made to contact holders of the copyright for other images used here. The author will gladly receive information that will enable him to rectify any inadvertent errors or omissions in later editions.

Chapter—1

HOME

Home is the place where, when you have to go there,
They have to take you in.
Robert Frost, "The Death of the Hired Hand"

*T*he wolves run on through the evergreen forests in their *eternal pursuit of the deer. For their part, the deer lead the wolves on a deadly chase. Each hones the other to perfection by natural selection. It is not only the weak and the old who falter and fall, but the inefficient—the ones who stray too far from the edge. To those who do the dance, whether deer or wolf, belongs the day and the future. It is not a good day to die. It never is. So, the wolves run on through the evergreen forests.*

Unannounced and unheralded, a dark form steps out of the endless green forest onto the snowy surface of a frozen lake. It is late afternoon, and the shadows are long, causing the moving form to appear larger than it is. Determined but unhurried in its pace as it progresses down the lake, the figure slowly morphs into a recognizable animal. Gusts of wind swirl the snow around him, haphazardly ruffling his fur. This happens with frustrating frequency. Emerging from an unusually large whirlwind of white, the shape materializes as a rare Algonquin wolf in his prime, master of his environment: long legs, large head, broad nose, and a shorter tail than most canids (the dog family). Up from millennia of evolution, he is the ultimate deer-hunting machine. But there are no deer here, and this wolf has a different mission. The sun is setting as he reaches the far end of the lake and pushes aside the lowest boughs of a white pine tree and stretches out on a thick bed of fallen needles. He slowly wriggles his bulky frame to shape a comfortable bed. The rustic color of the needles blends with the red on his legs, thighs, and ears to render him almost invisible. This wolf—we will call him Big Red—lacks perfect symmetry. One of the toenails on his right front foot is missing, the result of a leg trap he stepped on while outside the Algonquin Park's eastern boundary. His reaction to the released trap was so instant and so violent that he yanked one of his toenails from his foot.

Big Red—an Algonquin Wolf

Although it was not enough to fill his belly, he had somehow captured a snowshoe hare during the day. As he drifts off to sleep, his body starts to twitch convulsively, and the dreaming begins of his early life in his distant Natal Pack on the other side of Algonquin Park. While sleep comes easily to him, its progress is punctuated by more twitches and spasms.

🐾

It is dark—pitch black dark—like the interior of a deep cave. The ground beneath his belly is cold and damp, and this alien world is deathly quiet. With immense effort, he moves his small round body, and a growing sense of panic and hunger causes him to move ever more quickly as he meets only emptiness and silence. What is this place? Out of nowhere a warm soft object licks his head gently, picks him up, and moves him to one of her many feeding stations. He nurses and intuitively knows this is a loving place. Therefore, he lives.

As his belly fills with his mother's milk, his anxiety melts away replaced with the comforting scent of her body. Eventually, he feels other round objects near him who are nursing as well, three sisters and two brothers. It is the end of April, and outside the den, the temperatures can plummet to well below zero. Worse yet, each helpless pup weighs less than a pound and lives in a hole in the ground with a wolf. Death seems imminent! Still, such is evolution that wolves are rarely given a situation they cannot survive. "Whatever does not kill me makes me stronger," wrote Nietzsche. Yet how do they survive? The den is small so that the mother's body can warm it and the cubs snuggle for life itself. She licks her cubs to stimulate urination and defecation and then eats their feces to keep the den clean—surely this is premium daycare.

Mum at the Entrance of her Den

Earlier that same day, he and his littermates were in a long, wet membrane like sausages in a skin casing. After the moment of birth, his mother severed this casing (umbilical cord), and with an instinctive urgency, she hurried to release each sausage from its casing so that it might breathe then ate this skin (fetal sac). She was all things: nurse, mother, and protector. Gently, she licked these wet pups to stimulate breathing, and they did breathe—all of them. This moment of creation was the apex of her life, and after these six births, she rested.

Inside the den, there is no perception of time, no diurnal rhythm, just eternal night. Nevertheless, Little Red grows quickly and so do his fellow pups on their mother's milk and that of a lactating aunt who occasionally babysits. A runt sausage, however, does not thrive like his siblings and, on the eighth day, it dies. He disappears from the den, gently taken by his mother and placed, perhaps buried, somewhere in the immense green forest. The entire pack—mother, father, aunt, and two younger males—are in attendance for this pavane for a dead prince.

Red-tailed Hawk

High above in the blue dome of air, a large hawk makes easy circles in the sky. The sun shines blood red through his tail feathers as he watches the procession move through the speckled sunlight on the forest floor. The hawk pays attention to this queue in the hope of a meal, for he also has young to feed. It is doubtful the alpha female saw the hawk, but she hid her dead prince so well the bird never found it.

The hawk surrenders its search to scan the open valley for easier prey. The den is on the side of the valley close to an old wolf run and near a wintering deer yard sheltered by hemlock and cedar. A small brook bubbles up through cracks in the vast Precambrian Shield and trickles down the valley wall, forming a small ever-flowing stream. All the forest creatures great and small drink from it. The hawk makes a final circuit of this ancient valley and sees the funeral procession return to the den site. The wolves are still silent, each lost in their own sadness at the death of a prince. They mourned, and then they moved on.

If you wander the forests and fields of any land, you will soon find death. It comes in the form of the rigid bodies of those who have left us. Dylan Thomas says it touchingly when he describes, in *A Child's Christmas in Wales*, his search "for news of the little world": he would "find always a dead bird . . . perhaps a robin, all but one of his fires out." Closer inspection will reveal other fatalities: mice, partridge, turtles, snakes, frogs, and small birds that scavengers will carry away and recycle into new life.

Farther afield are the carcasses of moose and deer, wings of hawks, headless snakes, dead kangaroo mice, voles, weasels, raccoons, porcupines and, on rare occasions, a decaying bear. The dead litter this land. You cannot fall anywhere in the forest or the field without resting on the graves of the fallen.

🐾

Big Red grew restless in his dreaming and awakened cold and hungry. He got up, stretched, took a few steps to pee before returning to his bed. To conserve heat, he curled up in a ball with his tail over his nose and quickly returned to his dream.

🐾

Eventually, Little Red began to explore the den. His paws reached into nothingness, but occasionally struck the den's hard wall or the soft head of a wandering littermate. Although his eyes were open, there was nothing to see. His legs were growing now, so he no longer resembled a sau-

Little Red and Little Red Ears

sage but a regular wolf pup. One fine day, his mother led her surviving babies up a long dark tunnel toward a circle of light. Little Red sensed this was a rite of passage for him and his littermates, from darkness into light. When he reached the light and stepped forth from the den entrance, the color, sound, and the fresh fragrance of the forest overwhelmed his senses. He and his brothers and sisters bounced about with the joy of life and youth. Their mother lay satisfied on an entangled bank, admiring the life around her, thinking, "I, *Canis lupus lycaon,* made these things."

The hidden eyes on the hillside were quiet and attentive to the theater below. The pups, however, were anything but; they jumped, tumbled, and ran continuously. This field was their schoolyard where they played and prepared, on the edge of adulthood, practicing those behaviors needed to become grownups. To paraphrase Descartes, "they played, therefore they were!" On the hillside, the author could just hear their playful yelps and squeals. Otherwise, everything was quiet; time seemed to pass imperceptibly as the sunny field jumped with life, and these bouncy furry balls ran their heedless ways. The alpha male and female wolf had fulfilled their genetic obligations, and their genes are still running through these same forests and fields although the watcher no longer watches.

Wolf Pups Playing

> *In the sun that is young once only,*
> *Time let me play and be*
> *Golden in the mercy of his means,*
> Dylan Thomas, "Fern Hill"

No living thing was safe from these playful pups. They jumped at bumblebees, chased chipmunks and frogs, tormented mice, voles, and shrews—even wildflowers were targets of their endless energy. But, of course, their main goal was each other in an instinctive struggle for litter dominance. Big Red and his brother (we will call him Paws) were evenly matched, but their three sisters were easy targets. As with humans, there is a size difference in the gender of wolves, giving males a physical advantage.

Black Bear

There were other creatures here—much larger and stronger than either their mother or their father: black bears. Wolves and bears have been ancient enemies for millennia, but they avoid each other. On the other hand, given the opportunity, they will kill and eat each other's young and fight over the rights of a deer, moose, or caribou carcass. Each predator has unique attributes: bears are massive and robust, wolves are many and swift, so they are evenly matched, and the winner is seldom guaranteed.

On occasion, bears will devour squirrels and smash birdhouses to eat the baby birds inside, and for their part, wolves will claim windfall apples and plums from the author's orchard. But these are unusual behaviors. Black bears are herbivores; wolves, carnivores—mostly. Each stands on the pinnacle of its own evolutionary mountain.

In the den, the puppies are safe with their mother or aunt. Outside the den, the alpha male's presence deters all threats; in his absence, a proud pack member does the same. To successfully raise a litter of wolf pups requires the entire family. While their sisters were still nursing in the den, Big Red and his only surviving brother, Paws, were about to meet a large foraging black bear.

Their father was napping on a massive rock lookout in the dappled sunlight when he caught the first distinct odor of the approaching bruin. He bolted in the direction of the predator and found him rooting around a decaying tree stump in search of grubs and easily decoyed him away from the den site. Immediately their father returned to his patch of sunlight on the rock all the while his sons continued playing, oblivious to the danger that had just passed. For the alpha male, it was win or lose with the bear— wolves do not negotiate. Such is the banality of bravery!

The pups grew rapidly and gained so much in strength and size that they began to explore farther and farther from the den site and go to nearby rendezvous sites. This was distressful for the alpha male, for the pups it was exhilarating and part of growing up.

Inevitably something happened. A rare golden eagle (*see* photograph) abruptly plunged out of the sky and within seconds sank its massive talons into the spine of one of Little Red Ears' sisters and flew off to devour her. Its great wings quickly carried it up the valley wall to land in the territory of the Hill Pack wolves. This higher ground was mostly hardwood trees while the valley with the Natal Pack was entirely evergreens. The great bird with its bright golden head feathers and powerful beak ripped the soft flesh from the still warm body consuming everything except the skull. In a few days, maggots devoured the remaining scraps of flesh. After that, mice gnawed at the skull and slugs glided over the pure white dome to absorb minerals. By the next fall, she was all gone, even her parents and littermates had forgotten her in their struggle for survival. She no longer existed—or seemingly ever existed. Truly, death has littered this land with the fallen. You cannot place the palm of your hand flat on the ground anywhere without covering the grave of some fallen creature. *And then there were four.*

> *The golden sun,*
> *The planets, all the infinite host of heaven,*
> *Are shining on the sad abodes of death,*
> *Through the still lapse of ages. All that tread*
> *The globe are but a handful to the tribes*
> *That slumber in its bosom.*
> William Cullen Bryant, "Thanatopsis"

Golden Eagle

With each death, the likelihood of the continuity of Little Red's genetic river diminished. Now this litter of wolf pups was reduced to four, but this would not be the end of the dying. Two weeks later, Little Red Ears' other sister mysteriously disappeared. It could have been the golden eagle back for a second helping, a bear, or even a fisher—or something unimagined. All the ancestors of this small family had successfully passed on their inheritance for millennia—a mighty river of genes. Now this river depended solely on Little Red Ears, Paws, and Little Red. *And then there were three.*

Fisher

There are many who would say wolves have no morality, but this is false, foolishly false. In Western society, if you wish to conjure up a nightmare of drooling immorality, of heartless cruelty and mindless killing, the image is always that of the wolf. From nursery rhymes to adult fiction, the beast from the primeval forest is *Canis lupus*. Never was a creature more maligned than this great grandparent of *Canis familiaris*, the family pet. Yet there are only two authenticated cases of wild wolves killing humans in *all* North American recorded history.

Besides the devoted family structure we have seen, there are many more prosocial behaviors. For example, all the surviving pups will leave the natal territory to make a life and a family for themselves. This prevents incest, something humans also avoid. At 18 months of age, Big Red left his family, traveling all through Algonquin Park without achieving an alpha male position (the only breeding male in the pack). Paws and Little Red Ears also left for parts unknown, and Big Red felt he would never see them again. Family bonds are powerful among all canids. No matter what your rank—from the alpha to the omega—all family members stand and deliver in times of danger.

To survive, wolves are only as vicious as they need to be. Life selects those too meek out of the breeding population and, in an analogous manner, those too vicious as well. If you fight every few days, then in a few more days you are either injured or dead. Neither wimps nor warriors leave progeny. The survivors have the *required* degree of aggressiveness—they are the right stuff!

The first gray of morning filled the east when Big Red awakened on his bed of pine needles alerted by some signal. He looked between the large branches of his white pine tree to see two strange wolves coming down the lake directly toward him. He knew he could hold his own against this pair of hunters, but then he saw three more appear from the swirling snow of the lake's open surface. Fanned out in a shallow V formation, they were running straight at him. This was an unsuccessful night-hunting party that accidentally picked up his trespassing scent. If he wished to survive, Big Red had no choice. While still beneath the tree's lowest boughs, he went to the trunk's far side and left between its branches into the deep forest. He headed west—*he was going home.*

Big Red

If I ever go looking for my heart's desire again,
I won't look any further than my own backyard.
L. Frank Baum, *The Wonderful Wizard of Oz*

Chapter—2

SURVIVAL OF THE CUTEST

The lion and the tiger may be more powerful,
But the wolf does not perform in the circus.
Anonymous

This gang of five wolves pursued Big Red for hours until he entered the territory of an adjoining pack. Once these wolves caught the spoor of their neighbors, they slowed their pace and shortly returned to their own domain. The chase was never about killing and eating the trespasser, although on occasion, wolves are cannibalistic as are humans. Instead, they ran him off their territory. Land is life!

To find enough food to survive, each wolf requires a vast range. Since there are about five wolves per pack, this implies they hunt over an enormous expanse, running a marathon every day (*see* map on the next page). Wolves are tough, extremely tough! Pack size in Algonquin Park is relatively small, reflecting prey size. Five wolves will consume the average white-tailed deer together with most of the bones and the hide.

White-Tailed Deer

From Big Red's present position to his Natal Pack (*see* map), he had about 100 mi. (161 km) as the raven flies or 1000 mi. (1609 km) as the wolf runs. Our wolf knew that undisturbed, he could cover that distance in a week. From past experience, however, he also knew he would not be welcomed in any other pack's territory. The danger from other wolves and the need for food would slow his journey considerably. And since wolves hunt at night, Big Red wisely decided to travel during the day.

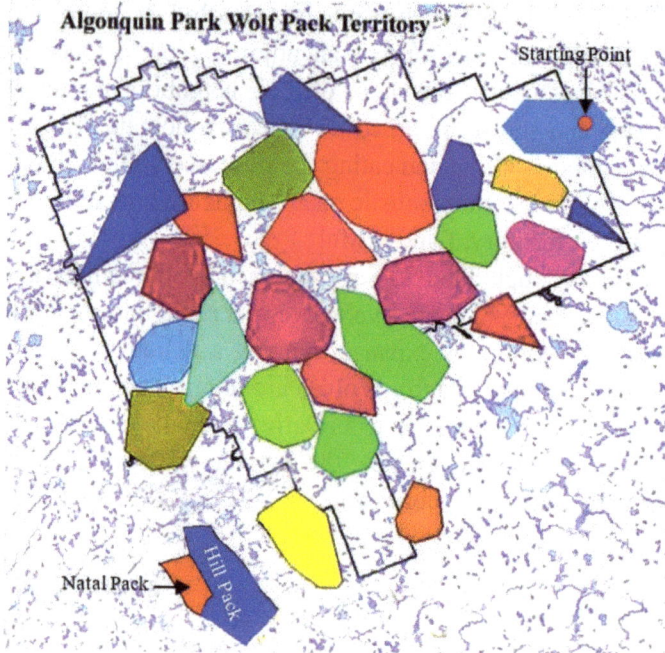

Now, he was ravenous. Fortunately, his acute sense of smell caught a faint whiff of a wolf kill as well as the cacophony from a jostle of ravens. Changing his direction toward this enticing odor, he soon saw the rib cage of a moose rising like a bombed-out building from the surface of a frozen lake. Since moose are the largest animal in the Park and immensely strong, the actual kill must have been an incredible struggle. Scanning the lake's shoreline with his keen eyesight, Big Red was aware that the pack that killed the moose would return for all the scraps, but at this moment, they were absent.

There is nothing ignoble in a predator scavenging—be it wolf, eagle, fox, fisher, or bear. Indeed, early man did the same.

Life dances precariously on the edge between maximizing resources and starvation, and early humans heard that drumbeat and knew that hunger. Since the agricultural revolution brought humans a great abundance of food, many have forgotten our hunter-gatherer-scavenger roots. Nonetheless, it would appear Big Red arrived too late at this site, for even the scraps are gone and the ravens were squabbling over nothing. Undeterred, he reached the remaining bones and with his immense jaws, crushed a femur of the unfortunate moose and devoured its life-giving marrow. This was an empowering meal and strength coursed through his body. Only wolverines, hyenas, and wolves have the jaw-crushing power to break bones and retrieve this valuable food source. Humans extracted the marrow with rocks and stone hammers.

After his meal of marrow, Big Red returned to the forest and his journey. Trotting was more comfortable now as this big wolf scouted for a place to spend his second night and avoid another pack of wolves in the morning. He passed many bedding areas, but he wanted a room with a view, a long view. A small island on a large lake would be perfect. Algonquin Park is a land of lakes, and his search was soon over. The crest of a small island crowned with a tormented jack pine afforded a panoramic lookout.

The lower part of Algonquin Park lies in an area called The Land Between—between the boreal forest to the north and the St. Lawrence Lowlands to the south. It has a biodiversity enriched from two vast regions. This is not Darwin's famous "entangled bank" from the last paragraph of *On the Origin of Species*; instead, this is an *entangled forest* of incredible life forms in countless varieties. Any list must include thousands of plants and trees, pages of different birds, abundant varieties of mammals, myriads of insects, several types of turtles and snakes, but only a single lizard (*see* photograph).

Five-lined Skink

At the pinnacle of this panoply of life stands the wolf, *lupus*. Big Red had met some of the residents of this entangled forest; little did he know how many more he would encounter during his homeward trek.

While moving in small circles, Big Red crushed the noisy snow beneath the jack pine into a bed. Even though he would lie on the snow tonight, his thick coat would prevent any melting under his weight and bodily heat.

Just as he was about to lie down, a lone raven croaked his hello. It circled low, tilting its head to get a better look at this wolf; surprisingly, it circled even closer a second time. When Big Red looked into its black eye, another consciousness stared back. This was not the blank, mechanical gaze of a robin but a knowing glance. And the sound of the air rushing through its wings evoked the wild freedom of the vast northern forests. Quickly, the moment passed, and the raven croaked goodbye and flew away to his night roost.

The silence deepened with the noisy raven's departure now only the occasional boom of a cracking tree due to the cold disturbed an otherwise soundless world. It was nighttime, and the ever-rising gibbous moon shone high in the winter sky, and its silver light covered the land. The austere beauty of this wilderness lake in the winter moonlight did not escape Big Red's awareness. This big wolf on a small island in a vast lake thought that this had been a good day. Curling in a ball, he sought sleep which, on this night, did not come quickly. Just as he was about to fall asleep, a booming call from the deep woods echoed across the unobstructed lake: "Who cooks for you? Who cooks for you all?" This was a barred owl (*see* photograph) declaring its territory or love—

Barred Owl

a night voice common to these forests. Almost immediately, this lone owl was joined by a chorus of others all around the lake. Big Red knew this bird because a family of them had a nest in a hollow tree near his natal den site. He and his siblings heard this talkative creature call on many nights. Finally, dreamless sleep overcame him.

It was well past midnight when he first heard them: the mesmerizing howls of a distant pack of wolves—undoubtedly the ones whose territory he was trespassing on. They howled for several minutes perhaps to celebrate a kill or to express joy at meeting each other again after a fruitless night hunt. At least he knew where they were, and it was not even close, so he drifted off to sleep until morning. For a soundless world, this was a noisy place.

Not known as one of the great masters of English, nonetheless, Charles Darwin in the last paragraph of *On the Origin of Species*—referring to evolution—wrote one of the most exceptional sentences in that language:

> There is grandeur in this view of life, with its several powers, having been originally breathed by the Creator* into a few forms or into one; and that, whilst this planet has gone cycling on according to the fixed law of gravity, from so simple a beginning endless forms most *beautiful and most wonderful* [emphasis added] have been, and are being, evolved.[1]

Why do humans judge some things beautiful and other things ugly? Why does the reader? Humans assess other humans as beautiful or ugly—seemingly without criteria. Are there any rules to guide our judgments, or do we know instinctively? Perhaps it is both. Although he had more to say elsewhere on this topic, Darwin, in the famous paragraph above, just assumed we knew which birds, fish, insects, and mammals were "most beautiful."

---

* Interestingly, this phrase "by the Creator" was not in the first edition of November 1859. Due to popular pressure for the mention of god, it was inserted into the second edition of January 1860 and subsequently retained.

An old cliché states that beauty is all in the eye of the beholder. That is partly true but not the whole truth. Beauty is something more, something objective we can measure. A one-antlered buck (*see* photograph) is not as attractive as his former self. His lack of symmetry hints at a certain diminished virility, as does the cane of an old man. In some societies, youth and manhood are synonymous with beauty. When your left side is identical to your right side (bilateral symmetry), people judge

One-antlered Buck

you to be beautiful and healthy. Many mothers realize their infants prefer looking at symmetric rather than asymmetric patterns. Or perhaps it is a form of imprinting; after all, the loving face that babies first focus on has bilateral symmetry, providing a reference for security and survival. In a broad sense, physical symmetry is related to health and beauty—at least as applied to the bodies of mammals. It is not much, just a toenail, but Big Red has begun his long passage from perfection to putrefaction, from a pup to a puddle of maggots. Show me an animal with *significant* asymmetry, and I will show you a sick animal.

Bilateral Symmetry

Admittedly, there is much more to what we find beautiful than just bilateral symmetry. Most cultures break this symmetry because they find it mundane, too common to be of any real interest. Children, however, are delighted with bilateral symmetry. Put a dab of paint in the crease of a sheet of paper, fold, press, and open it. They will squeal in pleasure at the design; adults soon tire of this too-obvious, too-simple pattern. Bilateral symmetry is everywhere in our society from teacups to toasters, and bicycles to birdbaths. It is part of the background; we hardly notice it. Historically, Japanese art and culture have tried to avoid the banality of this too-noticeable symmetry. In their ritualistic tea service, the cups and urn are placed to prohibit such an effect. Former supermodel Cindy Crawford kept a small mole on her upper lip just to avoid this symmetry. Even the one-antlered buck (*see* photograph) is a splendid creature, but within a few days, he will lose his remaining antler but regain his full symmetry.

> *Tyger Tyger burning bright,*
> *In the forests of the night:*
> *What immortal hand or eye,*
> *Dare frame thy fearful symmetry?*
> William Blake, "The Tyger"

The deep origins of what humans—and non-human animals—find beautiful is mysterious and goes well beyond simple bilateral symmetry. Some time ago, I read a review of a brilliant symphonic performance. The reviewer noted that after the concert had finished, the conductor did not turn around and bow to receive the expected applause. Exhausted, he slumped with his arms at his sides, and the baton dropped from his fingers—the concert hall fell silent. Everyone, the conductor, the orchestra, and the audience were transfixed by the incredible beauty and power of the music. It was some time before the spell was broken by the first person to stand up, clap, and shout "bravo." At that signal, all the revelers awoke and joined in the frenzy of applause. As I recall from the review, there were 12 curtain calls. Since musical tastes are acquired and individual to each culture and person, I decline to name this piece of music.

On a more mundane level, men find women's breasts attractive; women admire men's bums, or so I am told. Why? A specious argument suggests, bigger breasts imply more milk for the baby, but this is false. Breast size and milk production are unrelated. I can assure the reader that no man is thinking about milk production or babies while he is admiring a woman's breasts. I have no idea what women are thinking when gazing at a man's backside. As I said, all this is mysterious.

So much of life is explained by evolution that this is an excellent place to look for answers. In his book *Darwin's Dangerous Idea*, Daniel Dennett calls evolution by natural selection, "the best idea anyone has ever had." So consider this simple thought: *Anything you find beautiful, you will take care of.* And by caring for something, necessarily something alive, it is more likely to prosper and multiply. That is, it has an evolutionary advantage.

Consider the following unlikely animal (*see* photograph). When younger, I viewed this creature as the essence of ugliness— my attitude was like Darwin's toward the marine iguanas of the Galapagos, whom he called the "imps of darkness." The mole's nose has 22 protuberances like freshly extruded hamburger out of a meat grinder and claws so long and so sharp they are suited to tear apart the furrows of the fields of hell. Wolves find them delicious. You might guess I killed something that ugly, but I did not.

The Star-nosed Mole

Beauty truly is in the eye of the beholder: we see the star-nosed mole as butt ugly. But why? Some readers may think my question is frivolous because the mole with its digging claws seems a creature from the TV series *The Walking Dead*. Star-nosed moles, however, must see (yes, they have beady little eyes) each other as the heart of hotness or the entire species would disappear in a single generation. I repeat, beauty is in the eye of the beholder.

The question stays, "Why do *we see* one as ugly and the other as attractive?" The whole cosmetic industry rests on the answer.

🐾

It was deep into the night when Big Red got up to pee. The moon was higher in the sky, covering the whole land in silent silver. The barred owls had completed their chorus and were either hunting or sleeping; even the trees had ceased booming. Our wolf returned to his bed and slept until, as Dylan Thomas wrote, "the sun grew round that very day."

🐾

Young Raccoon: Essence of Cuteness

To us, the cutest infant in all creation is the human infant. In its presence, we get all mushy and gooey inventing a vocabulary of oohs and aahs. We adore the baby's large head and eyes, high cranium, short legs and arms, button nose, and, of course, its perfect unblemished symmetry. This baby is our gold standard for cuteness. So naturally, animals having the characteristics of human infants attract us most strongly—like this adorable raccoon (*see* photograph).

Consider the star-nosed mole and the young raccoon pictured above. You cannot even see the mole's eyes or its face because of the ornate branching nose. On the other hand, the baby raccoon has a large head, prominent eyes overarched with fur suggestive of eyebrows, short front legs reminiscent of arms, a button nose, and perfect symmetry. And the black mask—like women's eyeliner—is universally attractive to humans. All this regularity of features is set in a field of soft-looking fur.

This cuteness has high survival value. Our ancestors who initially found these characteristics appealing would clearly care for and so leave more offspring than those who did not. If natural selection favors a physical attribute, you will soon see more of it. For example, in the artificial selection of dogs (aka selective breeding), *we select* for cute, fluffy, adorable. For vegetables, *we choose* for sweetness, size, and texture. In both cases, we end up with what we want. Maltese terriers and diminutive Chihuahuas would not last overnight in the forest, but they thrive on your bed. And those large, sweet strawberries you buy in the supermarket never grew in nature's wild fields. Chipmunks pick the native varieties fitting several into their small mouths and cheeks at one time to carry back to their larders.

The late evolutionary biologist Steven Jay Gould [2] in one of his famous essays "A Biological Homage to Mickey Mouse" (free online) points out that even cartoon characters can evolve. Consider the images of Mickey taken from Gould's essay. The one on the left is from the first movie *Steamboat Willie* (1928) revealing a somewhat obnoxious rodent. This figure evolved to the juvenile Mickey on the right: bigger eyes, bigger head, large cranial vault, shorter arms, and incidentally much better behaved. Here we have the Mickey of today's Disney world enterprises—a cute, well-behaved, childlike creation. This evolution was viewer

Evolution of Mickey Mouse © Disney Productions

driven Gould speculates, and perhaps even the artists were unaware of this progression.

The sun was already up when Big Red awoke. As he stretched, he felt something light come in contact with his fur, and high-pitched chirping touched his ears. Small bits of pine scales were lightly showering the ground the result of a flock of industrious birds in the few pine trees this small island supported. These were red crossbills (*see* photograph)—the seed warriors of the immense northern forests—harvesting a bumper seed crop.

Red Crossbill

Red crossbills adapt not by beak *size* but by beak *shape*. Their strangely crossed bills appear to be a deformity. At first, critics of Darwinism—and they are everywhere—were delighted with this evolutionary blunder. But the essence of descent with modification, Darwin's preferred phrase, is that poor designs are selected out, and quickly. Extracting seeds from tight pinecones is no easy task, and the crossed bill is uniquely suited for this job. The bird inserts its sharply pointed beak under a pinecone's scale then moves the bill's top and bottom sections farther apart to extract the seed with its long tongue, thousands per day—a spectacular adaption.

Big Red was slightly annoyed as he shook himself to rid his fur of these unwanted pine scales. Scanning the lake for any wolves or deer, he saw neither. Unlike the crossbills, that he was now watching, he would have no breakfast this morning. For our wolf, the bright red colors of these birds appeared darker than for humans. Nonetheless, he thought these wandering warriors were beautiful. They soon stripped all the tiny black seeds from the cones and flew off into the dark green forest never to return.

Bird Watching

Crossbills come in two varieties, red and white-winged, and both have another incredible adaptation beyond their surprising bills that would have delighted Darwin. This second adaptation is so remarkable that no other small bird has copied it. If the seed crop is abundant, crossbills will nest even in January and February when the temperature might well fall to a life-destroying 40 degrees below zero. Their babies are born naked, blind, and helpless, yet such is the will to survive that they somehow do with the warmth of their mother's body and regurgitated seeds. Surely, just a few seconds of winter's steely blast should kill them. "Life finds a way" is a memorable quote uttered by the character Ian Malcolm in the 1993 film *Jurassic Park* and in the case of these Firebirds, it undoubtedly has.

> *Years and years ago, when I was a boy,*
> *when there were wolves in Wales,*
> *and birds the color of red-flannel petticoats*
> *whisked past the harp-shaped hills . . .*
> Dylan Thomas, *A Child's Christmas in Wales*

No one would say Big Red was cute, but most would declare him to be handsome. His mother loved him even before she could see him in the blackness of their den. All the wolf puppies were cute, even the runt sausage. Wolf mothers, like human mothers,

Big Red at Sundown

never forget their children. Big Red understood that if she were still alive, he would be honored at home as a prince returning from a heroic quest.

The snowshoe hare and the bone marrow of the last two days no longer sustained his great strength. He was ravenous. In the wilderness, it is all about food, always has been, always will be. He needed to take down a deer, a nearly impossible task for a lone wolf. He left his island lookout and trotted westward into the silent green forest in a desperate search of food.

Chapter—3

WOLF BIRDS

It is not the strongest of the species that survives,
nor the most intelligent that survives. It is the one
that is the most adaptable to change.
Attributed to Charles Darwin

*T*he green dark forest was too silent to be real* as it swallowed up Big Red with its countless trees, hills, valleys, ponds, and lakes. He was a puny creature, yet rolled out of stardust, baked in the furnace of creation just as you and I were—stars died that he might live. And his only antagonist is man, and before man ruled the earth, there were wolves. And just like you and me, he is a carnivore.

The snow was deep, but due to an earlier thaw followed by a hard frost, our wolf could safely run on its surface. He thought that the white-tailed deer, who walk on two toenails, might not be so fortunate. Big Red was searching for a deer yard, a relatively small area, about one-tenth of their summer range where they overwinter. Often a deer yard is in a valley sheltered from winter's cold blasts and surrounded by cedar and hemlock trees for forage. These ungulates (animals with hooves) trample down hard trails to avoid breaking through the snow crust. Once you discover a deer yard, you will soon find deer.

Big Red had been traveling for over an hour when he sensed something following him. Twice he heard them and realized they were close, awfully close. Since every creature in this vast land was after food, he wondered if these creatures were after him. When he heard them for the third time, he knew precisely who they were. What should have been a chilling situation for our wolf turned into a friendly encounter. From experience, he knew these birds and their trickster ways.

---

* Thanks to Gordon Lightfoot and his "Canadian Railroad Trilogy."

The Northern Raven

Two ravens, aka wolf birds, were shadowing Big Red hoping for a free lunch. These large birds mysteriously show up at every kill site looking for leftovers. Perhaps, one of them was the bird that had inspected him on the lake with the island lookout. Our wolf could not tell them apart. Every raven looked the same to him—just a big black bird with an enormous bill and a raucous voice. Fortunately, these two were quiet, virtually mute, and our wolf wondered why. He thought they must be mates. They flew silently from tree to tree, always keeping him within sight. They seemed aware that any noise from them would attract other ravens, many others. More mouths mean less food for each bird and food is the stuff of life.

Clearly, these intelligent birds must be able to distinguish each other, else half the population would be mated to the same sex. Possibly, they see further into the electromagnetic spectrum than we humans do. Nonetheless, now there were three on the hunt.

Our wolf may not have been able to tell ravens apart, but he could well distinguish one deer from another—the old from the young, the weak from the strong, the injured from the healthy. He did this as if his life depended on it. Humans, with a little attention to detail, can also do this. Consider the following two deer:

Old and Weary   Young and Alert

Descending into an unnamed valley, he at once saw signs of deer: cedar trees with the bark stripped away and many piles of their pellet scat. He had found a deer yard and he tried to hide where possible. His raven companions were forever mute, for they were part of the hunt. An unrestrained excitement surged through his body; he felt joyous with life and ready for anything. Just as he ascended a hillock and reached its summit, he surprised two deer, a doe and her yearling (*see* photograph). Without hesitation, he chose the doe. Although she was experienced, she was also old and lacked the great vigor of the yearling. Sensing his choice, the doe bolted away. And the race was on!

Just as he suspected, she was breaking through the snow crust, except where deer had beaten down the trail. Our wolf realized that if he could keep her within sight, victory would surely be his. He no longer felt tired or hungry; over millennia the Blind Watchmaker (*see* Chapter-9) had crafted his body with long legs for this chase. This is what he lived for; his was the greatest adventure of all time and he knew it. One of these two, pursuer or pursued, would die today so that others might live. Big Red knew it was not a good day to die. It never is.

In Algonquin Park, the authorities allow some limited logging during the winter and to access the felled logs, workers constructed temporary roads. The seasoned doe headed directly for one of these roads which, if reached, would allow her to quickly outrun Big Red. Our wolf was aware of this and realized he must reach her first. Tens of thousands of years of evolution had prepared each of them for this day. Both had seen other such days.

Yearling and Doe

With an extraordinary effort, he caught her while descending a steep hill and quickly made the kill. She was just half a body length from the road—a single step to life. But the death of the doe saved the yearling, and their genes are still running through this great land.

Wolves will eat 20 lbs. (9 kg) or more at a kill. In frustration and hunger, the ravens were beginning to break dead branches from an evergreen and rain them onto the snow below. *When do we get a meal?* thought his avian companions. To hurry the process, one of the ravens flew to the ground and pulled Big Red's tail. Just at that moment, however, three noisy ravens glided out of the wilderness and saw the whole scene. The two formerly mute birds erupted in a series of cronk, cronk, cronk calls (*see* photograph) and gave instant pursuit. But the fleeing ravens sang as they flew and soon scores of their friends arrived to overwhelm Big Red's two companions and claim all the leftovers:

Cronk, Cronk, Cronk

And thick and fast they came at last,
And more and more, and more —
Lewis Carroll, *The Walrus and the Carpenter*

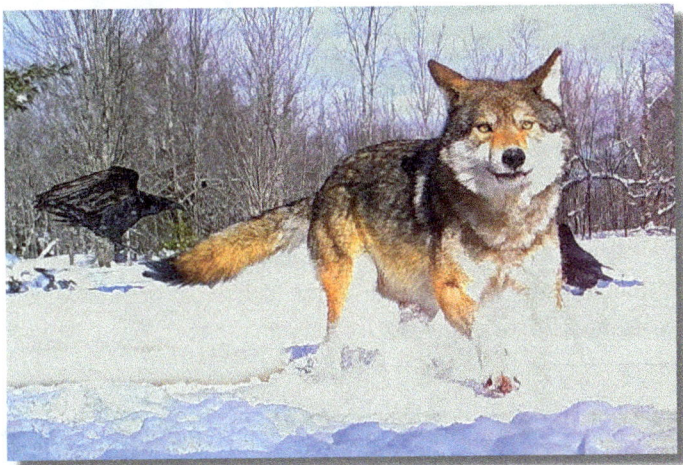

Big Red Chasing away Ravens

Big Red had his fill and retired under a pine tree to watch the chaos at the carcass. In this land without fat and very little lean, the ravens continued to appear as if out of nothingness to join in the feast. The doe, this once-proud animal, who died under an open sky in full sunshine, was now a jumble of bones and scraps. Our wolf recalled her grace and beauty during the chase and knew she was a worthy opponent. After all, he had beaten her by only a single step. With these thoughts in mind, his annoyance with the ravens grew until finally in the act of futility, he tried to chase them from her shattered remains (*see* photograph).

But he now had much more significant problems. All these avian voices had awakened the dark green forest from its slumber with an open invitation to a venison party. Our wolf knew he had to leave quickly before the resident pack of wolves arrived. With no further thought, he set off westward, the direction of his home territory.

He ran for an hour and was now distant from the deer carcass. Passing along a path less traveled bordering on a lake, he slowed his pace to a trot. Gazing in wonderment at the stars reflected in the lake's placid surface after rising from its depths, he took a deep breath. He felt like a mote in the eye of the universe, but he would at least be a defiant mote. Sleep overcame him and he sought shelter, as much shelter as a wolf ever needs. And that night he slept on the beach under the stars.

The northern or common raven (*Corvus corax = Genus species*) may well be the world's most intelligent bird; they are certainly one of the most widespread (*see* map). Crows, noted for their problem-solving abilities, are in the basket-weaving class compared to ravens. These large black birds thrive from the high Arctic to the hottest deserts, and everywhere in between. Cocky, swaggering, feisty, pugnacious, boisterous, irrepressible, mischievous, and with enough vigor to live 20 or more years in the wild and 70 in captivity, ravens are indeed one of nature's wonders.

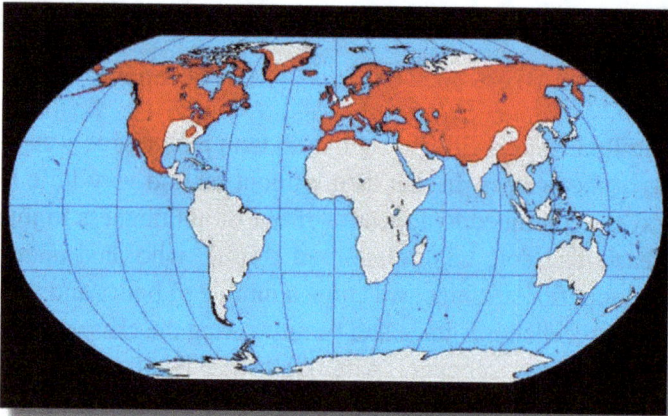

Range of the Northern Raven

Beyond the northern raven, there are more than a half dozen other so-called "species" of this bird, ranging from Mexico to Africa to Australia. If intelligence is proportional to distribution, then the raven caught the gold ring. Biologists define a *species* as the largest group of organisms capable of breeding and producing fertile offspring. These other "species" of ravens may be capable of interbreeding and producing viable young but for geographical limitations like the Inuit of northern Canada and the Aborigines of Australia—they never meet.

With such an enormous distribution, contact with humans was historically early and widespread. Western civilization has not been kind to these birds, usually seeing them in close association with dread and death. English poetry about ravens is universally forbidding and dark—witness the group noun for a flock of ravens is "unkindness." This term originated with their practice of flying over a battlefield to have the dead for dinner, unlike the Valkyries who gather the fallen heroes to Valhalla for eternity. "Conspiracy," a second collective noun for these birds, is equally forbidding. Both group nouns tell us nothing about ravens but much about humans. Remember these corvids did not kill anyone or anything; they are merely reaping the harvest of human folly.

Primitive people, or more correctly, less complex people, had an in-depth knowledge of ravens. They weaved these birds into their myths and legends. The Norse god Odin, father of Thor, had two ravens,* one on each of his shoulders. Every morning these birds, Huginn and Muninn ("thought" and "memory"), flew over the world to collect the news of the day and then return to whisper this knowledge in Odin's ears. These birds of legend and poetry were known as tricksters and were constant companions to wolves whether they liked it or not.

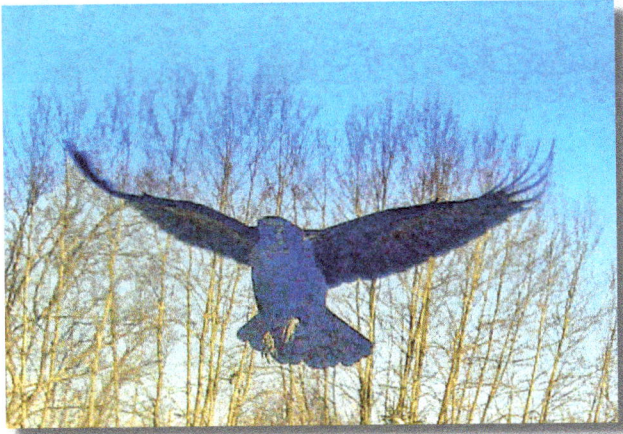

The Northern Raven: Ryder in the Whirlwind

Ryders in the Whirlwind

Come thou north wind great and strong
Swiftly blow my wings along
That I may scan the world below
And see all that there is to know
I am a Ryder in the whirlwind
I am nature's wild, chaotic force
That knows no bounds and follows no course.

---

* In addition to the two ravens, Odin kept two wolves, Geri and Freki.

In Christian mythology, or more broadly Abrahamic folklore, the raven is considered an "unclean" animal, meaning unfit to eat. Tradition says Noah released a raven from the Ark to determine if there was enough dry land to disembark. Now the raven because of its wild nature and the abundance of floating bodies for food did not return. Genesis 8:7 (KJV) says the following:

> And he [Noah] sent forth a raven, which went forth to and fro, until the waters were dried up from off the earth.

Scholars tell us the entire Genesis flood story was copied from the much earlier *Epic of Gilgamesh* (circa 2600 BCE). The incident of the raven uses almost identical language. Tablet XI says the following:

The Ark Raven

> I [Utnapishtim, the archetype for Noah] sent forth a raven and released it. The raven went off and saw the waters slither back. It eats, it scratches, it bobs, but does not circle back to me.

The *Epic of Gilgamesh* transports the reader five millennia into deep history—it is humankind's oldest known story. Yet its motifs are as fresh as this morning's rain: friendship, death, immortality, and the meaning of life. Following the passing of his best friend, Enkidu, Gilgamesh leaves his kingdom to find the mystical figure Utnapishtim and gain eternal life. His fear of death is a fear of meaninglessness and, although he does not win immortality, the quest itself gives his life meaning. Treasure the journey, not the destination.

🐾

Long before sunrise, Big Red heard them as they screamed across the sky as black arrows wrapped in crimson waves. These ravens were going to the deer carcass. Our wolf rose and shook himself to remove any sand lingering in his fur. Going to the lake, he waded in belly-deep before he drank with licks and slashes.

Because of yesterday's venison banquet, he needed no breakfast. He glanced around at the woods now grown silent, admiring its beauty. Yet, this was not his land, nor his home, so he headed westward toward Eden.

Wolves have a unique and ancient relationship with ravens. Find one and you will soon find the other. They help each other in ways I suspect neither would admit to. So close is this symbiotic relationship between wolves and ravens that many peoples call the latter the wolf-bird. And they talk to each other, or at least the ravens call, and wolves listen.

Let me explain a little of what I have learned about raven society from observation and from reading Bernd Heinrich's marvelous book *Ravens in Winter*. Raven society has two levels: resident pairs and roving bands of juveniles.* The resident couple, male and female, claim a vast territory as their own where they raise their family and gather their food. They can rule this territory for 20 or more years, vigorously driving out all intruders in spectacular aerial chases and fights.

Juvenile scouting expeditions cover incredible distances, but the birds regularly return to a roost tree for the night. Over the last two decades, a few of these temporary roost trees have been near my home, and the ravens that gather there, rather than rest let alone sleep, have what sounds like an all-night rock party. A honeybee that has found a large cluster of fresh flowers will lead its hive mates to them; surprisingly, ravens do something similar.

A Juvenile Jostle of Ravens

---

* *Google* Gordon Harrison "A Jostle of Ravens." Play with sound on.

In an act of apparent *altruism*, the bird who finds a carcass will lead his flock mates to the site from the roost tree. As you might expect, this unexpected altruism among unrelated birds aroused great interest in researcher Bernd Heinrich.

His explanation was cogent, but not easily discovered. It turns out that, if a roving juvenile finds a carcass, you can be sure the resident pair for that area has also found it. This pair would instantly drive off a single juvenile raven, but if a gang of ten or more arrives, the couple gives up and takes what they can from the carcass. If the wolves have not opened the body, no one gets much; even ravens' oversized bills cannot penetrate deer or moose hide. What to do? Well, ravens have an ancient solution! These birds produce a loud ruckus of chaos calls that summon any wolf within miles. Then everyone eats. As I said, ravens call and wolves listen.

Ravens have a vocabulary of 65 or more words, and we are just beginning to learn their language. Several times larger than crows and much, much smarter, they have extraordinary problem-solving abilities.

And they play, they play a lot. They will pull the eagle's feathers and the wolf's tail. I suspect the ravens that do these things are mostly males trying to impress females in the juvenile gang. These gangs are a kind of dating service until two mate and fly off to claim their own territory. I have seen them make repeated snow angels creating the impression of a giant dinosaur's rib cage. Like children, they tuck in their wings and slide down hills squawking happily all the way. In the sky, they dive, tumble, twirl, and do such things you dare not dream of. They are tricksters, daredevils, and acrobats. And, along with wolves, they are two of Darwin's greatest descendants.

The Raven sleeps when he wishes,
Wakes when he pleases.
Hunts when he must,
And plays when he can.
It's called freedom.

Chapter—4

THE JOURNEY

A foil'd circuitous wanderer—till at last
The long'd-for dash of waves is heard, and wide
His luminous home of waters opens, bright
And tranquil, from whose floor the new-bathed stars
Emerge, and shine upon the Aral Sea.
Matthew Arnold, *Sohrab and Rustum*

The snow felt firm beneath his massive paws as Big Red ran on through the evergreen forest toward home. Forged by a million years of natural selection, his large body moved with fluid grace. Listening carefully, he could still hear the raven chaos at the carcass in the distance. Little would be left for the blue jays and chickadees, and the late-arriving wolves would get only the thick deer hide, the bones, and the aroma. Since this was the middle of March, male raccoons would be out searching for still sleepy females to mate with. They would get nothing, not even the aroma.

Running Wolf

Everything was different now. When he was hungry, Big Red thought of nothing but food. Wolves are always one meal away from starvation, but with a full stomach, his mind wandered to other things. Gone were the ravens, the other wolves, and his fatigue. His mind turned to more pressing matters—his profound sense of being alone and his strong urge to have his own pack and family. Like humans, wolves are social animals; the lone wolf stories are anomalies, a passing phase, or lies.

Often, he wondered why no other pack had accepted him, for this is how wolf genes customarily disperse and avoid incest. Perhaps his enormous size was intimidating to other alpha males, so threatening that they never gave him even an apprenticeship position. He felt sure his brother Paws and his sister Little Red Ears had integrated into neighboring packs, perhaps achieving the status of breeding alphas.

In this immense winter wilderness with a full stomach, his sense of isolation weighed on him. He had felt this pain earlier on the island in the middle of the frozen lake under a bright canopy of sparkling stars, but wolves never cry on the outside. In some respects, our wolf was Gilgamesh, looking for immortality and the meaning of life. Having children, passing on your genes, is a form of immortality, the only kind open to living creatures. Tens of thousands of generations before him had done this exact thing; how could he falter now? It takes only a single generation to fail for the genetic river to dry up. And the great river of life locked away in his genes now depended on him.

Sleeping Wolf

As the sky darkened into evening, Big Red searched for a spot to spend the night. This had been a good day. In a thicket of fallen trees and brambles, he discovered an unoccupied bear's den. Crawling in, he curled up, closed his eyes, and after some thoughts toward the stillness and the solitude of the night, he slept.

Like the children of Ishmael, wolves are wanderers. Their only equal and sometime companion in this passion *to go where no one has gone before* is man. This wandering is inevitably for food or a mate. Big Red's Natal Pack controlled an area of 100 mi.^{2} (260 km^2). Big fierce animals are rare because they prey on a more abundant food base. For example, in Algonquin Park, there are at least 50 deer for every wolf. Deer numbers control wolf numbers, not the reverse.

Big Red's father came from afar in the northern regions of Algonquin Park while his mother and aunt came from the nearby Hill Pack. And his father's father back through the generations, where did he come from? Ultimately, where did wolves originate? To paraphrase Darwin, "Where is the origin of this species?" Fortunately, we know the answer, and surprisingly, it involves ice, snow, and a poem by Percy Bysshe Shelley.

Let me explain. Although presently the snow in the Park is only 3 feet (1 m) deep, during the last Ice Age, it was more than 10,000 feet (about 2 mi. or 3050 m) deep. Nonetheless, the depth of the ice sheet was exceeded by its breadth. Glaciers and the snow sheets covered Canada as well as the northern part of the United States. This incredible volume of frozen water ultimately came from the world's oceans via the water cycle. Unexpectedly the great English poet Shelley explains this cycle in the final stanza of his poem, "The Cloud":

> *I am the daughter of Earth and Water,*
> > *And the nursling of the Sky;*
> *I pass through the pores of the ocean and shores;*
> > *I change, but I cannot die.*
> *For after the rain when with never a stain*
> > *The pavilion of Heaven is bare,*
> *And the winds and sunbeams with their convex gleams*
> > *Build up the blue dome of air,*
> *I silently laugh at my own cenotaph,*
> > *And out of the caverns of rain,*
> *Like a child from the womb, like a ghost from the tomb,*
> > *I arise and unbuild it again.*

These ice sheets literally transformed the face of the earth. In North America, they depressed the Precambrian Shield so much that it is still rebounding. When the ice sheets retreated about 12,000 years ago, they left a deeply scarred landscape dotted with eskers, drumlins, moraines, and innumerable lakes. But during the ice age itself, with all this water locked in ice sheets, the ocean level fell 400 feet. Such was the decline that a land bridge called Beringia connected Asia and Alaska (*see* map) having its own distinct flora and fauna.

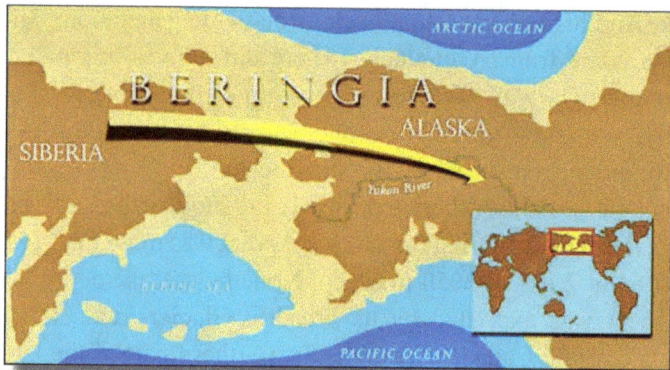

Beringia

Using this land bridge Asian gray wolves, the ancient ancestors of Big Red, migrated into North America between 70,000 and 24,000 years ago along with bears, deer, and people. Multiple migrations occurred with animals going both ways.

By virtue of an earlier migration, the massive dire wolf (*Canis dirus*), already a resident of the Great Plains and beyond, confronted these gray wolves. Terrorizing much of North America in large packs until the end of the last Ice Age, they were the most massive canine that ever lived. The famous La Brea tar pits in downtown Los Angeles has produced thousands of skeletons of dire wolves, and many are intermingled with the legendary saber-tooth tiger. Dire wolves (*see* drawing), weighing in at 200 lbs. (91 kg) for both males and females were at least 25 percent larger than the most massive modern dogs. Fate held their existence in a firm tether to the megafauna (horses, ground sloths, mastodons, bison, and camels) that went extinct at the close of the last Ice Age. Surely, they had encounters with early man; they may even have hunted each other.

Dire Wolf (*Canis dirus*) courtesy of Daniel Anton

Over time, every unique environment produces a new "species" of wolf. Consider the colder climate of Beringia that resulted in wolves with thicker, warmer fur, shorter tails and ears, a whitening of the coat, and distinctly larger bodies. The teeth changed as well with stronger carnassials for shearing through the flesh of the megafauna. The jaw itself became stronger with muscles attached along a higher sagittal crest resulting in a bone-crushing bite, and so on. This analysis makes sense, and this knowledge gives us confidence that we can know this place and these animals for the first time.

Photograph courtesy of the Beringian Wolf Diorama
at the Yukon Beringia Interpretive Centre,
Whitehorse, Canada

Both wolves, dire and Beringian, are thought to be separate species, hence incapable of interbreeding and producing fertile young. Presently, in North America, there are many so-called "species" of wolf. Here are four:

- Gray wolves of northern Canada and Yellowstone Park and surrounding states.
- The red wolf of central Ontario, parts of Quebec, and Michigan.
- Coyotes of the American West and the eastern states plus lower Canada and Newfoundland.
- Mexican wolf—less than 200 in the southwest and a few in captivity.

Since many of these "species" interbreed, producing fertile young, they *cannot by definition be separate species*. Latest studies* of DNA indicate there is but a single species of North American wolf—the gray wolf.

Appearance alone implies some hybridization among the gray wolf, the Algonquin wolf, and the coyote. This upsets racial purists. I wonder why? Mark Twain has the following to say on this topic concerning his dog, Jasper:

> He wa'n't no common dog, he wa'n't no mongrel; he was a composite. A composite dog is a dog that's made up of all the valuable qualities that's in the dog breed—kind of a syndicate; and a mongrel is made up of all riffraff that's left over.[1]

And, yes, composites are often hardier and stronger. All the dogs I had as a boy were composites with the strength and endurance of mules. In truth, all life forms are composites; we call the result evolution. Humans now wish to apply this nonsense of racial purity, which has poisoned entire civilizations, to the genus *Canis*, both wolf and dog. The search for racial purity is a search for unicorns—and they are composites too. And the belief in racial purity has led to some of the darkest places in the human heart.

---

* www.livescience.com/55586-wolves-only-one-species.html

If these groups of wolves are not different species, animals, or kinds, then we need a new definition for what they indeed are. Biologists have proposed the following term:

Ecomorph: A local variety of a species whose appearance is determined by its environment.

It is an interesting observation that as you go farther north the same species (i.e., different ecomorphs) get larger—consider the size progression from coyote to Red wolf to gray wolf: small to medium to large.

Medium-sized Ecomorph: The Red Wolf

Anything written about wolves and ecomorphs applies with equal force to humans. Consider the following. The Rwandans of the Congo (*see* photograph) exemplify adaptation to hot climates. Their body type produces the largest skin area for humans relative to total body volume. Therefore, surface radiation is maximal, so heat dissipation is maximal.

On the other hand, the short-limbed Inuit (Eskimos) with large, heavy torsos, exemplify bodily adaptation to Arctic climates. Their shape produces the smallest skin area for humans relative to total volume. Surface radiation is minimal, so heat loss is minimal. Both handsome racial types are products of natural selection. The direction of Inuit evolution has happened before in hominid history. To exist during the last ice-age in Europe, skeletal remains of Neanderthals indicate they evolved a similar body type, but millennia earlier than the Inuit—an example of *convergent* evolution at separate times.

We have just seen that body *size* and *shape* are significant factors in how efficiently an animal responds to hot or cold climates. Two 19th century naturalists, Carl Bergmann and Joel Allen formulated rules concerning these factors. In zoology, Bergmann's law is a principle relating external temperature to the ratio of body surface to mass in warm-blooded animals. Birds and mammals in cold regions tend to be larger than individuals of the same species in warmer areas. Bergmann proposed this principle to account for size as an adaptive mechanism to conserve or to radiate body heat, depending on climate.

Allen's rule is a corollary to Bergmann's, stating that warm-blooded animals in cold climates have shorter protruding fingers, noses, tails, ears, and legs than another race of the same species in a warmer environment. Consider the short, stubby digits of the Inuit compared to the long, slender fingers of the Rwandans.

 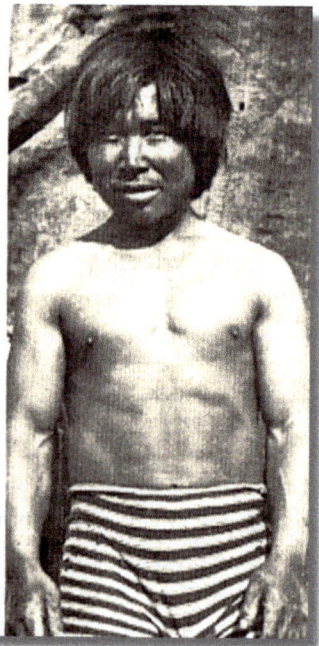

Rwandans   Inuit

Golden-crowned Kinglet

Nevertheless, in the hinterlands of Ontario lives a tiny bird—a very tiny bird—the golden-crowned kinglet. The common black-capped chick-a-dee of the same region weighs about three and a half pennies roughly double the mass of the kinglet at two pennies. When plucked, it is no bigger than the end of your finger. Heat flows from its body a hundred times greater than it does for humans. And kinglets are *permanent* residents of these forests where winter temperatures often fall to − 40°. For them to live in this ruthless cold is incredible!

Curiously, this reminds me of mathematician Ian Malcolm's comment in *Jurassic Park* after the park's creator, John Hammond, had declared his dinosaurs were genetically engineered to be utterly incapable of breeding. Malcolm countered with equal certainty that "Nature will find a way." And she often does. With the golden-crowned kinglet, she surely has—this bird somehow flourishes where it should perish. Its closest relative, the somewhat larger ruby-crowned kinglet, always leaves these regions for the winter months. The natural world is vast and full of wonders and exceptions to rules like Bergmann's and Allen's.

In the morning, Big Red noticed slivers of light penetrating through the brambles and branches into the old bear den. He stood up and stretched his long front legs to their full extent with his backside held high in a perfect downward-facing dog pose. He held that pose for some time until he pulled his front legs back in under his body. Then, with much diligence and care, he licked each of his paws to prepare for this day's journey giving special attention to his right front paw, the one with a missing toe. Occasionally, when he ran on ice, the absent toe hindered his ability to abruptly change direction. But this was a small inconvenience and he seldom thought of it.

Red Squirrel

Abruptly, a loud scurrying disturbed his morning exercises when a red squirrel propelled herself headlong into his sleeping quarters, instantly followed by three more. Snatching at the first, he hoped to have a squirrel breakfast, but the runaway bride and her suitors proved too swift for him. The wedding party exited the den to find a better arena for their amorous acrobatics. The suitors will, of course, eventually catch her, and they will mate, creating this year's first crop of baby red squirrels (*see* photograph).

The restlessness and energy these squirrels display as adults start from birth, for the babies are forever wiggling and squirming even in their sleep. These babies may be hugging each other in the nest, but as adults, except for the hour of estrus, they are quarrelsome loners.

Baby Red Squirrels

Big Red also went out from the musty bear den and surveyed the surrounding landscape. To the west was an immense body of water the humans call "Grand Lake" and to the east the shimmering emerald forest. Overnight the sublimated mist of the previous day had crystallized and now formed a thin blanket over the landscape. The fresh air tickled his large nostrils, and jewel-like crystals crunched beneath his paws. Such was his vigor and strength that he might have been Adam on his first day after creation in the Garden of Eden.

He had two choices. He could take the long way around the lake or go straight across saving the day's journey. The lake was pristine and silent with a sparkling haze hugging its surface.

If he crossed the lake, he would have the sun and the wind at his back but be visible to every wolf nearby. Reflecting for less than a minute, he then committed himself. Life is not without danger, so he stepped onto the lake's surface and trotted westward toward his luminous home.

Big Red on Grand Lake

Chapter—5

THE WAR ON WOLVES

Cast a cold eye
On Life, on death
Horseman, pass by!
W. B. Yeats, tombstone inscription

Big Red had been running for some time, but he still could not see the far side of the lake. Intuitively, he attempted to go in a straight line but slight variations in gait give *every* living creature an undulating path. He kept a fast pace so as not to expose himself on this large lake for any longer than necessary. The size of this lake made it an excellent arena for a pack of wolves to run down white-tailed deer. Once a deer is on the lake, the wolves can keep it in sight and ultimately surround it.

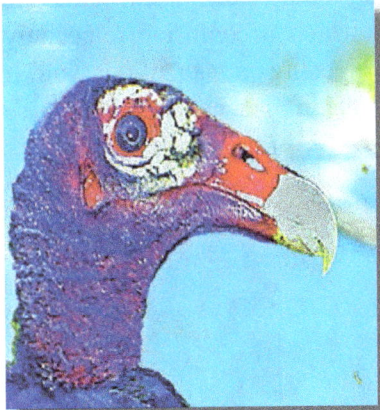

Turkey Vulture

Out of the corner of his eye, our wolf saw something large and black. Fortunately, it was only a turkey vulture, an early spring migrant from the south. Soaring effortlessly in a shallow "V" with barely a wing flap, this huge bird was searching for the dead or dying. "Bird, pass by" Big Red thought, "there will be nothing here for you today."

Nevertheless, he now ran a little faster! At that instant, four wolves emerged from the mist in a fanned-out formation. Big Red reasoned they had picked up his scent since they were downwind of him. His every decision now would be fateful. Nonetheless, he decided he could bust through their line and outrun the whole pack. Our wolf was nothing if not supremely confident. For a few seconds, the gang of four seemed astonished; they were expecting him to sprint away rather than toward them. Assuming he was foolishly overconfident, they moved in for the kill. Trespassers are not typically tolerated.

Big Red drove toward the gap between the center two wolves, trusting he would disappear in the fog directly behind them. He would never have done this had he known all the facts. The fog enveloped him as well as the two wolves at his heels plus two more closely following. He had no time to think he had fooled them when it happened—two more wolves popped up directly in his path, and a horrifying clash ensued. With six wolves surrounding him, Big Red had no chance of winning; the best he could hope for was to breakout and vanish into the mist. While circling furiously trying to protect his rear, he felt fangs puncture deep into his right thigh. He quickly returned the favor to one of the six who then withdrew from the frenzy. Now unable to run, he was surely finished! It would only be seconds until the remaining five wolves would eviscerate him.

With the kind of luck usually granted only to fools and children, a seventh even larger wolf appeared—the alpha male. Surveying the rage, he did something completely unexpected. He ferociously attacked his own pack which, in confusion, reluctantly withdrew to leave a battered and bleeding remnant of our wolf. It was then that Big Red recognized his rescuer was Paws, his

Wolf Fight—Fangs and the Fury

littermate and brother. Wolves never forget; blood is thicker than all other bonds—at least for wolves.

Although long separated by time and distance, these two wolves lay on the snow in the mist as if they had never been apart. Paws hugged his brother, licked his face, and was as attentive as he could be. Suddenly a frigid wind came up on Grand Lake and blew away the mist to reveal a desolate scene. Two constellations of wolves, star-scattered on the ice some hundred paces apart. The six in a wide arc, intensely watching the other two.

Blood flowed down Big Red's thigh, disappearing into the porous snow, creating a dark-red, fist-sized stain. In the other group, a similar mark appeared in the snow from the side of a young male. The brothers waited for the bleeding to stop, and after an hour it did. Wolves are tough—tough beyond anything humans can endure or even imagine.

The sun had reached its zenith before Big Red first moved onto his stomach to test his wound. Intense pain shot up his leg into his groin, but because this was not his first injury, he knew he could endure it. The wolves in the other group fixedly watched these two, not understanding their bond or past. Some relationships cannot be expressed in words, or songs, or even by Shakespeare himself.

The sun had progressed from its zenith halfway down to the horizon when Big Red finally staggered to his feet. All animals, human and non-human, try to hide their physical weaknesses. Yet as hard as our wolf tried, his rear end wobbled as he walked. Paws wanted to throw his legs around his brother's neck, but he felt sure this act would bring him to the ground. In a final gesture of goodbye, they licked each other's faces, and *Big Red started to walk.*

Soaring Turkey Vulture

The vulture returned, alerted by the blood, for they have the best sense of smell in the avian world. The other six wolves stared attentively at this wounded wolf.

Big Red could have walked in any direction, but he struck off directly toward the six wolves lying on the snow. Once again, these wolves looked at each other, wondering what to do as our wolf limped and staggered toward them. Paws watched admiringly for he well knew his brother's pride. Big Red was challenging these six to acquiesce to his presence! First, the youngest female stood up and moved back a few steps, then the other young female did the same. The other four refused to budge as he reached the halfway point between them. Paws realized he should not interfere. Big Red looked directly into the eyes of each of these four, a sign of aggression among wolves. With great difficulty, the young male whom Big Red had severely bitten stood up, leaving only two older males and the alpha female. Now twenty paces apart, the two males finally flinched and suddenly stood up together, leaving the alpha female alone on the ice. Big Red surmised she was already pregnant with Paw's progeny, and he

The Five Standing Wolves

decided to ignore her. The five standing wolves were still uncertain of what to do with this sizeable, crazy wolf. Try as Big Red might, he could not hide his limp and occasional wobble. He was almost upon them when something extraordinary happened, they moved apart and let him pass. The two young females had developed some admiration for this bizarre wolf who knew no fear and would not yield.

As Big Red walked away, the six wolves left behind were dimly aware that something remarkable had happened today on Grand Lake. Time and circumstance will call upon each of us to act heroically at some point in our lives. Today, Big Red made his. Over his shoulder, he could still see the vulture circling, and again he said to himself, "Vulture, pass by! There will be nothing here for you today." After another 30 minutes, he reached the forest on the far side of the lake and disappeared into the wilderness. The six wolves were still on the lake when Paws came to greet them.

With pretense no longer required, his limping and staggering increased. He needed a place to rest until he recovered. Crawling under the first white pine tree he could find; he lay on his left side. After a while, he licked his wounds bleeding again because of his extended walking. After a big kill, a wolf can go for three or more weeks without food. This was fortunate for Big Red because recently he had had an enormous meal of venison. His immune system and excellent health would be his doctor, and this white pine tree his hospital.

This may not have been a beautiful day, but it had been memorable. He had reunited with his brother and walked through the valley of death and shown no fear. With his massive head resting comfortably on a thick pillow of bronze pine needles, sleep came quickly with comforting dreams of home and his own family.

Do not go gentle into that good night,

. . . .

Rage, rage against the dying of the light.
Dylan Thomas, "Do Not Go Gentle into that Good Night"

Down through millions of years of evolution, no wolf had a flea collar, had his nails clipped, went to a groomer, received vaccinations, heart-worm pills, or a medication of any kind, least of all from a veterinarian. Their bodies either healed or they died, and this was true of all living creatures. And, of course, those that survived had better genes than those that died, and they passed these to their progeny. We call this the process of *natural selection*. Big Red was intuitively depending on these internal healing powers to be his doctor.

As I wrote previously, if you wish to conjure up a nightmare of slobbering immorality, of heartless cruelty and mindless killing, the image is always that of the wolf. From nursery rhymes to adult fiction, the beast from the primeval forest is *Canis lupus*. Never was a creature more maligned than this great grandparent of *Canis familiaris*, the family dog. Yet there are only two authenticated cases of wild wolves killing humans in all North American recorded history.

On the other hand, we have poisoned, trapped, snared, slaughtered, run down with snowmobiles, and shot from helicopters so many gray wolves that we virtually extirpated them from the lower forty-eight states. Under great protest, a few have been reintroduced into Yellowstone Park. But we know who the top predator is, the slobbering mindless killer—we need only look in the mirror.

The prevailing paradigm for wolf behavior comes from Tennyson's poem *In Memoriam* when it says, "red in tooth and claw." But if this were true, the pack would quickly disintegrate from death, injury, and animosity. You cannot gamble with your life every day, or you will soon lose it. Of all wolf-wolf interactions, 90 percent are prosocial. That is not to say that wolves, like our military or our entire social order, do not have a strict hierarchy, which accounts for the remaining 10 percent.

Apex Predators Displaying their Kill

In some sense, as I wrote previously, predator and prey have created each other. Each depends on the other for its health and long-term survival. The wolves run on through the evergreen forests in their eternal pursuit of the deer. And for their part, the deer lead the wolves on a deadly chase. Each hones the other to perfection by natural selection. It is not only the weak and the old who falter and fall, but it is also the inefficient—the ones who stray too far from the edge. To those who do the dance, whether deer or wolf, belongs the day and the future. It is not a good day to die! It never is. So, the wolves run on through the evergreen forests.

Without dissent, it is clear the top killer of wolves is man, not other wolves. In all places and all times, wolf and man have been ancient enemies. Yet, speak to a thousand people, and few if any will have ever seen a wild wolf. Wolves do not do well in zoos nor do they perform in circuses. An increasing number of people have become aware of the horrific cruelty inflicted on these sentient animals. Charles Darwin knew that the highest privilege that comes with free speech is using your voice to speak for those who cannot speak for themselves. I repeat his famous quote, "There is no fundamental difference between man and animals in their ability to feel pleasure, and pain, happiness, and misery."

This has not always been the view of non-human animals. According to the great French philosopher, René Descartes (1596–1650), animals are just machines that feel neither pleasure in eating nor pain in suffering. Descartes himself took part in live vivisections on dogs. As English philosopher John Cottingham comments in 1978, "To be able to believe that a dog with a broken paw is not really in pain when it whimpers is a quite extraordinary achievement even for a philosopher." Another Frenchman, Voltaire (1694–1778), agrees:

> *Barbarians seize this dog, which in friendship surpasses man so prodigiously; they nail it on a table, and they dissect it alive in order to show the mesenteric veins. You discover in it all the same organs of feeling that are in yourself. Answer me, machinist, has nature arranged all the means of feeling in this animal, so that it may not feel? has it nerves in order to be impassible? Do not suppose this impertinent contradiction in nature.*[1]

Darwin's position on vivisection is clear:

The love of a dog for his master is notorious; in the agony of death he has been known to caress his master, and everyone has heard of the dog suffering under vivisection, who licked the hand of the operator; this man, unless he had a heart of stone, must have felt remorse to the last hour of his life.[2]

To safely navigate this life requires luck, the kind of luck Big Red had earlier this day on Grand Lake when his brother Paws saved him from certain death. But in a broader sense, you also need to be born in the right place and at the right time. Without realizing it, our wolf did both.

The rangers in Algonquin Park—those trusted to protect the wildlife—trapped, poisoned, and shot 50 to 60 wolves every year before 1959. In retrospect, this seems completely immoral, almost preposterous.

Even if you are camping in the Park and have done so for many years, you may never have glimpsed a wolf. The Park is enormous, encompassing 3,000 mi.^{2} (7,770 km^2), but at winter's end—when wolves are at their lowest numbers—there are about 150.

Wolves Howling

That is one wolf for every 20 mi.^{2} (52 km^2). So, no wonder few campers or anyone else see them for they are wild spirits, the apex predators, and the real rulers of this vast land. On rare occasions, their electrifying songs fill the fresh night air only to let us know who owns this place and you best not forget it. Every August, thousands of people come to Algonquin Park* to hear their transfixing arias. Park officials take groups of hundreds out nightly on the off chance the wolves will sing. But wolves do not perform on demand; they do not negotiate and you do not get your money back. Yet when they do howl, your spine tingles and you can touch that ancient time when we roamed the forest with them.

After the rangers stopped slaughtering wolves in the park, something incredible happened. The number of wolves the following spring and each spring after that *did not increase*—it was still 150. Any reasonable person would have expected them to multiply significantly, but they did not. It was a paradox until you look closely.

The answer lies with wolf pup mortality. Fewer wolves in the springtime means more prey for the survivors, which in turn implies well-fed pups from their mother's milk and later from food scraps. It is always about food, and it always has been, or the prey base as biologists say. It is a mathematical equation: more food implies more pups survive to replace those the rangers killed. In Algonquin Park, the prey base is deer, moose, and beaver plus other odds and sods.

The prey base serves as a setpoint for how many wolves can exist in the Park, and that number is about 150. Change the prey base and the setpoint changes accordingly either up or down.

A Wild Boar in Winter

---

* *Google* "Algonquin Park public wolf howls"

Recently some wild boars escaped from a game farm in Ontario. They always escape because that is their nature, and that of all creatures born free—only those raised in cages consider it a sickness to run free. Now, these animals are well suited to Ontario's harsh winters, for they originated in Russia. And Russian wolves have long eaten wild boars as part of their prey base, so Algonquin wolves should be able to add them to their menu. You can count on it! Indeed, Ontario hunters and hikers have found several kill sites where the wolves dined on pork. Since wild boars breed prolifically, they may well become a regular item on the wolves' menu and so significantly increase the setpoint resulting in many more wolves. You can count on that too!

Wild boars maxing out at 200 lbs. (91 kg) with a vicious pair of long fangs, are a formidable foe. Plus, they often travel in large groups called *sounders*. The wolves must separate one from this group and attack its hindquarters to avoid the fangs. These encounters are horrific affairs where a wolf could easily be gored and if not killed, would endure a protracted death from an infection contracted from the boar's fangs. But such is pack loyalty that all members join in the fight from the alpha to the omega; they stand and deliver as one fighting unit. If successful, all will dine on back bacon and pork ribs.

🐾

Big Red had been recuperating on his bed of pine needles for some time. Finally, he forced himself to stand and test his leg, and although the pain was less, his leg was stiff. So stiff he still could not lift it to pee, so he reluctantly relieved himself like a girl and was glad no one saw him. He walked a little, stretched, ate some soft snow, but felt listless, so he returned to his hospital bed —it had now been six days.

🐾

Before Europeans came to North America, wildlife of all varieties was abundant beyond anything we can imagine today. This incredible panoply of life needed no varmint control, no harvesting, no culling, no wildlife management, or whatever euphemism you can invent for killing. Pre-Columbian life was doing quite well, thank you. In a couple of centuries, we exterminated four billion passenger pigeons and two billion Carolina parakeets. The last parakeet died at the Cincinnati Zoo, in the same cage as Martha, the last passenger pigeon. The plains bison (buffalo) went from 25 million to just a handful that a few hunters with full magazines could have exterminated forever. "Buffalo" Bill Cody slaughtered 4,000 in two years.

With our so-called God-given morality, we have driven hundreds if not thousands of species to extinction. Remember the Bible tells us God gave us dominion over all life, and we have taken it with a vengeance. To paraphrase Carl Sagan, to get a species back from extinction, you must first create the universe. As I have written elsewhere, we must speak out against the senseless slaughter of all those who cannot speak for themselves. The wolves of each species (ecomorph) had their own nation. The original territory of the red wolf ran through the southeastern US from the Atlantic and Gulf Coast, north to Ohio River Valley and Pennsylvania, west to Central Texas and southeastern Missouri (*see* map). Today the only place you can find the few remaining red wolves is in eastern North Carolina, and unbelievably there is a campaign to exterminate even these remnants.

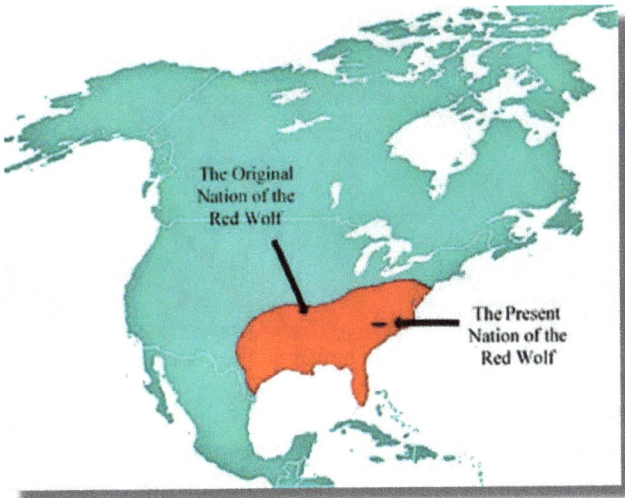

The Original Nation of the Red Wolf

The Present Nation of the Red Wolf

It is impossible to know how many red wolves existed before Europeans came to America—it may have been in the millions. But habitat destruction combined with poisoning, trapping, guns, and other horrors decimated their numbers. Slaughtering with Strychnine was the most common method of genocide where the victim convulses violently and dies from asphyxiation. By placing this poison in the carcass of a dead cow, say, you also killed eagles, foxes, fishers, and dogs resulting in a regular holocaust of living creatures. Today the Nation of the Red Wolf is gone, gone forever and of those millions, we now "allow" 40 to live in North Carolina. How generous of us. Released into this nature reserve in 1987, this small colony of red wolves is failing because of fierce opposition from game officials and hunters who are killing them.

The Nation of the Gray Wolf was more extensive than that of any other and its members more numerous. Nonetheless, guns, poison, and heartlessness extirpated every gray wolf from the lower 48 states in one of the greatest mass exterminations the world has ever witnessed. This was not *Dances with Wolves*,* but a waltz with the devil to extinction.

Kevin Costner as John Dunbar & Two Socks as Himself

The death scene of the gray wolf called Two Socks in the movie *Dances with Wolves* captures the pitilessness of this genocide. Six US cavalry soldiers are transporting a shackled and

---

* *Google* "Dances with Wolves and Two Socks" for the YouTube videos from the movie starring Kevin Costner and a wolf named Two Socks.

beaten John Dunbar, as played by Kevin Costner, in the back of an open wagon to his execution. Unexpectedly, Two Socks appears on the horizon searching for Dunbar, his human friend. For "sport" the soldiers—with that ageless machoism—take turns shooting at the wolf as he zigzags across the hilltop trying to avoid the bullets while keeping Dunbar in sight. The hero, realizing what the soldiers are doing, tries to strangle one of them with the chains on his wrists only to knocked unconscious. Because Two Socks will not give up his quest, inevitably one of the cavalry soldiers shoots him, and he cries in agony and is left to die in the prairie shortgrass under an open sky. Nevertheless, the reader or the watcher should not conclude this was a meaningless death, but a profound statement on the love of a man for a wolf and a wolf for a man.

Head Trap on a Live Wolf

Guns and poison were only two of the methods used to exterminate the Nation of the Gray Wolf. Those "men" who did this had an array of sadistic devices that would have gladdened the heart of any cretin in the Inquisition or the Gestapo—chief among these were a series of steel traps. These wretches bait the traps, leaving them for days, weeks, even months before they return to gather the dead. Most of the unfortunate wolves do not die at once, but blessed death comes only after hours or even days of agony. The wolf in the head trap (*see* photograph) is still alive and able to stand; this appalling device has certainly crushed his windpipe and death, if not easy, will be inevitable. Strychnine almost seems a blessing in comparison. The wolf in the leg trap appears to have been in a horrific struggle which he will surely lose. To spare the reader further horror, I decline to describe decapitating snares and other demonic devices.

Leg Trap on a Live Wolf

Wolf and Fox Hunt by Peter Paul Rubens circa 1616
Metropolitan Museum of Art in New York

Concerning wolves in Europe and Russia, although the methods were often different, the results were the same, more rivers of death. As if human hatred of wolves was not enough to eradicate these animals, governments offered *bounties*. This could be a significant sum depending on your circumstances. Solon of Athens (circa 600 BCE) was the first to offer a bounty for killing a wolf—not something to be remembered for. To claim your money, you had to present proof of the animal's death: its ears, tongue, tail, pelt, or a front paw. To a lesser extent, Canada and the US also supplied rewards for slaughtering wolves.

Any perfunctory search on Google of "Wolf Hunting" will uncover long dreary lists of wolves slaughtered, and prizes paid in every country across Europe and all through Russia to the Ural Mountains and deep into Asia. What follows are two examples (courtesy of Wikipedia) on wolf hunting and bounties:

In 19th century Spain, the Principality of Asturias passed an act between March and December 1816 paying out bounties for the death of 76 adult and 414 young wolves at 160 reales for an adult wolf and 32 for a wolf cub. The hunting of wolves represented a considerable source of wealth for local populations, with the "lobero" or wolf-hunter being a respected county figure.

In Communist Romania, up to 2,800 wolves were killed between 1955 and 1965. During the reign of Nicolae Ceaușescu, a reward equal to a quarter of a month's pay was offered to rangers killing wolf cubs. Full-grown wolves killed by any method at all resulted in as much as a half-month's pay.

Yet the number of wolves killed in Europe—especially before WWI—pales in comparison to the holocaust in the USA. There are two reasons for this. Hunting of any animal was the right and privilege of the mounted gentry, not the common folk and certainly not the surfs in Russia. (*See* the painting, *Wolf and Fox Hunt* by Rubens illustrating this point.) Secondly, these "common folk" had no Winchester rifles, Colt 45s, or firearms of any kind.

Everything about Russia is big. It is the world's largest country covering 11 time zones over two continents. Flag-wavers once said that the sun never set on the British Empire; that honor now belongs to Russia. So, with respect to killing wolves, they also win the coveted ring of blood. Their methods and results varied from czarist times to the USSR to present-day Russia. In 1858, the czarist regime paid $1,250,000 in bounties for *over* 1,000,000 dead wolves. These authorities, however, became suspicious that all the wolf tails the peasants submitted were not real, let us hope so. The USSR was relentless in its pursuit of wolves for they slaughtered 1,500,000 wolves at about a ruble a wolf. In today's Russia, wolf hunting continues minus any bounty with an average of 14,000 wolves a year taken mostly by trappers.

From all these countries, you get a whiff of Teutonic pride in the endless pages of bounties paid for killing wolves, like those lists from Auschwitz and Buchenwald. But for wolves, there was no Schindler's List of survivors, only agony and death. This mindless slaughter leads to some of the darkest places in the human heart. We either forgot or never knew that wolves are sentient beings who, like us, feel pain, know cruelty, and recognize love. Wolves may be just animals, but humans are just beasts.

Of all creatures great and small, wolves are closest to us socially, more so than chimpanzees, more than bonobos. Like us, they have a social structure with mates, mothers, fathers, brothers, sisters, aunts, and uncles; like us, they are tender and loving in their care of the young, and like us, they will defend their territory and their pups to the death. Furthermore, wolves care for each other and have a system of wild justice that we will explore in a later chapter. These complex animals have been our constant companions for millennia; they have trekked across continents with us; they came into the Americas with us during the last ice age. They were our first wild companions. Those humans who do not know wolves say they were the first *domesticated* animal. No, no, you do not domesticate wolves. If you are fortunate, they will accept you as a pack member. Wolves are the essence of the wilderness and are never truly broken.

Miraculously, despite two and half millennia of purges, poisonings, guns, traps, and spears remnants of Europe's original wolves managed to hang on in a few places. Down the spine of Italy in the Apennine Mountains and in the Spanish Pyrenes, you could always find wolves. These are special places. Humans have long ago extirpated wolves from England, Ireland, Scotland, and Wales plus Western Europe. There are still a few in Romania, Bulgaria, and Ukraine. Chernobyl benefited wolves and other wildlife. Humans moved out; wolves moved in and are doing exceptionally well with no signs of radiation poisoning.

Today, across Europe, there are numerous large eddies, those upstream swirls where wolves are making a comeback. The European Union (EU) in its humanity and wisdom protects wolves, despite a tide of hostility from some politicians. Incredibly, the first wolf in 100 years recently trotted into Belgium. Germany has 60 packs, and the Iberian Peninsula now has 3,000 of these beautiful animals. It would seem the EU has been good for the gray wolf.

Scotland has a program called *rewilding*: the reintroduction of extirpated animals to restore a balanced ecosystem inspired by the astonishing results of Yellowstone (*see* pages 64-65). It is already happening. The beaver—a keystone species—was introduced first and the lynx is scheduled next. Can the wolf be far behind?

Two private landowners, one who intends to import wolves from Sweden and the other who already has wolves on his property, wish them to run free in the glens and over the hills of Scotland. Whether these wolves are in cages or behind fences, they will escape, breed, and set up new packs in different areas. Queen Elizabeth may soon have them on her estates at Balmoral. And they will enter England by dancing over Hadrian's wall. Wales will be next! Dylan Thomas reflects wistfully on the passing of wolves in *A Child's Christmas in Wales*,

> *Years and years ago, when I was a boy, when there were wolves in Wales, and birds the color of red-flannel petticoats. . .*

One fine day, wolves will return to Wales—count on it!

Walt Whitman, in his arresting poem "Animals,"* makes some interesting observations:

> *I think I could turn and live with animals,*
> *they are so placid and self-contain'd,*
> *I stand and look at them long and long.*
> *They do not sweat and whine about their condition,*
> *They do not lie awake in the dark and weep for their sins,*
> *They do not make me sick discussing their duty to God,*
> *Not one is dissatisfied, not one is demented*
> > *with the mania of owning things,*
> *Not one kneels to another, nor to his kind*
> > *that lived thousands of years ago,*
> *Not one is respectable or unhappy over the whole earth.*

Wolves look neither to heaven nor earth. Their salvation lies elsewhere. They depend solely on their pack and on themselves. Plainly as history shows that if wolves were religious, humans would play the part of Satan himself.

We are puny creatures! We are parasites devouring the third planet of an ordinary star, one of 300 billion, in a small arm of an out-of-the-way spiral galaxy, a minor part of the Local Group of Galaxies, a minute fraction of the Virgo Super-Cluster, one of innumerable such clusters. Truly we are a mere mote in the eye of the universe.

Yet, science has given us a vision of the cosmos built on evidence. It is a world of such wonders as were never dreamed or deciphered by any astrologer or theologian. You and I, wolf and man, are splendid creatures! Both are rolled out of stardust, baked in the furnace of creation. "What a piece of work is a man and wolf, how noble in reason, how infinite in faculties, in form and moving how express and admirable, in action how like an angel, in apprehension how like a god!" (Hamlet, Act II, Scene 2.) All in all, man and wolf are beautiful species among many species on a little blue marble named Earth—the only known planet with life, and we must care for each other.

---

* Walt Whitman, from *Song of Myself*

I adopt the ethic of Albert Schweitzer as expressed in his cele-brated phrase *Reverence for Life*. James Brabazon said this elo-quently in his biography of Schweitzer:

> *Reverence for Life says that the only thing we are really*
> *sure of is that we live and want to go on living. This is some-*
> *thing that we share with everything else that lives, from el-*
> *ephants to blades of grass—and, of course, every human*
> *being. So, we are brothers and sisters to all living things,*
> *and owe to all of them the same care and respect, that we*
> *wish for ourselves.*

The Nation of the Gray Wolf cascaded down the river of death to the eternal sea of extinction. But rivers have eddies, those swirls, and whirlpools at the stream's edge that flow backward: the rein-troduction of wolves into Yellowstone on January 12, 1995, is one such eddy.

A small crowd of humans welcomed a long white truck as it drove through the Roosevelt Arch with its precious cargo of eight gray wolves from Jasper National Park in Alberta, Canada. After being absent for a biblical lifetime, wolves returned to Yellow-stone,* and things have never been the same.

In the years that followed, extraordinary events happened in the Park. As expected, the elk population declined and hence the dev-astation of their overgrazing. Unexpected events also occurred. As-pen and other trees, formerly eaten as pasture by the elk, began to grow along the edges of rivers and streams. This, in turn, attracted many long-absent birds and other creatures, chief among them, the beaver. Now these industrious rodents eat the bark from aspen trees and build damns. Beavers are what ecologists call a *keystone spe-cies* because so many other creatures depend on the pond formed by their damns: ducks, muskrats, otters, turtles, snakes, fish, frogs, minnows, insects, and so on. This must have been what the park was like before man exterminated the wolves, life in all its abun-dance.

Initially, the rangers housed these eight wolves in three large acclimation pens and fed them elk to get a taste for their unfamiliar

---

* *Google* "How wolves change rivers" for the YouTube video.

environment. But trouble started almost immediately upon their release. The alpha male, whom the park staff called "The Big Guy," with his powerful homing instinct, would have none of this pampering. He left the park shortly after his release and headed north into Montana on his way back to Canada. And his pregnant mate, "Natasha," followed him. As the crow flies, it is about 700 miles (1,125 km) from Yellowstone to Jasper National Park, or three or more times that as the wolf walks—Odysseus would be intimidated. Before long, the alpha female needed a birthing den, and her mate stayed to help her. Their pups were the first wolves born in the lower 48 states in a lifetime: four males and four females. Since the alpha was a phenomenal provider, the pups matured quickly, and their future looked bright.

Then a few weeks after this couple entered Montana, everything changed and that ancient human animus toward wolves resurfaced—a rancher for no reason but his primitive machoism, shot and killed this magnificent animal nicknamed The Big Guy. The government charged this "man" with slaughtering a protected species, and he eventually served three months in jail plus paid a fine. This was progress.

Fortunately, the park officials recaptured the alpha female with her eight pups and returned them to the safety of the park. To this day, over the rolling hills of Yellowstone and down its beautiful valleys the genes—those immortal coils—of The Big Guy and Natasha still run, hunt, and sing.

A Yellowstone Wolf of the Druid Pack

Before the millennium, conservationists placed gray wolves in several areas, and they were doing so well that their progeny had spread beyond the park's invisible boundaries into the river of death. Conflict with ranchers was inevitable, so the battle for the survival of gray wolves continues. A study in 2010 by the U.S. Department of Agriculture showed that out of 1.7 million cattle deaths that year, predators caused only 2.3 percent. And chief among these were coyotes, dogs, and mountain lions. Nevertheless, for centuries, wolves have taken on mythical status as a bloodthirsty killer. Except for a pitiful few, the Nation of the Red Wolf is finished, gone to extinction everyone. In the future you will only find them ceaselessly pacing in zoos—no fit place for a wolf and they know it.

🐾

It was now the *eighth day* since Big Red had sought shelter under a sizeable white pine tree. From a nearby marsh, he could hear male red-winged blackbirds calling to attract mates and establishing property—a classic spring sound of wetlands across this vast continent. Blackbirds arrive quietly in the dead of night by twos and threes. They hide until the first gray of morning fills the east, and the barred owls cease calling. Then at some unknown signal, they shake themselves, ruffling their feathers and expanding their breasts and tails. Their wings drape like a cloak, exposing large red insignia, fringed with gold, that flash from their shoulders. Then like some avian Pavarotti, they burst forth with their irrepressible aria *conk-a-reee, conk-a-reee, conk-a-reee!* To rivals, it asserts, "This land is my land,"

Red-winged Blackbird

but to everyone else, it declares, "Winter is dead," although the woods are still knee-deep in snow.

Big Red noticed the birds had stopped calling, deepening the silence of the forest, and he sensed this day would be different. The air was warm and muggy, which was unusual for early April when it happened.

Abruptly the sky lit up in a crystal light and the thunder followed, rolling between the clouds and the land awakening all sleeping nature. Majestic and powerful, this was spring's first storm. And when the theatrics had passed the rain came in cascading sheets melting the snow and quickening the land in rivulets of water. In the space of an hour, the water flooded Big Red's bed, causing him to move to higher ground near the tree's trunk. Several inches of snow had melted. Spring was coming in!

The air was warmer now when he thought he saw something move near the base of the tree. It was so small, he supposed he might eat it for a snack. And then it moved again! Big Red was sure it was dead for he had lived long enough to know that once dead no one returns—certainly not his two sisters and brother who died as pups. Again, this frozen blob* twitched something that might be a leg. This object—the size of your thumb to the knuckle—was not breathing, and without breath, there is no life. Then it twitched on its other side, mesmerizing our wolf—this was something he had never seen before. Slight movements, if that is what they were, continued for an hour. The ice crystals on its tiny body melted away, and its "head" rose slightly. And at that exact moment, its body expanded, and it took a breath! Big Red's eyes opened wide in wonderment because this bizarre thing that was dead was now alive. Since this blob had thawed, he recognized it as a frog common in the forest that he and his siblings often chased and pounced on. Big Red had witnessed the resurrection of a wood frog (*see* photograph).

Frozen Wood Frog

* *Google* "wood frog thawing"

He had been standing for some time watching this incredible amphibian, his leg felt strong but a little stiff from inactivity. Since the frog's transformation was complete, deep instincts directed it to the newly formed vernal ponds to create a new generation of these tiny creatures to wander the forest floor. *It hopped away, and as it did, Big Red walked away into the eternal evergreen forest in the direction of home.*

Big Red Walking

CHAPTER HEADER

Chapter—6

THE WARRAHS

Our task must be to free ourselves . . . by widening
our circle of compassion to embrace all living
creatures and the whole of nature and its beauty.
Albert Einstein, Letter reprinted in *The New York Times*, March 29, 1972

Dusk had come by the time Big Red stopped trotting and sought shelter for the night. His leg was no longer stiff but his entire body ached; he needed to rest. Those days of inactivity had taken their toll; he was not as strong as before, but he could at least raise his leg to pee like a true alpha male. His strength would return, but for now, he sensed he could not chase down a deer and certainly not a moose. During the day, he heard distant ravens giving their *chaos call* to attract other ravens and wolves to open a carcass. This was a good sign and he felt positive as he crawled onto a huge log to avoid the meltwater and spend the night.

Big Red Resting on a Log

In the morning, our wolf had a snack. While passing through a lowland grove, he easily caught the strangely unaware spruce grouse. This attractive bird employs an unusual defense tactic:

it relies on its camouflage and stillness to an extreme degree. So much so that it lets people and other predators approach within a foot or so before taking flight. This behavior has earned it the nickname "fool hen." Humans have killed them whenever they met.

Spruce Grouse

Nevertheless, this behavior persists, implying it works more often than not. Had it been otherwise, *natural selection* would have quickly assigned this stratagem to the dustbin of bad adaptations. This is not friendly behavior on the part of the grouse, just another survival strategy. On remote islands and in isolated places around the world, *friendly animals* do exist—places where man has rarely frequented.

Although his sleep was restless due to hunger, Big Red stayed on his log bed until the sun grew from red to round. Sparkling beads of ice covered his thick winter fur and the ground had frozen overnight, allowing easy walking. The air was incredibly fresh and crisp, tickling his nose. Despite his bed being hard—he had never known any other—he felt in prime shape, although still not capable of catching large prey. It had been a couple of weeks since his last big meal, and he was hungry. The spruce grouse was a small snack of mostly feathers and strange tasting flesh—no drumsticks, just two toothpicks, and some breast meat. He needed a real meal.

The forest all around him was coming back to life after its long winter sleep. From a nearby pond, he could hear the odd duck-like call of the thawed wood frogs. Overnight, the raucous purple grackles joined their cousins the red-winged blackbirds to take part in the morning cacophony. Other noises punctuated the typically quiet forest: red squirrels and northward-bound Canada geese together with sounds he did not recognize. In the distance, Big Red again heard the *chaos calls* of ravens and observed two turkey vultures slowly circling in the same direction. He trotted off toward them. Breakfast was nearby.

Our wolf was cautious, however, because anything large enough to attract a retinue of avian admirers must also attract other

An Eagle with Ravens

animals. What creature's death was causing such joy in this harsh land? Even when he was a mile (1.6 km) distant, his keen senses told him there were no wolves—but these same senses also told him there were other creatures there. Now treading quietly, he soon reached the site of all the commotion. He scanned for wolves, and as he expected, saw none. However, a bald eagle (*see* photograph) was busy trying to open a gigantic carcass when a fisher loping out of the forest caused him to take flight along with most of the ravens. Big Red was familiar with these giant weasels, and he knew they were a rough piece of business.

Yet, the moment Big Red showed himself, the fisher scampered up an aspen tree (*see* photograph) to wait his turn along with the bald eagle. Winter's deadly grip had long since frozen this massive carcass that heavy spring rains had recently revealed. Since he was uncertain what this behemoth was, Big Red dug around its still covered head.

Fisher

The snow was soft and he soon laid bare this animal's body. Our wolf was surprised he had not known this animal's identity instantly. Here was the carcass of a cow moose—a frozen bonanza for all the creatures of Algonquin Park.

What could kill such a majestic animal and leave no open wounds or overt signs of trauma? Little did Big Red know that the frozen bodies of more than 100 moose dotted the park, supplying a feast for all its birds and mammals. Fortunately for him, the local pack on whose territory he was trespassing, was dining elsewhere on another such frozen moose. But again, I ask the question, who was the killer here? The answer is small, disgusting, and on-going. The killer is a parasitic tick* that, even when engorged with blood and the size of a grape, the moose can tolerate. But when they come in tens of thousands, clustering in ghastly groups, they are a lethal force.

Ghost Cow Moose

The number of ticks on these animals varies from year to year depending on the fall and spring weather—global warming has made the situation far worse. Incredibly, a moose can endure 10,000 to 50,000 ticks over the winter without dangerous health effects. But tick loads of over 75,000 cause harmful effects lead-ing to death. These blood-sucking parasites sometimes cover the poor animal's eyes and the blood-rich areas on and around the genitals. Blood loss can be so significant that the moose develops anemia. The animal becomes so irritated by these ticks that they rub off their brown fur, revealing a white under skin inducing hy-pothermia. Appropriately, observers call these "ghost moose" (*see* photograph), and the angel of death is in close attendance. With their skinny necks and emaciated bodies and large hairless patches, these animals stagger through the forest like zombies from *The Walking Dead* and because of this, Big Red hardly rec-ognized them. At this place and at that time, this cow had lain

---

* Elsa the famous lioness celebrated in a series of books by Joy Adamson died from a tick-borne blood disease. See *Born Free*.

down to rest never to rise again. Every creature has a last step, a final beat, in a train of billions—all good things end.

Mercifully, all those horrible ticks were now dead together with the equally appalling lungworms caught in the throat of the moose while trying to leave the carcass like rats abandoning a sinking ship. Big Red knew none of this or needed to. The eagle and the fisher watched enviously from their separate trees as he expertly opened the carcass, and with the sideways bite of his carnassial teeth, he wolfed down chunks of moose flesh.

When he had taken his fill, he left the carcass to the fisher and the eagle with their retinue of ravens. The vultures sitting in the trees like sentinels would be the last to eat.

Algonquin Park rests on the Precambrian Shield, the remains of ancient mountains made small by time and fate to rolling hills and rocky outcrops. The soil is fertile, but thin like butter on bread, and in places entirely missing. Our wolf climbed a rocky knoll to avoid the spring melt and made his bed for the night under a scaggy jack pine. It was a good campsite, dry with a view in most directions. He fell asleep quickly, his full stomach soothing him— it was warm in the belly of the wolf.

Islands are strange places. They have fewer animals than the mainland, and those they do have are often bizarre and found nowhere else. Moreover, these animals are usually smaller than their mainland cousins. Consider the pygmy mammoths on the Channel Islands off the coast of California or the miniature humans from the island of Flores in Indonesia. For examples of island animals that are unusual and found nowhere else, consider the Galapagos with its marine iguanas and Mauritius with its dodos. Since these animals have never or seldom seen humans, they are overly friendly—always a deadly trait for them. Geographical isolation on islands is one of the vectors for "descent with modification" often called evolution.

A young man was hanging over the side of a Royal Navy ship retching with every roll. He pulled his coat snuggly around him for the ocean spray was icy and the wind frigid as the ship rolled onward to the Falkland Islands. Despite these dismal appearances, this was going to one of the greatest adventures of all time.

Charles Darwin

He would visit several island archipelagos, and his observations of their varied life forms would change our understanding of the natural world.

As the waters calmed and his stomach emptied, the young man turned away from the sea and revealed himself as Charles Darwin. His assistant Syms Covington* came up on deck to enquire after him. They greeted each other in a friendly manner and Darwin assured Covington his seasickness was normal when the ocean was rough. They did not speak any further but stood quietly in the spray and the darkness, each wondering what this voyage would mean to them, and what strange beasts they would encounter. They were from different worlds, but their lives would intertwine in unexpected ways. Necessarily each had some reservations about each other, yet they were friends.

When he was 15 years old, Covington became "fiddler & boy to the Poop-cabin" of the HMS *Beagle* during her second survey expedition voyage. Later, Captain Robert Fitzroy appointed him to assist Charles Darwin and be his personal servant—a position he retained after their return to England. Covington, who is all but forgotten to history, played a pivotal role in the collection of bird and animal species which afterward formed the bedrock evidence for Darwin's theory of natural selection.

Syms Covington

To be sure, there was an unavoidable air of an upstairs-downstairs relationship between these young men. Darwin's father was a doctor with a house full of servants while Covington's father

---

* See *Mr. Darwin's Shooter* by Roger McDonald. The *Wall Street Journal* wrote, "A gripping rendering of Covington's struggle to reconcile his faith with his contribution to the theory of evolution."

was a butcher with a house full of children. With some truth, we could say that the assistant provided the data that the master wove into his grand theory. Yet nowhere in any of his books is Covington mentioned by name. Instead, Darwin calls him "my servant," a designation Covington detested. To escape England's caste system, he emigrated to Australia, married, and had eight children. When his copy of *On the Origin of Species* arrived in Australia, he must have been disappointed that his name appeared only as "my servant." His simple tombstone in Pambula, New South Wales, correctly and proudly announces him as the "Assistant to Charles Darwin."

This young Charles Darwin was not the old man with the great beard in a long black cowl we are all familiar with. In Argentina, Darwin would ride 50 miles a day (80 km) on horseback, avoiding Indian attacks and camping with the Gauchos on the Pampas. In Peru, he climbed the Andes to 13,000 feet (3,960 m) to collect seashells. In the South Seas, he swam and dove in its beautiful atolls as modern tourists do. The author adorns his book *The Voyage of the Beagle* with references to the beauty of the native girls. No, no, this is not the domesticated Darwin of Down House, but an explorer of strange lands and innovative ideas. Unlike his friend Covington, Darwin was buried with the immortals in Westminster Abbey, beside Newton.

Darwin was not the first to visit the Falklands, but he was the first to arrive with a sharp eye for detail and biology. John Byron commander of HMS *Dolphin* landed on these islands in 1765 to encounter its unique animal. He dropped anchor offshore and lowered a rowboat with instructions to proceed up a small inlet to land on a sandy beach. The sailors expertly manned the oars and with swift strokes rounded a rocky point and aimed directly for the beach. For the animals watching from the grassy dunes, the sailors must have been a strange sight. Seeing they were coming, four of these animals bolted for the beach to welcome the newcomers. Terrified, the sailors thought these wolfen animals were fierce, not friendly. With no time to get in the rowboat, they retreated waist deep into the chilly water where these persistent animals followed them. Quickly, the water turned red, followed by floating bodies. How many of these creatures died, I cannot say, but the sailors all survived. The following day, Byron went ashore with his men and killed six more. These were the warrahs.

The Warrah by John Gerrard Keulemans

Darwin and Covington visited the Falklands twice, and they were astonished to find these isolated islands had a fox-like wolf with the classic white-tipped tail that the locals called the warrah. Before the Welsh and Scottish immigrants colonized these islands, they were uninhabited and hence the warrah had developed no fear of humans. The Falklands may have had two distinct species of this wolf. Darwin—always the close observer—wrote that the warrahs of the West and East Falkland Islands were but variants that differed depending on which island they came from:

> When I see these Islands in sight of each other, & possessed of but a scanty stock of animals, tenanted by these birds but slightly differing in structure & filling the same place in Nature, I must suspect they are only varieties. The only fact of a similar kind of which I am aware is the constant asserted difference between the wolf-like Fox of East & West Falkland Islands. If there is the slightest foundation for these remarks, the zoology of Archipelagoes will be well worth examining; for such facts undermine the stability of Species. [1]

The Falklands with its warrahs had all the ingredients that Darwin later found on the Galapagos Islands with its tortoises and finches. From his observations, Darwin predicted the extinction of the warrah; little did he realize it would happen in his lifetime. Consider the following entry from *The Voyage of the Beagle*:

> The Gauchos, also, have frequently killed them in the evening, by holding out a piece of meat in one hand, and in the other a knife ready to stick them. As far as I am aware, there is no other instance in any part of the world, of so small a mass of broken land, distant from a continent, possessing so large a quadruped peculiar to itself. Their numbers have rapidly decreased; they are already banished from that half of the island which lies to the eastward of the neck of land between St. Salvador Bay and Berkeley Sound. Within a very few years after these islands shall have become regularly settled, in all probability this fox [wolf] will be classed with the dodo, as an animal which has perished from the face of the earth.[2]

Warrahs are the only canid—a member of the dog family—to go extinct in recorded history. Some heartless cretin slaughtered the final one in 1876 at Shallow Bay, West Falkland Islands. As Darwin noted, they maintained their friendliness to the last animal. The final warrah ran to greet his executioner who rewarded him with a bullet to the head.

The genes inside this lifeless warrah had "lived" in an unbroken line for 3.8 billion years back to the first cells—back to the moment when life began. Now they were gone forever! Carl Sagan once remarked, "If you want to make an apple pie from scratch, you must first create the universe." What is true of apple pies is even more real of any living thing. But Sagan was mistaken! If you could create the universe again, you *would not* get another apple pie or another warrah. All the infinite contingencies of history are against you. Just as if your parents had another child, it would not be you. Why? The possible gene combinations are mind-bogglingly large. No, once gone, a species is gone for all eternity.

> *The Moving-Finger writes and having- writ,*
> *Moves on; nor all your piety nor wit*
> *Shall lure it back to cancel half a line,*
> *Nor all your tears blot out a word of it.*
> Omar Khayyam, *The Rubaiyat*

The warrah and you stand alone, unique in all existence, everywhere and always.

It is fortunate for the executioner of the last warrah that his name is unknown. What must he have thought of his bloody handiwork? I suspect that with his testosterone-flooded brain, he thought nothing at all. He kicked the carcass to be sure the warrah was dead and swaggered away to regale his mates with tales of his hunting prowess. As the executioner strutted away, a large hawk flew overhead carving small circles in the sky.

I wrote the following doggerel to commemorate this extinction event.

THE LAST WARRAH

Bleak, bleak land of sand and snow
Home where seals and seabirds go
Land without trees where only grasses grow
Home of the curious warrah.
Overly friendly and easy to know
When the last warrah met its final man,
There was death inside the warrah
And darkness inside the man.

A loud crash in the direction of the moose carcass abruptly awoke Big Red. On his feet and alert, he knew it was not wolves—the scent was that of a bear. A great bruin newly awakened from hibernation had been led to the carcass by its aroma. Since the bear had neither peed nor pooped for six months, it would take a week or more for his system to start running correctly, and so he was unlikely to eat. Unconcerned, our wolf relieved himself high up on the jack pine tree, walked in small circles over his bed, and went back to sleep.

Now that the warrah was gone, many wondered where it came from. The Falkland Islands are not visible from the beaches of Argentina, nor were they ever geologically connected. Stories abounded on the warrah's origin. Some thought they swam from the mainland, others mused that the natives brought them in boats, and still others proposed they originated on these islands. All these speculations were without evidence or merit.

The Maned Wolf of South America

Scientists unraveled the mystery of the warrah's origin using the marvel of DNA. The history—the deep history—of every living thing has a record written in their blood. Unexpectedly, it turned out that the warrah's closest relative is the maned wolf (*see* photograph), a long-legged, fox-like South American canid.

Knowing the warrah's closest living relative only deepened the mystery of how it arrived on the Falklands 200 miles (320 km) from the mainland. Evidence suggests, however, that during the last ice age, only 20 miles (32 km) of frozen ocean separated these islands from Argentina—a situation not unlike Beringia. And the warrahs could quickly have chased penguins across this frozen waste to the rich bounty of bird life on the islands.

The warrah's occupation of the Falklands acts as a precedent for the coyotes streaming into Newfoundland across the frozen Gulf of St. Lawrence in 1985. No other carnivore in modern times has expanded its range as successfully as the coyote, moving from the western United States throughout most of eastern North America in the last 100 years. The Nation of the Red Wolf (*see* pages 57-58) forms only part of their vast territory. Coyotes are the ultimate ryders in the whirlwind, making a new life in a new land; they went forth and multiplied. Coyotes are the warrahs of today.

Darwin called the warrah the Antarctic wolf, but modern researchers named it *Dusicyon australis*, the foolish dog of the south, which says more than they intended.

Ａ

The universe had been kind to a wounded wolf and Big Red knew it, as he rose from his bed just before sunrise. The raucous calls of ravens, already at the moose carcass, filled the chilly morning air. Fishers, martens, and foxes had fed on its bounty overnight. For once, food was abundant in this harsh land.

When he arrived at the carcass, the ravens left momentarily, but six huge turkey vultures scuttled a few steps away. Big Red took only a single bite since he was still stuffed. With a full stomach and his great vigor restored, our wolf's thoughts turned to home and his natal pack. His whole being longed for home, so he went westward toward a large body of water humans call Lake Vireo.

Big Red Going Home

This was an unfortunate choice! John and Mary Theberge, in their marvelous book *Wolf Country: Eleven Years Tracking the Algonquin Wolves,* detail the extraordinary life of a large wolf who claimed this area as his own and was known to kill trespassers. Big Red knew this lone wolf from an earlier encounter, but because of his overconfidence, he expected no confrontation he could not handle. Through the writings of the Theberges and others, this animal became known as the Vireo Lake wolf:

He seemed to have an aptitude for finding other pack's kills, which may have been crucial to his survival as a lone wolf. Only four days after taking advantage of the Jocko Lake pack's kill, he was inseparable from the air from a Jack Pine wolf at another deer carcass. At least twice that winter, however, he appeared to have made his own kills. Although old,* he was a big, strong wolf. [3]

As I said, this was an unfortunate choice by Big Red!

* By counting the annular rings in one of his incisor teeth, he proved to be 10 years old, the second oldest wolf recorded in Algonquin Park, the oldest known, Redpole 4, died at 15. And the record for wolf longevity anywhere goes to Madadh (Maddie), who lived to 19 in a UK compound.

Chapter—7

DEATH AT LAKE VIREO

Thou know'st 'tis common; all that lives must die,
Passing through nature to eternity.
Shakespeare, *Hamlet* Act 1, scene 2

For several days, Big Red had been aware that someone was following him, and this time it was not ravens. He thought he knew who it might be, but often the mind knows only that which lies near the heart. Twice he circled back to see his admirer. Nevertheless, his phantom follower eluded him both times. When the time was right, he felt, *she* would reveal herself.

Our wolf was close to Lake Vireo, but he was watching the ponds because they thaw out long before larger bodies of water. Their relative shallowness and the rotting vegetable matter bring heat to the surface ice, making it unsafe to walk on. But for the beavers, this was liberation from six months of total darkness and tired, tasteless food. On the other hand, Big Red fancied a beaver for breakfast. In the spring and fall, the beavers of Algonquin Park make up 40 percent of the meat menu for wolves.

A Beaver at Breakfast

Wolves typically find beavers by happenstance while wandering in the forest and crossing one of their trails. By cutting off the beaver's access to water, the wolves have an easy kill and a large meal—as much as 44 lbs. (20 kg). Today was different. Today, Big Red was actively hunting them. He had found a hole in the ice of a pond with fresh aspen branches scattered about (*see* photograph). Hiding behind a nearby rock, he patiently waited for the rodent's return. It was not long before a giant beaver, pulling some budding boughs, appeared.

Hushed, Big Red waited for the perfect moment. Almost! Almost! He was on the rodent instantly, crushing its skull and spine with his incredibly powerful jaws, but the beaver managed to emit a piercing death cry which echoed far through the forest. All creatures great and small who heard it knew what it meant—including the Vireo Lake wolf. Since Big Red was also aware that the beaver's death cry might have attracted others, he carried it some distance to a small clearing in the forest. He placed the beaver carcass under a spruce tree and settled in for breakfast.

As if on cue, the Vireo Lake wolf stepped silently out of the forest to confront the trespasser and steal his meal. Big Red rose to meet the challenge from this formidable Algonquin wolf. But our wolf, with his unpredictability and overwhelming confidence, did something quite bizarre. He picked up the carcass of the beaver and placed in the middle of the small clearing to taunt his adversary saying, *take it if you dare.*

Wolf with Radio Collar

Before a fight, there is a sizing up of your opponent. Each wolf stood sideways to the other, displaying their full size some 20 feet (6 m) apart, as they strutted in counterclockwise circles around the carcass. Their tails were straight out and the hairs on the back of their necks were erect. Each snarled and snapped, ferociously exposing fearsome sets of teeth.

Big Red instantly saw there was something substantial around the Vireo wolf's neck—a thick, wide leather collar with a black box* the size of a pound of butter hanging from it (*see* photograph). This was a radio collar and transmitter that researchers had attached to track this wolf's every movement. An ugly thing like a goiter on your throat. Our wolf realized this collar would make it difficult for him to get a firm grip on the other wolf's neck.

Despite Hollywood and all the nature documentary films the reader may have seen, *wolves seldom fight*. I have photographed and videotaped a thousand wolves without ever seeing a fight. *Why?* Quite clearly, if you fight every day, you will be dead or severely injured in a week. Wolves have no doctors, no hospitals, and no health insurance—just nature's natural healing powers. Within a pack, fights are more like squabbles for disciplinary purposes and quickly forgotten afterward, unlike dogs who hold a grudge.

So Big Red and the Vireo Lake wolf sized each other up and realized they were equals. By this time, each was wild with testosterone when the phantom follower who had been watching from the forest walked out and stood beside our wolf as if to say, "I'll stand by you." Big Red recognized her as the young female and the first to stand up and let him pass at Grand Lake—we will call her Phantom. This immediately changed everything for Big Red's adversary.

Watcher in the Woods

---

* *Google*: Gordon Harrison, radio-collared wolf

The Vireo wolf quickly left this makeshift arena, biding his time for another day.

Despite a troubled past, these two wolves quickly accepted each other—as I said, wolves rarely hold grudges. Big Red shared the beaver with her in an ersatz wedding banquet. After dining and with open displays of tenderness, their bodies cuddled and curled together as they tried to sleep. Since wolves, unlike humans—who are ready and eager for sex 24/7/365—reach estrus only once a year in January or February, coupling would have to wait. Nevertheless, our wolf had a mate—a beautiful, young, healthy companion, so he might yet be a father.

Their honeymoon at Vireo Lake continued for a week. By now, the ice on the lake was too soft and porous to allow them to cross on foot, so Big Red went south to get around this elongated body of water. On the sixth day, it happened! While our wolf was still asleep, Phantom went to the lake about 100 feet (30 m) away for a drink; the water tasted refreshingly cold. The Vireo Lake wolf, however, who had been shadowing them for days, caught her unaware and easily crushed her spine in one swift, powerful bite. But she too let forth a death cry, terrifying any animal still sleeping.

Instinctively, Big Red feared what it meant as he bolted toward the source of the sound. The Vireo wolf saw our wolf racing right at him. This time there was no sizing each other up just an epic struggle on the beach. Berserk with anger and anguish and perhaps because of his age advantage and quickness, Big Red managed to grip his opponent's neck with overwhelming force. Yet his teeth could not penetrate the leather collar, so he dragged the Vireo wolf deeper into the lake and forced his head under the water until all life escaped from his wildly writhing body. Afterward, he hauled the now floating

Big Red Berserk

corpse to shore and flung it like a rag on the sand. Staring in triumph and grief at the death all around him, he picked up the Phantom's still-warm body and carried her up the beach into the forest and gently placed her under a spruce tree. Turning away from her lifeless frame, he used his hind feet to kick fallen needles over her body in a futile attempt to hide it from scavengers. Yet he left the Vireo Lake wolf unmoaned, unattended, and uncovered on the beach.

He stood guard all through the night, preventing scavengers from eating Phantom's now rigid form. None appeared, but overnight, foxes and fishers found the Vireo wolf's corpse and devoured parts of it. Big Red had never killed another wolf before, and he refused to cannibalize it—just like humans, wolves rarely eat their own.

Early the following morning, a flock of ravens found the Vireo wolf carcass and consumed what they could. Just after sunrise, Big Red went down to the lake to get a drink. The ravens swooshed away in a flurry of wings, but he noticed something larger was approaching low over the water with enormous wings. These were not Valkyries come to gather the dead, but to eat them. From a great distance, six turkey vultures had picked up the stench of death and were coming to dine. It was too early in the year for the thumb-size black and orange carrion beetles to be out. But flies would soon find slivers of flesh and lay their maggot eggs, cleaning the bones to a glistening white in a few days.

Although Phantom was still intact because of her mate's diligence, internal deterioration went ahead at its inevitable pace. Unknown to Big Red, the same day the flies found the body of the Vireo Lake wolf, they also found Phantom. They laid their eggs in her mouth, eyes, ears, and anus. And soon her body began to smell, so our wolf scraped aside some of the spruce needles, and it was then that he saw the horror—hundreds of maggots wiggling in her mouth and eye sockets. He jumped back, aware of what this meant; he had seen it many times. This was the way of all flesh, and he could do nothing more. Now she was alone in the universe going back to her elemental forms. Walking away, he glanced back one last time.

Because he had not eaten for many days, he was thinking with his stomach. Another beaver? Several of their now ice-free ponds were nearby. The first he visited had a recently refurbished beaver lodge (*see* photograph) with bark-free sticks and mud. A wolf must catch a beaver on land to have any chance of killing it, and typically beavers are active at night not at noon.

Nonetheless, with his keen eyesight, Big Red noticed something on the left side of the lodge, low down, that the reader may have missed: a Canada goose sitting on her nest (*see* arrow). She did this every year and without protest from the lodge's builders. It was the right place for a nest, safe from most land predators. Geese, however, are not helpless but vigorous defenders of their nest and territory—a foolish fox that approaches a nest is sure to receive a beating. These large birds have two nasty weapons: the bite from their beak and the bruising from their wings. However, Big Red was not a fox, but he was a good, if slow, swimmer with

Classic Beaver Lodge

his dog-paddle strokes. On the side of the lodge opposite the goose, he silently entered the water swimming the short distance to the beavers' home. He scrambled up the lodge to its peak overlooking the goose. The bird being accustomed to the beavers' noisy repairs paid little attention. Big Red could see her clearly huddled low on her clutch of eggs, as he bounded down toward her. But the goose, aware of something we could neither see nor hear, flew off at the final moment. Yet, our wolf still had his dinner, a fine meal of six large eggs. The goose and the gander would have to build a fresh nest elsewhere and trust to better luck.

In the evening after sundown, Big Red went to that same pond. Now a pond at night in the springtime is a unique, even spiritual, place—a place beyond human and animal powers and control.

The spring peepers were in full chorus, creating the loudest sound for their size of any living creature. Only the male peepers sing; the females judge their performance. These tiny frogs—they can sit on your thumbnail—are easy to identify by the faint cross on their back, yet they are incredibly difficult to find.

Beavers, forever at work it seems, cause ripples on the black surface of the pond and the moon shivers. He could hear whip-poor-wills call in the distance as a night squadron of Canada geese honk their goodbyes northward bound for the tundra. Something splashes at the water's edge, perhaps a deer or bear taking an evening drink. Others join the peeper chorale: western chorus and wood frogs. A barred owl shouts out his curious call and two foxes bark at the slowly rising moon.

As this empowering oratorio of sound rolls over him, our wolf stands transfixed. It lifts him up; his spirit soars, and he knows he can do anything, anything at all. Just as he realizes this, the beavers stop swimming. The luminous body of water opens, dark and tranquil, from whose floor the new-bathed stars emerge, and shine upon Eden's pond.

Energized, he left the pond and sought higher ground to spend the night. High points allow for good vision and hearing of other wolves. Finding a treeless promontory overlooking the lake, he stretched out on a bed of soft moss growing in the cracks of the granite rocks. The vault of heaven was cloudless, and despite the moon, the stars shone with startling clarity. Big Red knew nothing about the stars, nothing at all. Yet they made him feel insignificant:

> *Looking up at the stars, I know quite well*
> *That, for all they care, I can go to hell.*
> W.H. Auden, "The More Loving One"

Instinctively he knew that any meaning he would have in life must come from within himself. For a few intense days, he had a mate who stood by him giving unexpected joy and purpose to his existence, but she was gone forever. And, he had justly killed her murderer, the Vireo wolf, who had been terrorizing this area for years. Sleep, troubled sleep, came slowly as starlight bathed his massive frame by an isolated lake, on a lonely planet, in a merciless universe.

♣

WHACK goes the beaver's tail, scattering the birds from the trees and the bushes. The spring peepers cease their incessant song; a once-sleepy muskrat plops below the pond's dark, glassy surface. And the painted turtles sunning themselves on a floating log slip silently into their watery realm. A few birds hold their ground crouching low on their nests while the bittern disappears into the bulrushes. By now, the beaver has reached the lodge greeting her two kits.

The cause of this disruption in the daily life of the pond is a canoe carrying two people, a man and a woman. Since it is spring and the beavers have babies, the young woman *pleads* with the man not to trap. But he says they need the money the fur will bring, so the trap is set by the lodge's underwater entrance. They paddle away without speaking, and the pond returns to its timeless ways.

The following morning the two canoeists return to discover both the trap and the beaver missing. The man knew he had securely staked the device to the pond bottom, placing it at the underwater entry to the lodge. Yet in her desperation, the mother beaver had pulled the stake out of the mud and died an agonizing death elsewhere, the trap's steel jaws clamping inexorably on her soft body while water flooded her lungs.

The trapper is disgusted at this outcome because not only had he lost the fur, but also the beaver had lost its life, and all for nothing—nothing at all. He unsuccessfully drags the water for her body. And, as a last resort, he destroys the dam partly draining the pond, but to no avail. All the life of this pond will now die; the dam buster has become the destroyer of worlds.

The trapper was an Englishman, Archie Belaney (aka Grey Owl), and the woman was a Mohawk, Gertrude Bernard (aka Anahareo), and their story was only beginning. But I will let Grey Owl speak for himself from his book *Pilgrims of the Wild* [1] in which he recounts this scene and its astonishing sequel:

So, we turned to go, finally and for good. As we were leaving I heard behind me a light splash, and looking back saw what appeared to be a muskrat lying on top of the water along side of the house. Determined to make this wasted day pay, I threw up my gun, and standing up in the canoe to get a better aim, prepared to shoot. At that distance a man could never miss, and my finger was about to press the trigger when the creature gave a low cry, and at the same instant I saw, right in my line of fire another, who gave out the same peculiar call. They could both be gotten with the one charge of shot.

They gave voice again, and this time the sound was unmistakeable—they were young beaver! I lowered my gun and said: "There are your kittens."

The instinct of a woman spoke out at once. "Let us save them," cried Anahareo excitedly, and then in a lower voice, "It is up to us, after what we've done."

And truly what had been done here looked now to be an act of brutal savagery. And with some confused thought of giving back what I had taken, some dim idea of atonement, I answered, "Yes; we have to. Let's take them home." It seemed the only fitting thing to do.

For the beaver and the two people in the canoe, that was the day everything changed. Anahareo encouraged Grey Owl to author books and articles on conservation and, with the help of their two pet beavers, they became worldwide celebrities. Fame followed! David and Richard Attenborough attended one of Grey Owl's conservation talks in England and were impressed. Much later, Richard Attenborough directed the film *Grey Owl* starring Pierce Brosnan. Belaney sat for a portrait by Yousef Karsh, met the king, and was feted everywhere.

After he died suddenly at age 49 of pneumonia, a newspaper article exposed his double life, yet in retrospect, none of that mattered. What remains of his life is monumental, as if a sculptor had blown away the chips from his marble or the nonsense from his existence to reveal its core. What remains is the restoration of the beaver that faced extinction when he and Anahareo picked up their cause and their babies. Not only were the beaver restored but also their dams and the incredible variety of life that the beaver encouraged all over this land.

We should thank Grey Owl and Anahareo—the names they preferred—for the return of the beaver and the existence of these ponds with all their remarkable beauty and life.

There are many who see little or no value in nature, certainly none in swamps, marshes, or beavers. I claim these people are dark inside—people who live for what we see in the film *Manufactured Landscapes* (a 2006 documentary film about the work of photographer Edward Burtynsky, free online): colossal factories, mega-quarries, and mammoth recycling centers. Henry David Thoreau was the patron saint of swamps and all wild places because he relished being in and writing about them, as this excerpt from his *Journal* reveals:

> *I seemed to have reached a new world, so wild a place...far away from human society. What's the need of visiting far-off mountains and bogs, if a half-hour's walk will carry me into such wildness and novelty?* Journal, August 30, 1856.

Beavers (*see* photograph) are what biologists call a keystone species. Without them, entire ecosystems would cease to exist including a multitude of birds, fish, frogs, insects, and mammals. Beaver dams, unlike most human concrete barriers, allow water to pass through. These furry creatures desire to keep the water at a fixed height to protect their lodge, not submerge it. So, every beaver dam has an outlet forming a rivulet or small stream.

A Keystone Species: The Beaver

As noted earlier, these rodents can grow to unexpected sizes with 44 lbs. (20 kg) not being unusual, and they make up 40 percent of the Algonquin wolf's diet. If Grey Owl and Anahareo had not saved the beaver from extinction, we would have lost many of our wolves—another reason the beaver is a keystone species. So, beavers help wolves. And as we saw in Yellowstone Park, wolves help beavers; they depend on each other.

Evolutionary biologist and gadfly Richard Dawkins* famously wrote, "The chicken is only an egg's way for making another egg." This is not as senseless as some may think. The egg holds all the genes for the chicken—we call this the genotype. These genes control the sum of the physical characteristics for the new-born chicken—we call this the phenotype. Essentially, the geno-type is in the egg; the phenotype is the chicken. This dichotomy fits all living things.

Over time, the genotype changes slightly due to natural selec-tion, and this, in turn, changes the phenotype. Again, this is true for all living things. The environment can change the phenotype during an individual's lifetime. For example, flamingoes are not born pink; they get this color because of the food they eat. This color change, however, has no effect on the genes.

Consider the deep ancestors of the beaver. In the Pleistocene period, which ended about 12,000 years ago, there were giant bea-vers—part of the megafauna. These rodents were *ten times* the size of the present ones weighing in at over 400 lbs. (180 kg). Appar-ently, they did not build dams, but may have dined exclusively on water plants for their incisors were six inches long, top and bot-tom. These teeth were better suited to digging than chewing off bark. Since their tails were not flat, they could not slap the water to warn of danger for *they were the danger*. This change in pheno-type came about through *minute* changes in the genotype to meet the conditions of the age they lived in. These genes—thousands of them—are the closest thing we have on earth to immortals, and most have existed for millions of years entirely unchanged. Daw-kins said he should have called his book *The Immortal Gene* rather than *The Selfish Gene*. It is humbling to realize we are merely throwaway survival machines to replace molecules (genes). This is just as true for wolves and beavers as it is for humans. To acknowledge this takes strength, courage, and wisdom.

---

* *See* YouTube video "Richard Dawkins *The Selfish Gene* explained."

🐾

The following morning, Big Red slept late awakened by something cold wriggling on his belly. Jumping to his feet, revealed three garter snakes who had slithered up from their hibernaculum to enjoy the warmth of Big Red's body. They reminded him of the maggots in Phantom's mouth, so he moved some distance away to avoid these serpents and reflect on his present situation. It was clear there were no other wolves around Vireo Lake and that he might inherit this territory. Should he stay? More directly, why was he still here? Was he in some strange sense still guarding Phantom's corpse?

Garter Snakes in a Woodpile

The sun had turned from deep red to yellow when he first heard distant murmurs from his promontory lookout. Something was coming! In the distance, the trees grew right to the water's edge hiding all life from his view. Closer to his lookout, sheets of granite cascaded down the incline to disappear beneath the waves. The sounds grew louder and seemed to come from near the forest's edge. These noises were foreign to him, so his alertness intensified, and he stood up. What was coming? He quickly trotted from the promontory and hid behind some cedar bushes.

The sounds became louder and more distinct, and then suddenly two creatures* exited from the trees onto the rocks. Walking upright on just their hind legs, they strutted like the lords of creation. When our wolf was a cub and living in the den on the hillside, one of these creatures occasionally walked by. Since then, Big Red was familiar with these creatures and did not fear, nor did he

---

* John and Mary Theberge

see them as food. These two had a black box in their front paws and appeared to be following some signal Big Red could neither hear, see, nor smell. He shadowed them. Before long, it became clear they were searching for the remains of the Vireo Lake wolf. When they found them, they picked up the goiter that had been around his neck and placed it in a sack. They even picked up his glistening white skull, wrapped it in something soft, and gently put it in another bag. Big Red thought, "Who are these aliens that do such bizarre things? Were they the ones who first put the goiter around the Vireo Lake wolf's neck? Why would any wolf let them do that?"

Unlike the man near his den (the author) when he was a pup, he feared these two. In that instant of clarity, he decided to leave this place and continue his long journey home. Somewhere deep in his heart, he knew he would always go. Not for a moment had he *truly* considered staying. Turning westward, he fled from this lake of horror and death without looking back.

The stars are fixed, but the planets wander. The woods are quiet, but the whip-poor-will sings. The forest is still, but the wolf runs on.

Chapter—8

OUT OF ASIA

All stories are about wolves.
All worth repeating, that is.
Anything else is sentimental drivel.
Margaret Atwood, *The Blind Assassin*

When he stopped running, the sun had already dropped below the horizon. All was still, almost lifeless, but that would prove to be the view of the tourist. Although he was hungry, he was also too tired to hunt, so he made his favorite bed under a white pine tree. All he could hear was his breathing and the snapping of twigs beneath his feet as he made his bed. After some time, he listened to a few frogs calling from a distant marsh and a lonely whip-poor-will who kept saying his name over and over again. This somnolent background soon lulled Big Red to sleep, into a deep, rewarding sleep.

Sometime after midnight, it happened. Without warning and without fanfare, the forest all around him burst forth in a tsunami of howls, the wild call of the Algonquin wolf. It sounded like a dozen wolves. What hell had he stumbled into? There was no question they were aware of his trespassing, and he needed to move instantly. Their calling was to flush him out of his hiding place.

Will-Poor-Will: Bird of Mystery

Although wolves can hear from a surrounding area of more than 100 mi.², these voices in the night were much, much closer. Instinctively, he ran westward. The forest was bright and clear, at least to a wolf with night vision and a gibbous moon. Within half a mile he encountered his first pack member, a small female who wisely let him pass for she knew wolf strength lay more in numbers than in individuals. But she followed, and others soon joined her. Never lacking self-assurance, our wolf felt confident he could outrun the entire pack. Nonetheless, something lay ahead he had not counted on—an enormous lake. Running along the shore, looking for a way around this obstacle, he was soon standing belly-deep in ice-cold water with a semi-circle of wolves on the beach advancing toward him.

With the pack of wolves within striking distance, our wolf made the fateful decision to swim across the frigid lake at night. The other wolves thought they might swim as well. He could not see the far side, but with most of his winter fur still intact, he floated high in the water. These outer hairs are hollow to retain heat; however, his genitalia and the area between his back legs had no such protection. By the time he had dog-paddled 100 yards (91 m), his pursuers realizing this was a bad idea, returned to the shore. Alone now swimming in the freezing waters of a large lake in the Algonquin wilderness at night, what else could go wrong?

The surface of the water was an enormous sheet of black glass, and the merciless stars rose from its bottom to shine upon this lonely, nameless lake. Periodically, something broke the surface of the water only to disappear into its black depths. Instinctively, Big Red tried to dog paddle in a straight line without being able to see the far side of the lake. It is impossible, however, for any creature to walk or in this case to swim in a straight line—there are always some slight undulations. These undulations can accumulate to walking or swimming in a circle and the distinct possibility of death. But right now, he had another setback. Some 20 minutes after he entered this icy water, one of his back legs stopped working and locked in a cramp—the leg bitten at Grand Lake. Apparently, this leg had a residual problem that revealed itself when under stress.

Now just as a man cannot row a boat with a single oar, a wolf cannot swim in a straight line using three legs. So, our wolf gave up on his back legs and paddled using only his strong front legs (*see* photograph). This slowed his progress, but at least it was more linear. Unlike his canine cousin the Labrador (yellow, black, or chocolate) his tail just floated behind him and was of no use as a rudder. He dog-paddled on through the night and the freezing dark element with the help of the webbing growing halfway up between his toes. Eventually, he thought he saw something in the distance; he was sure it was the far shore. The freezing water was inducing what humans call hypothermia, and he instinctively knew he must quickly get out of it and onto dry land.

Big Red Swimming & Not Happy

He paddled faster as the outline of land approached. Ringing the shore, however, were slippery black boulders blocking his way and with his exhaustion and only two good legs, he could not scale them. Swimming desperately along the lake's rocky edge, he discovered a marshy inlet. And using his front legs to push aside the floating logs left by beavers, he pulled himself from this frozen death. He struggled up a slight incline dragging his backside, trying to escape all wetness before collapsing on some dry moss covering yet more rocks.

He wanted to howl victorious to let his pursuers know he had made it across, but he could not. He wanted to tell them he had evaded them, but he could not. He wanted to tell them to make a dream they had killed a wolf, but he could not. He just lay there shivering convulsively, exhausted—close to death.

Every living creature has a genetic history revealing that it is a transitional form on a hidden path going nowhere. Trace this lineage back far enough, and you will discover the origin of this species.

Several hundred thousand years ago somewhere in the vast continent of Asia, a new species appeared and met the times and its challenges. It was smaller and weaker than cave bears, hyenas, or saber-tooth tigers, and certainly than mammoths—but perfectly evolved to hunt all varieties of deer. Its strength lay not in individuals but in groups, although some animals were awesome. They hunted in packs like the velociraptors of the Jurassic period, killing cave bears, hyenas, and even giant wooly mammoths. We call these creatures wolves! They went *out of Asia* into Europe, Africa, India, the Americas, and Australia living by the following credo— this was Sparta, not Athens:

> *Respect the elders*
> *Teach the young*
> *Cooperate with the pack*
>
> *Play when you can*
> *Hunt when you must*
> *Rest in between*
>
> *Share your affections*
> *Voice your feelings*
> *Leave your mark!*
> Del Goetz, "The Wolf Credo"

Dogs* are just friendly wolves . . . mostly. In Asia, about 30,000 or more years ago, some wolves began following our hunter-gatherer ancestors, and a few went over to the human side. The hunters had been fortunate and killed several deer, so scraps of meat and bones were plentiful around the camp. A few brave wolves crept close to take advantage of this unique ecological niche. The hunters recognized their value as an early warning

---

* *Google* "Cosmos: A Space Time Odyssey S01 E02 (Part 1)"

system against bears, cats, hyenas, and other predators. Soon the hunters purposefully fed them leftovers. And then one wintry night it happened; a wolf less afraid than the others came closer to the fire for warmth. And a young man less afraid than the others reached out his hand and stroked the wolf's back, and with that, the family dog was born! Still, not all canids can be tamed; the African wild dog is one such. Even if you get one as a pup, they are unmanageable.

Without realizing it, our deep ancestors practiced *artificial selection*. Out of a litter of wolf puppies, they kept the cutest (*see* Chapter-2), the friendliest, or the strongest, and so on. The changes were so seamless it is impossible to say this is a wolf, and that is a dog; so, I call these intermediate forms wolfdogs. Over the generations, wolves did become dogs, all 300 different breeds of them: from Chihuahuas to Great Danes. The human companions of early wolfdogs immortalized them in the cave paintings at Font-de-Gaume, France (*see* photograph). Such was the devotion of humans and wolfdogs to each other that they were often buried together. Prized animals were buried wearing decorative collars right beside their owners and treated like humans in death as in life. Ancient graves at Lake Baikal in remote central Asia show such closeness. Wolves were the first animal humans "tamed," thousands of years before cattle, sheep, and pigs. Wolves are the companions of hunters; cattle, sheep, and pigs are the food of farmers.

Wolf in Font-de-Gaume Cave circa 12,000 BCE

Man & Wolf Traveled the World Together

Man and wolf went everywhere together. There is evidence that the first humans to trek across Beringia and between the two opposing glacial ice sheets to finally arrive in the vast plains of

North America were accompanied by wolves. This trek was so perilous that research reveals only 10 people—10 extraordinary people—survived it. This was man's first journey to the Americas,* but wolves had made this trip many times before. Within just 800 years, man and wolf traveled the entire length of the Americas right down to Tierra del Fuego. Theirs was an age of heroes, man and wolf, even if they did not realize it.

🐾

After an hour, Big Red stopped shivering and fell into a deep sleep and slept until noon the following day. Fortunately, the moss-covered rocks he had pulled himself up onto were in a sunny patch surrounded by dark forest. This sun dried his thick fur and dissolved the leg cramp, so he stood up and took a long, long stretch like a woodchuck after hibernation. He felt both weak and ravenous, so he crouched on the edge of a beaver trail not far away, and he waited for his supper to arrive. Sometime after sundown, he fell asleep again, lulled by the hypnotic calling of whip-poor-wills.

As at Grand Lake, the gods of good fortune blessed Big Red with the luck normally given only to fools and little children: a big beaver ambled right up to his nose. When he had finished eating much of it, he went back to sleep for the remaining night-time. Now his body must restore itself, so he can continue his homeward journey.

A Beaver at Night

Had he been a poet (my apologies to Tennyson and his famous poem "Ulysses"), he might have thought:

> All times I have traveled greatly
> both with those that loved me and alone.

Among all the mammals, wolf and man are the greatest travelers; as companions, they traveled the world together. They were a formidable pair. One trotted out of Asia; the other walked out of Africa. But, of course, when man first left Africa, he had no wolf companion—that was about 65,000 BCE, and it was long a profound mystery where these first humans went and when wolves joined them. It is one of the most remarkable discoveries of all time that science can now answer the first part of this question with certainty. The original humans to leave Africa went all the way to Australia. This epic journey required extraordinary intelligence and greatness of the human spirit—they went where no one had gone before. These first travelers were fearless! Absolutely fearless!

None of this journey is conjecture; unique mutations called markers* by geneticists support it. The DNA in your blood holds the most fabulous history book ever written—a kind of time machine. And it proves we are all one tremendous family; ideas of race are false, totally false! Only a few times since we came down from the trees, have humans made such a discovery. The genographic map of humankind verifies that Afghans, Nordic people, Russians, Arabs, Chukchi, Inuit, San people, indigenous North Americans, Mongols, Slavs, Tierra del Fuegians, Chinese, Europeans, and the Amazon forest people are all *Africans.*

Similarly, I predict that when the genographic map is completed for these canids out of Asia, it will prove that coyotes, gray wolves, Algonquin wolves, Mexican wolves, African wild dogs, warrahs, maned wolves, European wolves, Indian wolves, Abyssinian wolves, golden jackals, and dingoes are all *gray wolves.*

Africans were in Australia for 50,000 years before the dingo arrived. Genetic research shows the dingo came through the Malay Archipelago around 4,000 years ago. Even when the glaciers were at their maximum and hence oceans at their minimum, it was still a 30 mi. (48 km) boat ride from New Guinea to Australia. Who brought them? Surprisingly, it was common for the people

---

* If your DNA is unravelled and stretched out, it would reach to the moon and back 7,000 times. And a *genetic marker* is somewhere on this incredibly long road, and finding it is the work of high-speed computers.

of the Malay Archipelago, to visit north Australia, so common that the Australian government forbade it in 1900.

The dingoes brought by these seafaring people must have liked the varied menu this continent offered for many decided to stay. They were companions of these seafarers, *not pets*, and they are not another breed of dog but a different creature altogether.

These immigrants realized the benefits of a partnership with the aborigines because they went everywhere together. Even aboriginal Dreamtime art reflected this relationship (*see* photograph).

Rock Painting of a Dingo from Laura Region, Queensland

Whether with the natives or alone, dingoes explored the entire continent with its unique marsupials. Dingo and man were the only non-marsupials in the Land Down Under. Although dingoes ate few snakes, after all this was Australia, they and the aborigines were the top predators hunting everything from the biggest kangaroos to smallest wombats—the Australian version of grazing animals and woodchucks respectively.

But who filled the ecological niche of the top predator on the island continent before man and dingo arrived? Evidence suggests it was the Tasmanian tiger or wolf (aka thylacine) who was not originally confined to that island. The thylacine was the largest known carnivorous marsupial of modern times. The top dog you could say. Native to continental Australia, Tasmania, and New Guinea, the last one died in the Hobart zoo in 1933.

Multiple reasons exist for the passing of the Tasmanian wolf. Top predators hunt and kill each other unless they work as companions like the aborigines and the dingoes. So, dingoes undoubtedly played a role in the extinction* of this unique marsupial. It is of note that the final holdout of the thylacine was Tasmania, the one island dingoes never reached.

Now the Tasmanian tiger is a most curious creature. Remove the stripes from its back and hindquarters, and you have what appears to be a wolf (*see* drawing). But how is that even tenuously possible? Vast periods of time and distance separate wolves and Tasmanian tigers on the tree of life. Why from an infinity of forms do they look so similar?

Tasmanian Wolf courtesy of Google Images

Scientists will tell you that animals—no matter how distant genetically—who fill the same ecological niche come to look alike, even if separated by vast distances and great periods of time. This happens because of the nature of their employment. Biologists call this process *convergent evolution*, the independent evolution of similar features in species of different lineages. Compare the woodchuck, a mammal of North America, to the wombat, a marsupial of Australia. They look like close cousins, but they are extremely distant on the evolutionary tree of life. Their job descriptions, however, would be identical: "Stubborn loner wanted to build impressive burrow and consume tender young plants." Closer to home, swallows and swifts look like twins— they both catch insects on the wing—but they are on entirely different branches of life's tree.

---

* Rumors of sightings persist on the Australian mainland.

With the Tasmanian Tiger gone, dingoes were the masters of their entire domain—continental Australia. When they reached the southern shores of the Land Down Under, like the Fuegians at the tip of South America, their great wanderings ended. They had come through China, down the long Malay Peninsula to the magnificent Archipelago of the same name, and on to New Guinea and ultimately Australia.

Wolves conquered the world—the world of wilderness that is. Joyous with life, they raced out of Asia into Europe, India, and Africa. The danced across Beringia into the Americas down to Tierra del Fuego and the Falkland Islands, and at last to Australia and its southern shores via China and the Malay Archipelago. All the civilized and hence dull places, they left for man. As Thoreau wrote in his essay *Walking*, "Wilderness is the preservation of the world." If we civilize all these wild places in our headlong rush to "develop," we will have cut the spirit out of the earth and left a land unworthy of life. Clearly, wolves will not live there.

But here on Australia's southern shores, with the soft sound of waves breaking up the beach, faced with 2,500 miles of open ocean until Antarctica, dingoes finally ceased their restless exploration. All good things . . . end.

Dingo on the Beach

🐾

Wolves are tough beyond anything humans cradled in the comforts of modern materialism can understand. Big Red awoke refreshed and ready to move on. His body may have healed, but his spirit was in pain. He had an emptiness deep inside and was tired of being alone, hearing only the sound of his own breathing and muted vocalizations. It was now more than two years since he had left home on a futile quest to establish his own pack and family.

In the wilderness of Algonquin, the average life expectancy of a wolf is six or seven years. His father is likely dead now, but our wolf had confidence that his mother and his aunt were still alive. And perhaps his sister Little Red Ears had come home. He licked his paws, arose, looked around, and headed westward with an impatient trot.

What Does the Wolf Say?
He declares, "I'm going home."

Chapter—9

THE WATCHMAKER'S GIFTS

*The last word in ignorance is the man
who says of an animal or plant,
"What good is it?"*

Aldo Leopold, *Round River,* from his Journals

Big Red had been trotting for three days without seeing or hearing another wolf; he welcomed the change. By this time in the spring, the white-tailed deer had dispersed from their winter deer yards, and the does were seeking out secret places to drop their fawns.

Our wolf had seen six deer in these three days but was unable to make a kill. Less than 15 percent of all wolf attacks are successful when done by a pack, and less than 5 percent of attacks by a lone wolf succeed. He had eaten two red squirrels, but they were just appetizers; he needed the entrée. It seemed as if even the ravens had stopped following him.

Deer do not live in the deep forest where no sunshine reaches the ground. They live on the edges of forests, farms, lakes, and the sides of roads. Big Red sought out such places, and finally, he found prey.

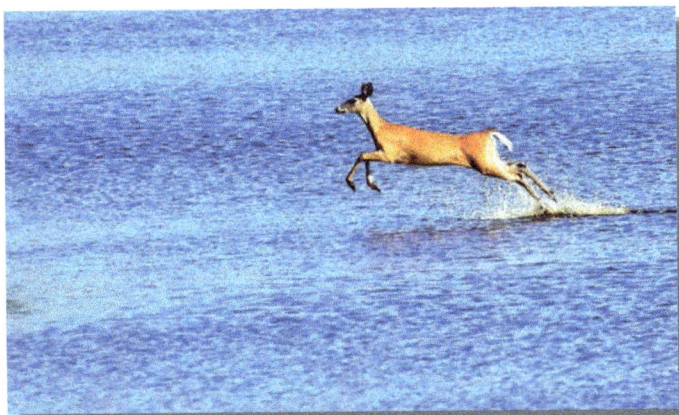

Fleeing Deer in a Lake

Big Red saw a doe swimming in the water where a creek emptied into a large bay. The previous night had been freezing, causing ice to form around the shoreline of the bay. He watched as the doe repeatedly tried but failed to get up on this thin layer of ice. Since he was uphill, she had not caught sight of him yet.

Over the next hour, Big Red slowly angled down the hill toward the deer standing in ankle-deep water. When he reached the halfway point, his behavior changed. Each time the deer looked away from the partially hidden wolf, he would stalk closer. When the doe looked in his direction, Big Red came to an immediate halt. His stalking behavior was that of a leopard or a tiger, not a wolf, but as a single attacker, he had little choice. To adapt your hunting strategy to changing conditions is a sign of intelligence while doing the same thing repeatedly with negative results is undoubtedly not.

Despite a steady cool breeze from the bay, not even a hair on his body moved. This stop-and-go stalking continued at a painstaking rate. Only once did it vary, when our wolf briefly sat down. But, when the deer looked away again, he instantly rose to all fours and closed the distance between him and the deer with another step or two. Eventually, it became plain that the deer could see Big Red, and at this point, she raised a front hoof and vigorously stamped it back into the water. Over the next several minutes, the deer repeated this behavior with her front hooves, but our wolf slowly continued his approach—although with much shorter increments and at a much slower rate.

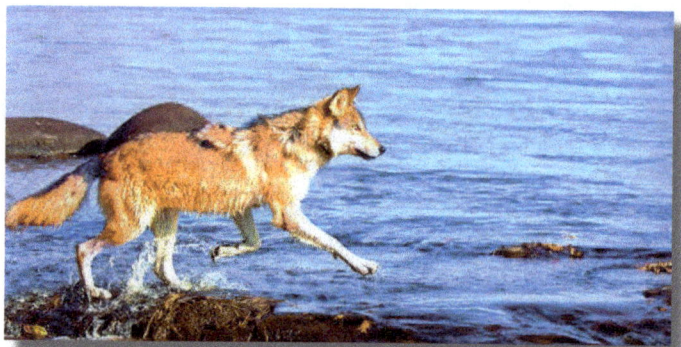

Big Red Pursuing the Deer into the Bay

Finally, Big Red placed himself behind a large shoreline rock about two body lengths from the deer and waited, motionless. Then, after what seemed like ages, he made a burst toward the deer, which was still standing in the shallows. With one bound, he was in the water (*see* photograph). The deer instantly reacted and lunged toward the deeper water of the bay. With our wolf's second bound, he made contact near the neck and shoulder area of the deer, almost submerging her in the water.

From this instant, the next five minutes seemed to happen quickly. The deer and wolf thrashed around violently in these decisive moments. In the first seconds of the attack, Big Red inflicted several effective bites to the deer's neck and mouth area, drawing large streams of blood that coated the hair on her right side and flowed freely from her mouth into the water. Recalling his recent icy swim and leg cramp, Big Red climbed onto the deer's back at least three times in a furious struggle. Several times he completely submerged her below the surface while continuing to inflict wounds to the neck and back of this already bleeding animal. Just as it seemed clear that Big Red would prevail, the deer broke away into deeper water. From that point forward, our wolf was able to inflict only minor wounds to the deer's rump as he tried to claw his way up onto her back. Then, about five minutes after the attack had started, the deer turned and swam toward the middle of the open bay, while our wolf went back to the shore, trotted up the hill, and disappeared into the forest.

The injured deer swam around the bay trying to get up on the ice but failing each time as the ice broke under her weight. Finally, after much searching, she found a place where she could touch bottom. Soaked in freezing water, the deer repeatedly licked the wounds. After some time, she closed her eyes and seemed to sleep while standing in the ice-cold, shoulder-deep water. Meanwhile, Big Red reappeared up on the hill and bedded down in an area of tall grasses and shrubbery. Only his ears were visible above the vegetation except when he stood up to see the wounded deer. He was still there when the sun went down.

Bald Eagle

Somehow and sometime during the night, the doe emerged from the freezing water onto the dry land where Big Red was waiting. With her loss of blood from the wounds and the hypothermia from the icy water, our wolf delivered the coup de grace, and he ate until morning. Just after sunrise, three long-absent ravens found the carcass, and turkey vultures soon followed. Even a majestic adult bald eagle flew in across an intense cerulean sky to join the feast (*see* photograph). The forest was hungry—the forest is always hungry. And these wolf birds at once began their "chaos call" attracting other ravens and wolves, so Big Red left with a full belly.

He trotted westward until midday and then quickly found a thick bed of pine needles to have a well-earned rest. Once again, good fortune had favored him; this, combined with his unique gifts from natural selection had given him a healthy doe.

🐾

It is often said that wolves *kill only* the old, weak, and sick. This is utterly false. Wolves kill whatever they can get, and on occasion, as today with Big Red, this included a young, healthy deer. As I wrote in the first paragraph of Chapter-1:

It is not only the weak and the old who falter and fall, it is the inefficient—the ones who stray too far from the edge.

This doe put herself in a vulnerable position—alone in the middle of a bay with an icy rim. Wolves do take a preponderance of the old and weak, merely because they are usually easier to catch. As will become clear, it is a good thing that Big Red captured a prime doe during her reproductive years. Why? Let me explain.

Before Europeans arrived in the Americas, predator-prey systems were in equilibrium. The deer died off from predation, hunger, disease, and so on at about the same rate as they were replaced every spring. Ditto for wolves. A balance point had been achieved, and unless something new was introduced into the system, such as humans, wild boars, or moose, it stayed there.

Experiments on animals in the wild are nearly impossible. Fortunately, man's stupidity and nature's bounty have already done tests for us. In Chapter-5, "The War on Wolves," we learned of the immense and beneficial effects of reintroducing wolves into Yellowstone Park: the return of beavers, rabbits, and many birds, regrowth of long-absent trees, and so on. Consider an analogous situation: the introduction of white-tailed deer to a previously deer-free area.

In the Gulf of St. Lawrence (*see* map) is an immense island called Anticosti larger even than Algonquin Park. It is a land of high cliffs, waterfalls, and evergreen forests. Initially, it had no deer and only five native animals; one of these was the American black bear. A hundred years ago, the owner of the island imported 220 deer; after that, everything changed. Today Anticosti has only a handful of permanent residents, no towns, and no roads, but it has deer, lots of them: at last count a staggering 120,000 in the fall.

In the absence of wolves, the ecological impact of ungulates is immense. The deer have transformed the forest by eating some trees and avoiding others they find unpalatable. All the shrubs and berry bushes are gone, resulting in death by starvation for every black bear on the island. Who would have imagined that

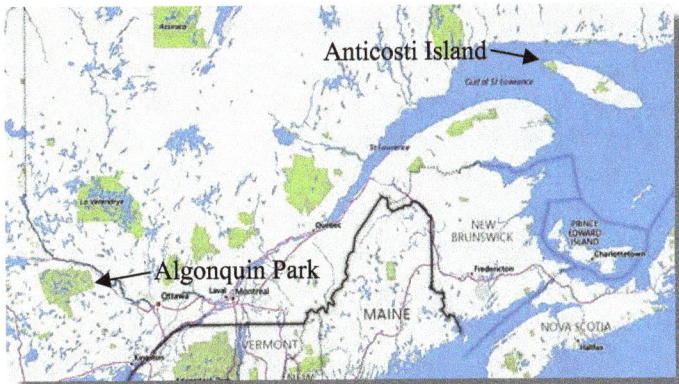

Anticosti Island and Algonquin Park

white-tailed deer could kill off the magnificent *Ursus americanus*? But what they have done to themselves is much worse. Approximately 20,000 die an agonizing death from starvation *every winter* even with the killing of 9,000 in the fall deer hunt.

So, when Big Red or any other wolf kills a prime deer, they are to some small extent preventing the fate of Anticosti from occurring in Algonquin. It is interesting to guess how many years it would take for the deer of Anticosti Island to reach a balance point with wolves if they were introduced.

Many people are horrified by one wild animal killing and eating another wild animal. I wonder how many of these people have seen how their dinner is prepared at the abattoir (aka slaughterhouse)? Few or none, I suspect. We do not need to admire how natural selection works; nor should we apply its laws to human society. But we do need to see the world as it is.

Aldo Leopold (1887-1948) was one of the legendary founders of the American environmental moment. A renaissance man of prodigious accomplishments: conservationist, forester, philosopher, educator, writer, professor, and outdoor enthusiast. I took the following five paragraphs from his most famous book, *A Sand County Almanac*,[1] where he unknowingly foretold the fate of Anticosti Island:

> *Only the mountain has lived long enough to listen objectively to the howl of a wolf. . . .Those unable to decipher the hidden meaning know nevertheless that it is there, for it is felt in all wolf country, and distinguishes that country from all other land. It tingles in the spine of all who hear wolves by night, or who scan their tracks by day. Even without sight or sound of wolf, it is implicit in a hundred small events: the midnight whinny of a pack horse, the rattle of rolling rocks, the bound of a fleeing deer, the way shadows lie under the spruces. Only the ineducable tyro can fail to sense the presence or absence of wolves, or the fact that mountains have a secret opinion about them.*

> *My own conviction on this score dates from the day I saw a wolf die. We were eating lunch on a high rimrock, at the*

foot of which a turbulent river elbowed its way. We saw what we thought was a doe fording the torrent, her breast awash in white water. When she climbed the bank toward us and shook out her tail, we realized our error: it was a wolf. A half-dozen others, evidently grown pups, sprang from the willows and all joined in a welcoming melee of wagging tails and playful maulings. What was literally a pile of wolves writhed and tumbled in the center of an open flat at the foot of our rimrock.

In those days we had never heard of passing up a chance to kill a wolf. In a second we were pumping lead into the pack, but with more excitement than accuracy: how to aim a steep downhill shot is always confusing. When our rifles were empty, the old wolf was down, and a pup was dragging a leg into impassable slide-rocks.

We reached the old wolf in time to watch a fierce green fire dying in her eyes. I realized then, and have known ever since, that there was something new to me in those eyes - something known only to her and to the mountain. I was young then, and full of trigger-itch; I thought that because fewer wolves meant more deer, that no wolves would mean hunters' paradise. But after seeing the green fire die, I sensed that neither the wolf nor the mountain agreed with such a view.

Since then I have lived to see state after state extirpate its wolves. I have watched the face of many a newly wolfless mountain and seen the south-facing slopes wrinkle with a maze of new deer trails. I have seen every edible bush and seedling browsed, first to anaemic desuetude, and then to death. I have seen every edible tree defoliated to the height of a saddlehorn. Such a mountain looks as if someone had given God a new pruning shears, and forbidden Him all other exercise. In the end the starved bones of the hoped-for deer herd, dead of its own too-much, bleach with the bones of the dead sage, or molder under the high-lined junipers.

It was well past midnight when Big Red awoke. The forest was without sound, not a whisper. He got up, stretched, lifted his leg high, and peed on the tree he was sleeping under. The tree took no offense nor was one intended. The forest seemed brightly lit to our wolf although the moon was a mere sliver in the night sky. Aware morning was distant, he returned to his bed.

Wolves and deer are in an "arms race" that has gone on for tens of thousands of years. They have evolved together in a deadly dance biologists call *coevolution*. The genes of each animal have created a phenotype best suited to pass on their genotype. This has resulted in some fantastic features and behaviors. I call these gifts from The Blind Watchmaker* that is, natural selection. Let us consider three of these gifts:

The eyes of all animals—this includes yours and mine—are highly evolved. Charles Darwin acknowledged in *On the Origin of Species* that it seems absurd to think the eye formed by natural selection. Yet he believed it did evolve, despite a lack of evidence at that time. Life provides a stunning array of different eyes, implying the eye originated many times, from the compound eyes of insects to the unique vision of octopuses.

In the natural world, nocturnal animals have developed a "straight-back" concave reflector. This reflector—a layer of cells behind the retina called the *tapetum lucidum*—gives the animal "white-eye." Since this cellular layer is absent in humans, we get "red-eye" from a network of blood vessels in the retina. The purpose of the *tapetum* is to reflect light back through the rods of the retina a second time, thereby giving creatures like wolves and deer excellent night vision. Each photon is reflected straight back to the same photocell that missed it coming the other way, so the image is not distorted. If the photon is missed on this second try, it escapes the eye socket and becomes part of the white-eye phenomenon.

---

* *See* Richard Dawkins book *The Blind Watchmaker* for the best explanation of natural selection ever written.

Wolf with White-Eye

White eye implies a creature of the night. We have all seen this phenomenon while driving after dark. The classic case is the "caught in the headlights" look of a deer, wolf, or rabbit (*see* photograph).

Wolves originated in snow country. They are animals of snowscapes with long legs for running through deep drifts. In the winter they flourish, often running and playing like dogs in the white fluff. When the snow is deep, they tread with great care, conserving energy however possible. Big Red's track pattern is unusual for a four-legged animal; he leaves less than the expected number of paw prints. His smaller hind paw lands in the impression just made by the front paw on the same side. That is, he double prints (*see* photograph), as we do when following a friend through heavy snow because it is less arduous. Many other animals such as coyotes also double print. Artificial selection and a full food bowl have rendered dogs incapable of doing so—they make a four-print pattern. Through a hundred thousand years, natural selection pressures have favored energy-conserving behaviors. In a million-year march, a minuscule pebble in a boot can be crippling.

Wolf Double-Print Track

Crater-1   Crater-2

Consider these two photographs of moon craters (courtesy of NASA). The one on the left is empty, and the one on the right is a solid mound. This, however, is a well-known optical illusion. Please turn this page upside down. Voila! The situation is reversed: the empty crater becomes the mound and vice versa. Looking closely reveals these are identical photographs of the Webb crater rotated 180° relative to each other. The left crater is countershaded (dark top, light bottom) and, it appears empty. The right crater (light bottom, dark top) is the reverse and seems full. In large part, the reason most but not all creatures have white bellies is to take advantage of countershading.

When an animal is darker on the upper side and lighter on the underside of the body, biologists believe countershading is a form of camouflage. Many creatures—mammals, birds, fish, reptiles, insects, even the family dog—have white bellies. This pattern has existed since at least the Cretaceous period and perhaps longer

Porcupine   Skunk

(145 to 65 million years ago). Richard Dawkins, in his memoir *An Appetite for Wonder*, maintains countershading allows the wearer to appear flat or empty and hence of no food value.

"This is the exception that proves the rule" was never more proper than in *reverse countershading*. In this situation, natural selection has worked its magic to make the animal more visible as a warning sign. Any animal that issues such a warning needs a robust defense system to back up its bravado. The skunk and the porcupine (*see* photographs) have such mechanisms. These two animals not only have black bellies but also have white fur or quills on their backs. You cannot miss them, but you should. Skunks and porcupines do not run away; they stand and deliver.

🐾

The night is vast and full of wonders. Well before dawn a distinct sound roused Big Red. It was the sound a living creature makes. It was close and growing louder. He looked around intently, but even with his night vision, he could not find its source. When the night is still, the least noise can be mistaken for an elephant—like a mouse in the house before sunrise. Finally, he saw the creature "flying" from tree to tree with several others in hot pursuit. The object of this chase was surely a female and her many pursuers, ardent males.

Northern Flying Squirrel

The Creature

Our wolf had seen these creatures many times, but always at night and rarely on the forest floor. Often, he had tried to catch and eat one, but they were incredibly quick and arboreal. This secretive animal is the *northern flying squirrel* (*see* photographs), intermediate in size between a chipmunk and a red squirrel. It is as abundant as the latter but entirely nocturnal and mostly arboreal. This is a splendid mammal, matchless and mysterious gliding from tree to tree with unnerving accuracy. Big Red decided to leave these acrobatic lovers to their bacchanalia.

He got up, stretched, and peed again on the unfortunate tree. In recompense, he pooped (*see* photograph) on the roots of the tree to fertilize it. Satisfied with himself, he resumed his journey.

Wolf Poop mixed with Deer Hair

This morning was remarkable: his belly was still full, and no wolves were pursuing him. A sense of profound malaise settled over him. Predators are more intelligent than their prey. They must be. And intelligence needs to be challenged and stimulated. With a full belly and no challenges, Big Red might as well have been in a zoo pacing back and forth behind its bars.

For some time, he had been ashamed of himself. All this hiding and traveling during the daytime to avoid confrontation. He was especially disappointed with himself for not howling out his defiance at the world. His strength was a point of immense pride for him, and his cleverness was such that he was never at a loss.

He scouted out a high point of land overlooking this post-glacial landscape. When he found it, his deep pride almost arrogance caused him to do something incredibly foolish like the time on Grand Lake when he challenged six wolves to give way. He would let his entire world know who and where he was. A challenge saying, "Catch me if you can."

From deep down in Big Red's chest, a rumble grew and swelled up through his throat and flowed from his mouth—this sad song rolled across the valley and echoed from the hills to ultimately die as a whisper to the distant darkness. It is a wild, unconquerable call of defiant sorrow and disregard for all the adversities of this world. For miles around, all creatures great and small heard his song, and many shivered in fear and crouched lower in their beds. For the deer, it was an alarm call, and for a few minutes their boredom vanished, and they were again conscious of their treasures. Several moments passed after his song, and then from far off a lone voice answered his defiant call with a soft, almost happy howl. Big Red wondered what it could mean.

Night Song of the Algonquin Wolf

Chapter—10

THE WRITTEN WOLF

April is the cruelest month, breeding
Lilacs out of the dead land, mixing
Memory and desire, stirring
Dull roots with spring rain.
T. S. Eliot, *The Waste Land*

A road less traveled weaved a path through the forest, avoiding rocks and marshes where it could. The cedars, tamaracks, and balsam fir trees reached across the road as if to greet long-lost relatives on the other side. In a few places grass still flourished in the dappled sunshine between these trees as Big Red trotted its easy trail.

Eventually, the road opened to a long-abandoned farm reclaimed by nature. Here and there were moldy remnants of human activity in the form of massive logs cut and piled for some ghost reason. Rock fences and stone piles were everywhere—the echoes of long-ago back-breaking toil. Having passed through the bowels of bears and birds, pin cherry and apple trees dotted the "fields." And between these, berry bushes and wisteria flourish reclaiming the open land. Deer had been grazing on the bright spring grass as if they were lawnmowers. Near what may have been the house, lilacs grew luxuriantly filling the field with a fragrance beckoning bumblebees to dine.

Nothing else remained. No colossal wreck just weeds and wire bush. Where horses and cows once held sway, fields of wild raspberry canes now hold court. And when the berries ripen, bears roam where the horses' stalls once stood. No one would know anyone had lived here. Everyone had forgotten how green was their valley!

In the last two centuries, a new creature has lived on the land, an animal who by labor and passion thought to mold this rocky wilderness closer to the heart's desire. Like Sisyphus, these creatures rolled the rocks into piles and fences, cut the trees into houses and barns, and scratched the fields with shovels and plows to grow a few vegetables. Since time is the overlord of all ventures, these hardy, brave, and foolish pioneers are all gone now, as are their houses and fields. And but for a few books and this poem by Canadian writer Al Purdy, they would not even be a memory:

> And where the farms are
> it's as if a man stuck
> both thumbs in the stony earth and pulled
> it apart
> to make room
> enough between the trees
> for a wife
> and maybe some cows and
> room for some
> of the more easily kept illusions—
> Al Purdy, "The Country North of Belleville"

Big Red was looking for a snack, though his recent venison feast still sustained him. He knew what he wanted from this abandoned farm. Hiding behind some wisteria bushes, he surveyed the open grassy areas, and it was not long before he saw it—a large woodchuck enjoying the sunshine and the grass (*see* photograph).

Woodchuck in April just out of Hibernation

Our wolf charged this hapless ground squirrel, but it quickly plummeted into its nearby hole. Yet, the chase was not over; Big Red recalled a trick he had seen his father use. Dashing to the burrow, he waited on the side *opposite* the entrance path. As he expected, less than a minute later, the rodent popped its head out with his back exposed to Big Red—death was instantaneous. Our wolf thought it was an excellent snack, and he might enjoy another. He had no idea these creatures were squirrels; he just knew they were delicious.

The woodchuck is Algonquin Park's largest squirrel. He can climb trees if the occasion requires, but, as his other name—groundhog—implies, he prefers to touch the earth. Robert Frost commemorates this member of the squirrel family in his poem "A Drumlin Woodchuck." Here are two stanzas:

> *My own strategic retreat*
> *Is where two rocks almost meet,*
> *And still more secure and snug,*
> *A two-door burrow I dug.*

> *All we who prefer to live*
> *Have a little whistle we give,*
> *And flash, at the least alarm*
> *We dive down under the farm.*

Woodchucks are true hibernators. This animal sleeps away winter's terrible hardship, taking just a single breath every six minutes and maintaining a body temperature of 37° F (3° C) while wolves run on through fields and forests of snow. He appears dead. Yet, his photograph—taken in April during the first days of the spring—reveals an animal in good condition just out of hibernation. We forget how fantastic hibernation is! Many animals such as bears and chipmunks are said to hibernate, but they are just winter sleepers. They wake up often, sometimes daily, move about, and then return to sleep.

Hibernation is like "stasis" from the *Star Trek* franchise, the state in which someone passes prolonged periods entirely unaware in a special chamber. Any unfortunate woodchuck brought out of stasis for amusement on February 2 knows that, whether he sees his shadow or a dinosaur, there will be six more weeks of winter in Canada. Natural selection created hibernation as a perfect method to escape the ravages of winter. With this gift, plus his warning whistles to littermates and the ability to climb trees or go to earth to avoid danger, this squirrel appears not to need countershading, and, indeed, he has none.

Upward Facing Chuck   Downward Facing Chuck

Big Red continued through a series of abandoned fields each more derelict than the previous one. On a mound of earth, he noted some unusual activity, a woodchuck practicing his yoga exercises (*see* photographs) After a long winter's nap—about six months—it must have felt good to stretch. He had hibernated curled up in a tight ball. This yoga session lasted some time, with the woodchuck repeating various positions over and over. Our wolf decided to leave him to his exercises.

It was already evening when Big Red discovered a large abandoned barn. Always curious, our wolf explored its exterior before entering through a missing board. A lower area was littered with rusty plows, harrows, and rakes, all long unused. The owner of these ancient implements had long ago piled a slightly higher area with hay still soft enough to make a bed on.

A Barn Being Eaten by the Forest

Not long after he had curled up in a ball, he realized he was not alone in this colossal decay. There were bats, flying squirrels, hordes of mice, and several raccoons. But this was probably the first time a wolf had spent a night here, although foxes often denned under the barn floor and porcupines could always be found here. In the peak of each gable end of the barn, the farmer with an eye for beauty had cut decorative entrance holes so barn swallows could enter at will. These swallows swoop under the lowest strand of a wire fence and routinely careen into a barn through a vertical crack in the boards that would have wedged your hand. They are all gone now. Only their old mud nests still cling to the beams of the barn the way the ancient Anasazi adobe homes clutch the cliffs of the Canyon de Chelly.

Curiously, our wolf felt comforted by the other guests as he drifted off to sleep. As a pup on his natal territory, he had often seen the barns owned by the farmer whose property they lived on, and who occasionally walked by their den. Sleep came quickly, and dreams followed.

ODYSSEY BY HOMER

Woodchucks may have poems written about them, but the Canidae—wolves and friends—have been buried beside their masters and had marble and limestone carved with their images. And stories

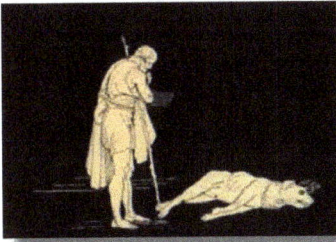

The Death of Argos

about wolves and dogs occur early in Western literature. Both the Bible and the Qur'an mention dogs in less than complimentary terms, but religion never did understand the natural world. Yet the Greeks, well, they were different! The account of Odysseus' dog Argos near the end of the

Odyssey rings true. Edith Hamilton tells this story in her marvelous book *Mythology: Timeless Tales of Gods and Heroes*:

They [Odysseus and his son] reached the town, they came to the palace, and at last, after twenty years, Odysseus entered his dear dwelling. As he did so, an old dog lying there lifted and pricked his ears. It was Argos, whom Odysseus had bred before he went

to Troy. Yet the moment his master appeared, he knew him and wagged his tail but had no strength to drag himself even a little toward him. Odysseus knew him too and brushed away a tear. He dared not go to him for fear of arousing suspicion in the swineherd, and he turned away that moment the old dog died.[1]

Both master and hound recognized each other without a gesture and without a word. Argos was faithful to his master—that pack instinct which binds wolves in a tight family and hunting unit. Since antiquity, readers have recognized Argos as a parallel for his returned master, both are aged and mistreated. This is literature's first story about a dog, and Homer—three millennia ago—got it right, precisely right. Art transcends time.

DOCTOR ZHIVAGO BY BORIS PASTERNAK

Whether you read the book or saw the movie, *Dr. Zhivago* is an enthralling story of deep passions and sweeping grandeur. The Nobel Committee awarded Boris Pasternak, the Prize in 1958 ostensibly for his poetry but really for this epic book. Ultimately, the communist authorities forced him to refuse the prize. He later ironically said of these bureaucrats, "They don't ask much of you. They only want you to hate the things you love and to love the things you despise."

Since this artfully crafted tale takes place in Russia, there will be wolves somewhere in its pages. These are the "infamous" steppe wolves of legend, myth, and literature. Consider the following excerpt from the time Lara and Yurii Andreievich (Dr. Zhivago) spent in the Ice Palace (*see* photograph) on the Russian steppe.

The Ice Palace from *Dr. Zhivago*

At three in the morning Yurii Andreievich looked up from his papers. He came back from his remote, selfless concentration, home to reality and to himself, happy, strong, peaceful. Suddenly the stillness of the open country stretching into the distance outside the window was broken by a mournful, plaintive sound.

He went to the unlit adjoining room to look through the window, but while he had been working the glass had frosted over. He dragged away the role of carpet that had been pushed against the front door to stop the draft, threw his coat over his shoulders, and went out.

He was dazzled by the white glow playing on the shadowless, moonlit snow and could at first see nothing. Then the long whimpering, deep-bellied howl sounded again, muffled by the distance, and he noticed four shadows, no thicker than pencil strokes, at the edge of the clearing just beyond the gully.

The wolves stood in a row, their heads raised and their muzzles pointing at the house, baying at the moon or at its silver reflection on the windows. But scarcely had Yurii Andreievich realized that they were wolves when they turned and trotted off like dogs, almost as if they could read his thoughts. He lost sight of them before he noticed the direction in which they had vanished.

"That's the last straw!" he thought. "Is their lair quite close? Perhaps in the gully? How terrible! And Samdeviatov's horse in the barn! They must have scented it."

He decided for the time being not to tell Lara, lest he upset her. Going back, he shut all the doors between the cold rooms and the heated part of the house, pushed rugs and clothes against the cracks to keep out the draft, and went back to his desk. The lamplight was bright and welcoming as before. But he was no longer in the mood to write. He couldn't settle down. He could think of nothing but the wolves and of looming dangers and complications of every kind. Moreover, he was tired.

Lara woke up. "Are you still burning, my precious light?" she whispered in a husky voice heavy with sleep. "Come and sit beside me for a moment. I'll tell you my dream."

He put out the light.[2]

As you might expect, the writing is compelling and imaginative, but the sentiment toward the steppe wolves is ancient. We learn nothing new that other writers had not written centuries earlier. The wolves are aggressive, dark, menacing—positively something not to frighten Lara with.

There are other perspectives. I saw the movie version as a young man. The scene at the Ice Palace with the silhouettes of the wolves moving effortlessly through the trees in the moonlight transfixed me by its power and beauty. This memory is now 50 years old, yet it still evokes emotions in me. This is a scene to write about. Perhaps a poem on these extraordinary creatures living in punishing conditions of cold and ice, yet somehow enduring. May I suggest the first line:

Furious with life, dark figures run in the moonlight. . .

Some poet can finish this or form it into something nearer to their heart's desire.

Instead of doing this, Yurii Andreievich no longer felt like writing poetry. He used phrases like "That's the last straw!" and "How terrible!" referring to these wolves. Below is a photograph of a "terrifying" young steppe wolf. There are those, but they will not be many, who find this canid vicious and threatening. Pasternak had fallen victim to the power of myth—the myth of the Big, Bad Wolf. Look for yourself! Judge for yourself!

Young Steppe Wolf

NEVER CRY WOLF BY FARLEY MOWAT

All cultures are not equal! Some value birds, bears, deer, and wolves. Some do not. Some would conserve these creatures; others would consume them. Some seek birds in the woods, others find them dead at the foot of skyscrapers in the city with all their fires out. Some cannot live without nature; others cannot live with it. As I said, all cultures are not equal.

Wolves are galvanizing creatures of deep controversy always depicted in Jekyll and Hyde terms. Yet forests need wolves; otherwise, a wilderness becomes a city park—just a tea party for rabbits and squirrels. Nature does not need man. Indeed, life thrives in the absence of man. Consider the Americas again, before Europeans arrived, with their guns, germs, and steel as Jerad Diamond wrote. The land overflowed with life in phenomenal abundance: flocks of passenger pigeons darkened the skies; Carolina parakeets were almost as abundant. Herds of bison (buffalo) and caribou of unimaginable size stretched to the horizon covering the prairie and the tundra in their epic journeys. And these herds were trailed and preyed upon by thousands of wolves. All this is gone now, never to return. Man changed all that and then blamed the wolves for the disappearance of the vast herds of caribou. Top predators detest each other.

Fortunately, cultures can change. It is a remarkable event when a book is the agent of that change. Farley Mowat, a recently deceased Canadian writer, is one such agent with his renowned book *Never Cry Wolf*. This work started a movement to protect wolves in all the circumpolar countries.

In a 2001 article of *The Canadian Historical Review entitled Never Cry Wolf: Science, Sentiment, and the Literary Rehabilitation of Canis Lupus*, Vol. 84 (2001) Karen Jones lauded the work as "an important chapter in the history of Canadian environmentalism":

> *The deluge of letters received by the Canadian Wildlife Service from concerned citizens opposing the killing of wolves testifies to the growing significance of literature as a protest medium. Modern Canadians roused to defend a species that their predecessors sought to eradicate. By the 1960s the wolf had made the transition from the beast of waste and desolation (in the words of Theodore Roosevelt) to a conservationist cause célèbre. . . .. Never Cry Wolf played a key role in fostering that change.*

The Canadian Wildlife Service flew a young man, Farley Mowat, into the Barren Lands of Canada's North to study wolves. He was to gather evidence that the wolves were destroying the vast caribou herds. The Canadian Wildlife Service called their policy "wolf control," which meant death by cyanide poisoning. If the wolves could speak or write, however, they would call it lupicide.

What follows is an excerpt from *Never Cry Wolf.* Luckily, Mowat had found an active den site and, laden with equipment, he decided to observe it and the surrounding area:

Glumly I went back to my unproductive survey through the telescope. The esker appeared deserted. The hot sand began sending up heat waves which increased my eyestrain. By 2:00 P.M. I had given up hope. There seemed no further point in concealment, so I got stiffly to my feet and prepared to relieve myself.

Now it is a remarkable fact that a man, even though he may be alone in a small boat in mid-ocean, or isolated in the midst of a trackless forest, finds that the very process of unbuttoning causes him to become particularly sensitive to the possibility that he may be under observation. At this critical juncture none but the most self-assured of men, no matter how certain he may be of his privacy, can refrain from casting a surreptitious glance around to reassure himself that he is alone.

Arctic Wolves Relaxing

To say I was chagrined to discover I was not alone would be an understatement; for sitting directly behind me, and not twenty yards away, were the missing wolves.

They appeared to be quite relaxed and comfortable, as if they had been sitting there behind my back for hours. The big male seemed a trifle bored; but the female's gaze was fixed on me with what I took to be an expression of unabashed and even prurient curiosity.

The human psyche is a truly amazing thing. Under almost any other circumstances I would probably have been panic-stricken, and I think few would have blamed me for it. But these were not ordinary circumstances and my reaction was one of violent indignation. Outraged, I turned my back on the watching wolves and with fingers which were shaking with vexation, hurriedly did up my buttons. When decency, if not my dignity, had been restored, I rounded on these wolves with a virulence which surprised even me.

"Shoo!" I screamed at them. "What the hell do you think you're at, you . . . You. . . peeping Toms! Go away, for heaven's sake!"

The wolves were startled. They sprang to their feet, glanced at each other with a wild surmise, and then trotted off, passed down a draw, and disappeared in the direction of the esker. They did not once look back.

With their departure, I experienced a reaction of another kind. The realization that they had been sitting almost within jumping distance of my unprotected back for God knows how long set up such a turmoil of the spirit that I had to give up all thought of carrying on where my discovery of the wolves had forced me to leave off. Suffering from both mental and physical strain, therefore, I hurriedly packed my gear and set out for the cabin.[3]

With experiences like this, spun together with self-deprecating humor, Mowat became a staunch defender of the wrongly named "Big, Bad Wolf." Yes, wolves kill and eat *some* caribou, mostly the old, the sick, and the young, but they also consume mice and lemmings. With 14 million copies sold in English as well as being translated into 24 different languages, *Never Cry Wolf* has become a powerful voice for those who cannot speak for themselves.

Mowat visited the Soviet Union on two occasions and wrote a rollicking story of his adventures there titled *Sibir*. He loved the peoples of the vast northern areas of far eastern Russia, and they had respect for him. So, when *Never Cry Wolf* was translated into

Russian, it found a broad and favorable audience, especially among the young. This book singlehandedly rehabilitated the status of the wolf on its home ground, Russia.

POSTSCRIPT

After Mowat left Wolf House Bay where he had met and habituated with five curious Arctic wolves, the Canadian Wildlife Service returned for another purpose. An official of this "service," sworn to protect wildlife, sprinkled strychnine-treated baits like candy all around the still-active dens. He never returned to see the results of his labor. The inevitable death of this family of wolves—three adults and two pups—must have been . . ..

> *Wild wolves who caught and sang the sun in flight,*
> *Rage, rage against the dying of the light.*
> *Do not go gentle into that good night.* *

OLD THREE TOES: AN AMERICAN LEGEND

In the time before Netflix, Spotify, and DVRs, people went to see first-run movies and listen to live concerts. In days even before that, we read books and newspapers. Back further still, in the pre-Gutenberg era, people talked to each other and told stories. In the evening around a glowing lantern or in the forest close to campfires people huddled and told tales, *tall tales*. Stories of heroes on a quest confronting wild beasts that harassed the land slaughtering livestock and people. These stories are universal, with identical themes, but often different animals depending on the location and the time.

Let me tell you a story: In Russia, Europe, and North America, the villainous animal was usually a wolf of exceptional cunning, size, and age. The last of these was Old Three Toes who roamed North and South Dakota into Montana from 1912-25 ravening livestock. Depending on which account you read, he lost two toes on one paw and one on another while escaping from leg traps. Others say, as with Big Red, he had a missing toe on a right front paw from one of those merciless devices.

---

* My apologies to Dylan Thomas and his poem "Do Not Go Gentle into That Good Night."

The Internet has a wealth of stories, legends, and letters about the career of Old Three Toes. The following titled "South Dakota's Killer Wolf" by Katie Hunhoff is one of the best or worst:

One of the last was a wolf named Three Toes that achieved great notoriety in the hills and plains of northwest South Dakota. Archie Gilfillan, a sheepherder, and writer were intrigued by the local ranchers' mixture of respect and hate for the wild and wily creature. In his book Sheep, Gilfillan noted that Three Toes "for 13 years laughed at poison, traps and guns, lived in and off enemy country with the hand of every man against him, a cunning, bloodthirsty killer, a super wolf among wolves and the most destructive single animal of which there is any record anywhere."

So, named because he had lost a paw[sic]in a trap early in his life, Three Toes gained a reputation as a bloodthirsty killer by 1912. He left his unmistakable paw print at ranches throughout Harding County. Infuriated ranchers tracked his whereabouts and devastating destruction. They estimated that his lifetime of kills exceeded $50,000 in cattle and sheep.

Three Toes lived to an old age and reached the peak of his destruction in the 1920s. Gilfillan wrote, "For first, last, and all the time, Three Toes was a killer. Other wolves might kill one cow or sheep and eat off that and be satisfied. But Three Toes killed for the sheer love of killing. He would kill on a full stomach as well as when hungry. On one occasion he visited three different ranches in one night, killed many sheep and lambs at each one, but ate only the liver of one lamb."

Officials bumped the bounty for Three Toes to $500, but no hunter could catch the cunning old wolf. In July of 1925, federal wolf hunter Clyde F. Briggs settled on a ranch near the center of Three Toes' hunting range. For weeks Briggs set his traps, and Three Toes carefully eluded them. But he was tricked on July 23 by a hidden trap. The earth around him was scratched and plowed by his frantic efforts to escape from the trap's grasp by the time Briggs arrived. The trapper muzzled and hog-tied the big wolf and put him in the

The "Hero" Standing over
Old Three Toes

back seat of his car, intending to deliver him to Rapid City alive. But soon a passenger cried, "I think he's dying."

"Briggs stopped the car, and looking around, found the wolf's eyes fixed on him. But the eyes did not see him, for the wolf was dead," wrote Gilfillan. "Call it a broken heart, or what you will —something of this sort is what killed the old wolf. He was resting easily when found, his wounds were superficial . . . but there was something in his grand old spirit that could not brook capture, and Nature, more merciful than he had ever been, granted him his release." [4]

As I said, I would tell you a story, and this story was about a wolf written by a human. What follows is a different story written by a *wolf about humans*. The wolf is Old Three Toes, but it could just as well be Two Socks, the Custer Wolf, or a million others we have slaughtered:

You came to our land, uninvited. You took it from us as if you were the lords of creation. You gave us nothing. Your arrogance was so staggeringly immense that you seemed unaware that others live here: the Cheyenne, Lakota, and the Crow, the bison, deer, elk, fox, black-footed ferrets, prairie dogs, golden and bald eagles, black and grizzly bears, magpies and ravens, and gray wolves. Our family was large, healthy, and interdependent. You brought disease so that the Cheyenne and their brothers died in high numbers their bodies covered in horrible red sores. You brought boomsticks so like a coward to kill us from a distance. You brought terrible devices with iron teeth that grasp our legs and will not yield until we die in horrific agony. You also brought poison, so animals—all birds and all animals—that eat it die in anguish, and death is a blessed release. And you looked at your works, and you saw that it was "good."

You build your large dens above ground and put fences everywhere to separate us from our brothers and sisters and our prey. You kill everything you see. And after you killed all our animals, you bring in your own—those poor domesticated beasts that do your bidding, and then you eat them. Those few of us who are left, what are we supposed to eat when all our food is gone?

After you have poisoned millions with your pellets and killed others with your boomsticks, you claim victory. You murdered my entire family: my mate, my only sister, and her two brothers. You even killed my mother and father, and you claim I am the "wild animal."

A Pyramid of Bison Bones

I judge you to be unfit to rule over us as a god-king. You are the most potent force for evil I have ever known. Your history, your behavior, lead to some of the darkest places in the animal heart.

You say I killed 50 sheep in one night yet ate the liver of only one lamb. But you murdered millions of bison and ate just their tongues (see photograph), and often you poured poison on the uneaten carcasses so no one else could feast. Consequently, every living creature, bird, mammal, and mouse, in the surrounding area died an agonizing death. And ultimately when all your poison had been eaten, flies laid their eggs, and only maggots have their fill.

You said I was an enormous wolf, but at death, I weighed only 84 lbs., barely a wolf almost a coyote. You said I was 20 years old, but no wolf lives that long in the wild. I had no birthdays; I never counted the few years I had.

You finally caught me in two of your fiendish traps with iron teeth, although they do not kill, they inflict appalling pain. You left me in agony for days before you returned to claim your prize. Then, helpless as I was, you bound me with sturdy ropes and threw me in the back of one of your noisy smoke wagons. You thought to put me in a cage for public display and ridicule. But know this, I was born free in the land of the big sky, and I died free, denying you your victory. I am a wolf, a fierce ryder in life's whirlwind. You may kill me, but you will never tame my spirit.

Now I am a memory in the minds of those who love me. Once you hated me, but now you build statues to me (Buffalo, South Dakota). And like a legend, I am immortal. No one remembers you, and I refuse to repeat your name here. You are lost to memory and history as just another heartless executioner. Books* are written about me, and all you have are a few yellow newspaper clippings. We are both gone now: one to oblivion, the other to legend.

The Last Wolf: A Ryder in Life's Whirlwind

PERSONAL POSTSCRIPT

You are your memories; your memories are you. I mean that literally. If you woke up tomorrow morning with no memories, you would be an alien in an alien land.

A caring teacher in grade five—who somehow knew my past—recommended a book for me to read. Now to that moment, I had never read an entire book, so this was my first. I do not recall much detail from this story, of course, but the emotions it kindled are as bright and real to me as yesterday. Recently I searched for this young person's book on Amazon, BookFinder, and elsewhere but to no avail. In some ways, I am the living embodiment of those black letters on white paper. That book was *Old Three Toes*.

---

* *The Last Wolf* by Gary Enright 204 pages ISBN-10: 1882159659

It was well after midnight before Big Red grew restless. Being accustomed to the freshness of the forest, the odor of decaying hay and rotting timbers was new and grew annoying to him. And without the light from the stars, it was black inside the barn but for a few slivers of light slipping in between the boards. He arose, did the downward facing dog position to stretch and passed from darkness to light by way of the missing board. Peeing high up on the barn, but not to claim ownership, he then moved away from this crumbling structure toward a large sugar maple tree.

Remembering clearly how his call from a few nights ago had been answered by a soft, almost happy howl, he had a need to sing once more of his pain to this dark, mysterious world. Turning toward the barn, he released a torrent of defiance letting the world know who and where he was. And out of the darkness, the universe answered *at once*. Startled for an instant, he howled again, and as before the answer was immediately returned.

He then realized the voice from the darkness was his own. When in his natal territory, he had experienced this previously. His parents had taken Little Red Ears, Paws, and himself on a fall training run. They were near the barns of the farmer who lived about a mile (1.6 km) distant from their den. Big Red recalled how those echoing barns had answered as well.

Turning his back to the barn, he sang again with the most exquisite, deep voice that spread over the forest like wildfire before the wind. He waited for an answer, then he called again even longer and lower than before. Again, he paused, and an answer came out of the darkness, the same happy howl from several nights ago, but it was closer now. In response, he sang a friendlier song, and a soft voice replied. They continued for some time, and our wolf knew this boded well.

With no desire to return to the barn, he found a dry area under the maple tree. It was a moonless night in early May, so the tree was still leafless, and the stars shone like diamonds through its branches leading to the infinite sky. After some soft and warm feelings toward the night singer from the darkness, he slept.

WOLVES: RYDERS IN THE WHIRLWIND

I am presently writing the book you are now reading. And my need to write about wolves comes from deep memories in early childhood, even before I went to school. We had a farm in the hinterlands of Haliburton, Ontario. The house was large and rambling with two staircases, the barns numerous and filled with animals of all varieties. Most importantly, there was love. I wish to share some of these early memories with you so you will understand my motivation:

An amber glow shone from the window of the house with the two staircases on a warm summer evening; four children huddled around a man, listening to his stories. Their only lamp cast no heat, but that did not matter for they were listening intently as he recounted another of his hunting adventures. It could have been a scene out of central Asia with everyone gathered around a campfire telling tales of the day's bear hunt, for the broad outline of these tales is always the same. The hero goes forth on a dangerous quest; he meets his adversary, engages him in battle, and defeats him, returning home in triumph.

In much of the world, the evil adversary has been the wolf—top predators always dislike each other. My uncle was a superb teller of very tall tales; his enthusiasm and conviction were contagious. Whether the stories were true really did not matter to us children. Yet, in all his many encounters with wolves—and he spent his life outdoors—he never spoke of killing one. If I close my eyes, I can be there again lost in rapture with my imagination, adding the color and sound to his Homeric tales.

The Algonquin Wolf

At the dramatic climax, my cousin's sisters would often become frightened and run to their mother, who was putting away the supper dishes. Although my cousin and his sisters were all the same age—they were triplets—the girls rarely went outdoors by themselves and never into the forest. They had a different life.

After an hour or so of these narratives, we would become aware of the slight hiss of the Aladdin mantle lamp. My uncle always returned the hero by just surviving the wolves tracking him or surrounding him at his campfire. He had no hatred toward wolves just respect for a worthy adversary, so my cousin and I had none as well. But of all creatures on the farm, the wolves gripped our imagination in a way words cannot express. After the stories, many of which we had heard before, my cousin and I would go to bed, stroke the stuffed owl's head at the top of the staircase, and lie down to dream of our quests and encounters with wolves.

Outside the house, all the farm animals were sleeping. The barns bathed in the gray stillness of moonlight while the faint glow of the stars appeared otherworldly. The horses in their stanchions rested standing up with locked knees. In another barn, the geese and ducks wiggled a nest in some straw while the chickens and turkeys took to the highest roosts they could find. The pigeons were asleep in the loft of the post-and-beam barn. And the pigs, after having rolled in more mud against late-summer mosquitoes, "cuddled" in a small group in their huge outdoor enclosure. But the cows were elsewhere on the farm no doubt at the crest of some rise lying in a rough circle, sleeping but aware of predators. Wolves particularly spooked them.

Nonetheless, not every creature was sleeping: the barn cats were stalking mice while the mice were searching for food. Some milk snakes in the haymow were also hunting mice. Life was everywhere, but it was quiet, secretive.

Beyond the barns, in the spring field, the slash, the little fallow field, and further still was a noisy quietness. Nighthawks flying over the meadows would occasionally see a ghostly figure move from grove to forest—possibly a bear, deer, moose, fox, fisher, or even a wolf. At the furthest end of the farm in a valley we called the back-barn flat, we had another sizeable two-story structure in which my grandfather stored hay. On this August night just after midnight, a pack of wolves joyous with life rushed out of the tall hemlock forest to the south to cross this open area. There were seven; this year's pups were on a training run.

Sleeping, we knew nothing of this. Yet in coming decades when I had built my home at the top of the hill, above the back-barn flat (see map page 273), I began to realize this area was a well-used runway.

A Young Algonquin Wolf

On hundreds of nights, wolves would wake me with their astonishing howls*—and this vast wilderness song moved me profoundly. Here was a creature that did not need us and lived free in a way humans had not for ten millennia. They have their own families, their own moral values, and as we will see in a future chapter, their own wild justice.

And eventually, Big Red's family renovated a den in the rusty-colored soil near the red pine trees that I had planted as a boy. I felt protective of this den and the wolves that lived there, so periodically I would walk by to check up on things. We were acquaintances. I laughingly called them my "outside dogs."

Big Red awoke well before dawn in his free home under the maple tree and the stars. It had been a comfortable night because the mosquitoes were not yet out, and the air was fresh. Sensing other life nearby was comforting even for a wolf who did not care for the sound of his own voice.

---

* Listen to these wolves on the website *The Science Behind Algonquin's Animals* and be astonished (www.sbaa.ca/projects.asp?cn=314).

The constellation of Orion the Hunter was rising in the east accompanied by his two wolfdogs, Canis Minor and Canis Major. To the Greeks, dogs were so noteworthy that they placed them in the sky as a remembrance. Here on earth, however, Big Red strode across the field under the uncaring stars, neither savior nor Satan, just a wolf on a Homeric quest.

The Wolf and The Stars

Chapter—11

WOLVES VS. BEARS

A bear's days are warmed by the same sun,
his dwellings are overdomed by the same blue sky,
and his life turns and ebbs with heart-pulsings
like ours and was poured from the same First Fountain.
John Muir, naturalist, "Finding a Dead Yosemite Bear," October 1871

When I was younger, I would take my dog out every evening for his last walk. Most nights brought some new sight or sound, and I marveled at nature's variety. Many evenings, shortly after sunset, my dog would stop, sit, and stare intently into the darkening wilderness. This stopping and staring would happen several times, and I quickly learned to pay attention—something extraordinary was about to happen. Before long, a pack of wolves would howl from the direction of the valley, and both man and dog would listen up smartly.

When you are in the forest or the field with a dog, you need fear no living thing. Your dog will stand by you to the death, at least that is my experience. Besides, wolves should not be feared. Nonetheless, this wolf song touches something primitive within us, and the hair stands up on the back of our necks. These howls

The Three Noses

always came from the valley near my home, which was situated on an enormous plateau. My dog was a composite of bearded collie and Irish wolfhound—huge, gentle, and restrained, and certainly not on a leash. He never returned their calls, but he would glance at me as if to say, *I told you so*. Later I discovered these wolves had a den in this valley halfway up the far side, so they were broadcasting warning calls: stay away—this land is our land. This was the den where Big Red was born. In decades past, my grandfather had a barn in this valley to store hay, but just the foundation stones remain. I knew this valley well. As a boy, I had played there with my cousin, and we ran through the fields like foxes.

My dog and I continued our walk, listening and learning. The wolves knew we were here, my dog knew they were there; I knew nothing. Such are the secret abilities of canines both *lupus* and *familiaris*. It seems evident that these canines could smell each other (*see* photograph). That big snout they have is not a perch for spectacles, but for a unique gathering of olfactory glands. A wolf's sense of smell is better than a dog's and 100 times that of a human.

🐾

Big Red was still a considerable distance from the valley of his birth but moving swiftly. Although he had started trotting in the starlight, it was daylight now. Not long after sunrise, he picked up a sulfurous smell, a whiff of decay while more than a mile away. This foul stench increased as he walked and soon, he saw something lying on the forest floor dappled by the sunlight. Here was the rotting carcass of a once-great bruin of the north woods. Yet death was alive with a million maggots. Our wolf was both repulsed and mesmerized! There was nothing here he wanted, even the vultures turned away in disgust. Most of the bruin's enormous skull was bare and therefore free of maggots. His remarkable eye teeth were now on full display (*see* photograph).

Why did this bear perish in this place at that time? Now without evidence, you must make an educated conjecture. Consider, however, this bear was only a couple of weeks out of hibernation, which inevitably left him weakened. In the wild, black bears can live upward to 25 years but rarely reach that age. Hunger, hunters, and cars kill most before they are ten. I guess this bear died of old age. He appeared to be on his way to pick nearby spring leeks (ramps), and, at this place and at that time, he had lain down to rest never to rise again. As I noted elsewhere, every creature has a last step, a final beat in a train of billions—all good things end.

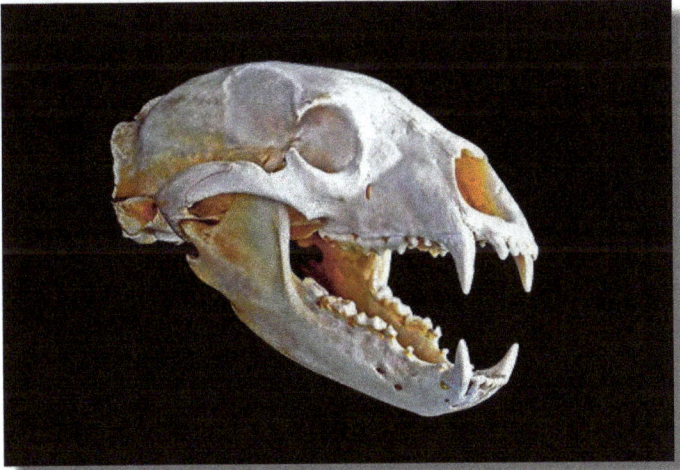

Skull of a Black Bear

I have referred to this bear as "he" because of his enormous size: males are often twice as large as females, both as cubs and adults. And they need to be large to defend their territories from competing boars (male bears). Also, the older the bear, the bigger. The large boar had his paws neatly folded, seeming to imply "Yes, I have been a very good boy" (*see* photograph). All authoritative texts refer to *Ursus americanus*, the black bear, as "a shy woodland creature." But that is only part of the story.

Big Red hurriedly left this scene of death and transformation. He was in search of something more appetizing, a venison dinner perhaps. And since most deer were in a weakened condition after their harsh winter ordeal, they were easier to catch than in the summer or fall. Perhaps good fortune awaited him.

For some time, our wolf had been hearing unusual noises coming from up ahead. Unknowingly, he was approaching Algonquin Park's single, sizeable paved road—a place of danger and death. Both deer and moose tend to congregate along its grassy sides in the spring to enjoy the runoff from last winter's road salt.

I Have Been a Very Good Boy

In the predawn, a doe, who had survived the cruel winter in good condition, cantered up a steep grade to reach the roadside at the moment a pickup truck approached. With just a single hoof on the pavement, the oncoming vehicle lights mesmerized her. Seconds later, the truck's rear-view mirror shattered the side of her head—from life to death in an instant. Her limp, warm body tumbled down the embankment coming to rest out of sight of the road.

Her bodily gasses soon escaped from both ends of her digestive tract into the air, and the odor of death wafted through the nearby forest, awakening the thumb-sized black and orange carrion beetles. Within hours, Big Red encountered this faint odor, and he quickly found the carcass—she was cold now but still prime venison. Our wolf smiled at his good fortune and began to dine.

He had been feeding for a few minutes when an uninvited male black bear thought to join him at dinner. Wolves and bears are near opposites; the former is a pack animal, the latter a grumpy loner. On this occasion, it was Big Red who was alone and stood no chance of defeating a giant bear by himself, and he knew it. In his first winter out of the den, our wolf had witnessed his father, mother, and aunt attack a bear. And his father, who led the charge, never entirely recovered. Today, neither bear nor wolf had any intention of sharing!

This was their decisive moment. Without fanfare or a human audience to cheer on either animal, only their genes would "remember" this day. The wolf was faster, the bear stronger. The deer was too heavy for Big Red to carry away, so he stood over it defiantly. To display his anger, the bear snorted and huffed while advancing. When he reached the deer's shattered head, he engulfed it in his enormous mouth dragging the carcass from between the wolf's legs. Big Red clamped his teeth on the doe's rump resulting in a tug-of-war splitting the animal into two pieces. Despite their size, bears are surprisingly quick and agile. The bruin dropped the doe's head and lunged at our wolf who just avoided the bear's jaws but felt his enormous claws pass effortlessly through the thick fur on his haunch. Then they circled around the dismembered deer, each trying to intimidate the other, one growling the other huffing. Their dialects were different, but they understood each other.

Big Red vs. Black Bear

By now, an audience of turkey vultures and ravens had arrived, each ornamenting their own dead pine tree at the forest's edge. Their black silhouettes blended with the dark cobalt sky. They took the side of neither bear nor wolf. Their job was to patrol the park's ribbon of death to clean up the roadkill.

Big Red's unbelievable confidence in the face of near death was absurd. Undoubtedly, the bear was going to eat venison today; the only question was how much? The circling and lunging by the bear continued for some minutes. At each attack the wolf barely avoided death. Finally, the bruin realized this weird wolf was not going to give up, so he made his decision. Once again, the bear grasped the deer's head in his mouth, but this time he walked off the field of combat, neither winner nor loser, just a quitter. Big Red smiled once more and dragged the hindquarters into the forest to feed. There was more than enough meat here for one wolf.

Our wolf ate and rested until near sunset before he left to find lodgings for the night. Trotting quickly along the road's grassy edges, he hid behind bushes whenever bright lights approached. Uncertain why he did this, but his instincts assured him those lights did not bode well for wolves. After a few miles, he left the road seeking higher ground in the forest to made a bed. Near midnight a young wolf found the hindquarters Big Red had abandoned, and she also fed.

Sleep came quickly to our wolf, but uneasy dreams of bears followed close behind.

The Black Bear, *Ursus americanus*

Black bears can grow to enormous sizes—some exceed 800 lbs. (363 kg). Nevertheless, the cubs will be born the size and weight of two oranges. Worse yet, each helpless cub lives in a hole in the ground with a hibernating mother in early February. At that time of year in Algonquin Park, temperatures can plummet to $-40°$.

As I wrote about wolf pups, death seems imminent! Still, such is evolution, that neither bear cubs nor wolf pups are put in a situation they cannot survive.

Yet how do they survive? First, hibernation for bears is not a vegetative state but more of a torpor, inducing only a slight drop in body temperature. One glance inside a bear's den and the full, unblinking stare of a sow (mother bear) will convince you of this fact—and of the wisdom of a speedy retreat. The burrow is snug so the mother's body can heat it, and the cubs snuggle for life itself. Although the sow neither urinates nor defecates all winter, she will lactate such creamy milk that the cubs develop quickly. The mother licks her cubs to stimulate defecation and then eats their feces to keep the den clean—as with a wolf bitch, the sow provides premium daycare.

Wolves and bears typically give each other a wide berth. Exceptions to this rule are rare and usually deadly. A wolf, for example, would be beyond foolish to confront a mother bear with cubs (*see* photograph). One is an omnivore specializing in shoots and leaves; the other a carnivore focusing on deer and beavers. Bears have been around much longer than wolves; they live longer and have an easier time than their canine forest neighbors. Each is at the peak of an evolutionary mountain, but these are different mountains with a deep valley between them.

Mother Bear & Cubs

During Little Red Ears, Paws, and Big Red's first winter hunting with their pack, the deer were missing. Because of the extreme cold and deep snow, these animals migrated to a distant deer yard. Here the Ministry of Natural Resources (MNR) fed them a rich mixture of oats, corn, and molasses. Near the wolf pack's home, all the rooms in the snow-white mansions of the forest were empty of life. In retrospect, our wolf's family should have followed the deer, but wisdom after the fact is pointless. During that forbidding time, they "lived" on mice, red squirrels, one fisher, and two porcupines. But this pack was not alive; it was barely breathing.

Deer Mouse   Red Squirrel

Fisher   Porcupine

Desperate times require desperate measures, so Big Red's father decided on a perilous plan to save his family and himself. This was a plan so dangerous and bizarre that it may never have been attempted before.

From previous years, this alpha male knew of a den on the side of an ancient glacial lake where bears hibernated (*see* map). It was about a mile (1.6 km) as the crow flies or several as the wolves struggled single file through the deep snow double printing where they could. Upon arrival, the family members realized this was an inauspicious setting. The den was on a slope composed of loose gravel, providing poor footing for an attack. The entrance to the lair was ringed with ice crystals, showing there was a beast inside. Since the den entrance was narrow, Big Red's father would have to go in alone. As noted, before, bears are not sleeping during hibernation, just in torpor, and they can be swiftly aroused. Unaided, it was impossible for the alpha to kill this imposing animal. So, he resolved to antagonize it to such an extent that the bear would pursue him out of the den where this desperate family of six could confront *Ursus americanus*.

Fortunately, the den was shallow, allowing in a little light and a quick exit for the wolf. The alpha had to confront the boar three times before he could sufficiently infuriate the beast to chase him from his lair. The great bear burst from the den in a shower of snow and furiously attacked the wolf pack. The six wolves reciprocated in kind as the bear circled frantically to catch one of his tormentors. The wolves were attempting to exhaust the bear sufficiently so that one of the three adult wolves could inflict a deep neck wound. The bear's stamina was formidable, but the wolves, although weakened by starvation, were unrelenting. The bear realized their stratagem, so he clawed his way up the lake's embankment and clambered up a tree. Safe now, the wolves retreated out of sight, but they did not leave. Sometime after sundown, the bear descended the tree and returned to his den.

The wolf pack saw this, but they waited until morning before returning. Once more, the alpha male entered the den by himself. This time the bruin chased him out instantly, and a horrific fight ensued. Here, lost in a wilderness of snowy cathedrals, a struggle for life occurred between one bear and six wolves. Leading the attack, Big Red's father sustained a hard wallop to the left side of his head that sent him flying, causing the loss of two teeth. At that instant, Paws and Big Red each sank their teeth deep into opposite sides of the bear's throat so that the beast suffocated. In this place, at this time the brothers had proven themselves worthy of the species *lupus* in the family *Canidae*. This was their rite of passage.

One died so that six might live—some say the lives of the many outvalue the life of the one. This massive meal sustained the pack for a month, and by that time the deer were returning to their usual yards. Although he did survive, the alpha male was never the same, and he fathered no more sons and daughters.

🐾

Abruptly, Big Red awakened from a nightmarish memory. He rose, watered, and fertilized the land before tightly curling up for the rest of the night. In the distance, he could hear the unnatural sounds of the highway.

🐾

Bears are plentiful, wolves are few. Algonquin Park has 2,000 black bears yet just 150 wolves. All reference books say bears are loners; I have said so myself. This is true, but there are fascinating exceptions.

Unless you have children, you cannot fully know the remarkable bond between parent and child—both human and nonhuman. Bear cubs stay with their mother for 17 months; all the while she is protective and affectionate. During the first summer, they nurse every day cradled between mum's legs as she licks their bodies. And, in the fall, they will take a long "sleep" together, snuggling for warmth, with mother's body blocking the den entrance. But next summer everything changes!

The following June, the sow becomes intolerant of her cubs and tries to drive them away—or so the textbooks say. Yet this is not what I have seen from my home above the valley of Big Red's birth den. Instead, the parting is more like the one that occurred between the "Little Lady" and her mother. The mother commanded her obedient cub (*see* the photograph of the "Little Lady with the Pancake Bum") to stay in the middle of my field. Then she shuffled off into the forest only to return in 20 minutes to see her cub again. Then, once more, she left. This coming and going repeated itself half a dozen times throughout three hours. It had every appearance of a long, sad goodbye. Finally, she left forever! Now was her time to find a gentleman caller—not a hard task I might add. Boars impregnate sows every two years.

Remarkably, the still-obedient cub stayed in the field until sundown obeying mother's command. It may have waited hours longer, but I could not tell on that moonless night. She was gone in the morning. Now, obedience by itself will not help her survive, although it has taught her many lessons. Life now required a new paradigm. Some learn, some do not; some live, some die. Life's challenge is always the same—adapt or perish.

Little Lady with the Pancake Bum

In her hunger, our young orphan tackled a porcupine—always a poor menu choice (*see* the photograph, white arrows show three quills). Unlike some dogs we had on the farm, she will never repeat this mistake. I was cheering for her survival, although half of all such castaways die before fall hibernation.

Porcupine Problem

The reader has already realized bears have fantastic physiology. Neither urinating nor defecating, they lie in a dirt hole for five months with no ill effects and no bone density loss. Somehow, they reprocess the urea in their urine to create new proteins. I know of no other animal that can do that. Scientists are studying this incredible ability to help the bedridden and astronauts, both of whom lose considerable bone density from lack of exercise or weightlessness, respectively.

If the fall berry and apple crop should fail, a starvation year ensues, and the sow's body will absorb any developing fetus(es) to preserve her life—nature's birth control. So that winter, she will have no cub(s). This unusual phenomenon will synchronize the estrus periods for female bears over the entire crop failure area. I became aware that these periods were in sync in my region.

Because of this phenomenon, the unfortunate little lady with the quills in her face had much competition for food from other orphans. One sow I knew had two large male cubs that she had turned out into the world. Whether she left them at various times or whether she cast them out together, I cannot say. What I do know is I would see one or the other every few days.

Much against the advice of my friends and everyone else, I decided to feed these three orphans with cracked corn and dog kibble. I marvel at the wonders of evolution—this book celebrates its creations—yet that is not a moral or intellectual imperative to imitate its severity. So, I stepped in and fed these foundlings who quickly learned to come to my free kitchen several times a day. Both they and I were amply rewarded. The dejected female orphan, who was left in my field, grew into a beautiful animal. In the years that followed, she had many cubs of her own. She always brought them to dinner. Clearly, she did not bring her progeny to show me, but she did manifest a presence and a sense of pride that said, "I, *Ursus americanus*, made these things." She grew to become the bear I called "Mother Courage" in Chapter-13.

The two male cubs I mentioned earlier finally met at my food kitchen. To me, this chance meeting was extraordinary for solitary animals. They greeted each other with hugs—yes, bear hugs—and kisses (*see* photograph "Bear Brothers United"). Their chance encounter was nothing less than joyous. No longer alone and afraid! Stand by me they implied to each other, and they did all that summer.

Since they were young and carefree in the forest and the fields, they marched to no drummer but their own. Every day was endless and the summer an eternity. Although they were not in search of moose, wolves, or other bears, they did on rare occasions find one.

Bear Brothers United

On this fine day, they went into the forest behind my home and turned east toward the rising sun. Perhaps they looked for berries—they were always looking for berries.

Friendship between two animals of the same species is the way of the world. Friendship between two animals of different species, however, is the stuff of myth and legend and justly celebrated in renowned stories: *Androcles and the Lion, Charlotte's Web*, and *The Yearling*. Dogs and humans form the closest and most perfect interspecies bond. But, I repeat, the universe is vast and full of wonders, and what Finnish photographer Lassi Rautiainen captured in the wilds of northern Finland was extraordinary. For ten days, he recorded a profound partnership between a gray she-wolf and a brown he-bear. Rautiainen witnessed the strange pair meeting every evening to share food after a grueling day of hunting. No one knows when or how this relationship formed, but by now each needed the other.

It is noteworthy that these peak predators were of opposite genders, and both were young like the bear brothers. When not hunting, they were together and unbelievably sharing their food. Even dogs in the same household rarely do this. Clearly, their bond was not

Stand by Me

about food or procreation, but it seems clear they just enjoyed each other's company. **The sound of silence is the sound of loneliness.**

The forests are dreary dark and deep,
And we have fears we quietly keep.
Wolf and bear need not their fate bemoan,
If they stand together, they are never alone.

This Evening the Wolf Brings Dinner

Big Red awoke to a forest coming back to life. The scent of buds breaking into leaves on every tree and bush was an elixir for his senses. He felt as he did at Grand Lake before his fateful crossing of the ice—he might have been Adam on his first day in the Garden of Eden. But here there were no forbidden fruits, just foolish choices. Springing to his feet, he stretched briefly and began a fast trot through the forest. Leaving the highway behind, he headed southwest toward home.

Eventually, the highway noise dissipated, but a different and gentler sound flooded the forest, like the wind in the trees. This crisp chattering attracted our wolf, and shortly he discovered its source: a stream, past full flood, yet flowing swiftly to a nearby lake.

A long shallow stretch of water caught Big Red's eye where a late run of white suckers sparkled through the froth and foam to lay their eggs in the ecstasy of creation. Their silver backs caught the sun in flight and sparkled as they deposited eggs in the gravel where attendant males quickly fertilized them. The wolf had seen

The White Sucker

this fish before, and although they tasted fine, their bodies were a vast labyrinth of sharp bones. He would not eat them; besides, he was full of venison—but nearby was someone who would. On the opposite bank of this narrow stream, a giant black bear was ambling toward this fishing spot. The bear smelt the wolf from a far distance, but neither was willing to leave. Big Red continued down his side of the stream, and the bear shuffled up the other.

Now they were close, but neither flinched nor sprang into the forest. It was not in Big Red's nature to give way or show fear, and apparently, the bear was similarly made. Both were deadly silent, although they secretly glanced at each other. The massive bruin advanced to the start of the school of egg-laying suckers.

At this point, wolf and bear were mere paces apart, yet each proceeded carefully, deliberately choosing every step. At the exact instant they were closest, both animals raised their heads and stared directly into the eyes of their challenger. They took the measure of each other—and then walked on by. The bear wanted fish; the wolf did not.

Bear Going Fishing

Chapter—12

WILD JUSTICE

*Man in his arrogance thinks of himself a great work, worthy
the interposition of a deity. [Yet it is] more humble and,
I believe truer to consider him created from animals.*
Charles Darwin, *The Descent of Man*

S ince noon, Big Red had detected a pungent stench coming
from the surrounding forest. This odor was not just foul; it
was foreign. A nose as large as our wolf's is a deep repository of memories, and this stink was not one of them. In the forest,
you can only see as far as the next tree or bush, so wolves and bears
came to rely on their noses more than humans. Odors can slide
around trees like a river around rocks. Our wolf was sure the stench
came from scat, but the scat-terer was unknown. He thought no
more about it; he had other concerns.

For several days, Big Red was aware he was being followed
again, and it was not by ravens—it was by another wolf. The wolf
that had been answering his night songs, perhaps? Should he circle
back and see her, or should he let her find him? At Vireo Lake, he
had vainly circled back trying to find the she-wolf called Shadow.
Within the hour, however, this dilemma would resolve itself.

Sound in the forest travels faster and farther than odors. And
from a distance, piercing squeals and yelps alerted Big Red to
some calamity. Most run from danger, few run toward it. Within
minutes, he arrived at an astonishing scene.

A lone wolf was fighting off three bizarre creatures (*see* a
photograph of "The Three Big Pigs"). Yet, at any time, she was at
will to just leave. Staying hidden to preserve the element of surprise,
Big Red had every intention of helping this audacious, persistent
she-wolf. From his hidden place, he determined the ringleader
among these three hairy forms before emerging from the forest. His
jaws clamped inexorably on the neck of the most massive beast,
snapping it quickly. As he did this, the animal released a stream of
the pungent stench that Big Red had smelt earlier in the day. After
this, the beast's two backups swiftly faded into the forest.

The Three Big Pigs

The other wolf, a young female, was still here, but now standing at Big Red's side. Our wolf had been so lonely for so long that had this beautiful animal looked like a junkyard dog, he would have loved her. They shared their affection, and although wolves only breed once a year in the winter, Big Red knew he had found his mate.

He came to realize these wild boars had not attacked her— she had attacked them. She was a fierce animal who, like our wolf, knew little fear but brought much. In his mind, he called her *Spitfire* for she was a wild, free, and joyous creation.

Spitfire, Big Red's Mate

There was no marriage ceremony. There were no witnesses. No papers to sign, no marriage license, no wedding party. No bridesmaids, no best wolf. No gifts, no honeymoon trip. No male parent to give her away. There were no wedding vows and no wedding bells. But there would be no divorce—wolves mate till death do them part. Like humans, however, on occasions, alpha males will practice polygamy. Nonetheless, these two were just as much joined as two royals married with pomp and circumstance before the world rather than alone in this quiet place under the vast canopy of Algonquin Park.

The Snugglers

But there would be a wedding supper of back bacon and pork loin. To prepare for this, the wedding couple kicked sand and soil over the wild boar's foul scat. They considered their dinner delicious and ate much. Afterward, they left this scene to find a place to spend the night. Spitfire willingly followed Big Red's direction. She moved with such grace and lightness that her paws barely kissed the earth. Her gaze like his was one of happiness and serenity. Together their movements, unlike the stumbling of dogs, are smooth, refined, and choreographed flowing effortlessly over forest and field.

The shadows were lengthening before they came to a small silver lake and made their bed together on a rocky abutment. Their affection for each other was all-consuming as they rubbed their bodies together and pawed one another (*see* photograph). When his mate laid down under the stars, Big Red spooned her body with his. He was no longer alone. And now there were two.

INCEST AVOIDANCE

Big Red and Spitfire were dispersing wolves or emigrants as humans say. By leaving their natal pack to find a mate and a new territory, wolves spread their genes and prevent inbreeding. In their essential book, *Wolf Country: Eleven Years Tracking the Algonquin Wolves*, John and Mary Theberge mention Redpole 4, a wolf who had progeny, hence genes, in at least five different packs.[1]

Yet there is something else happening here well beyond gene dispersal, something so profound that it touches close to our heart. By dispersal, wolves are avoiding incest—a universal human taboo—so these canids are practicing a high moral code. And wolves have been doing this long before we came down from the trees to wander the African savanna.

This moral code originates from natural selection. Genetics tells us that inbreeding is detrimental to the gene pool. Inbreed long enough, and paradoxically you will cease to exist. Consider the royal families of Europe where hemophilia was common—three of Queen Victoria's children had it as did seven of her grandchildren. Wolves and moral codes are not a pairing we would have expected. We grew up with tall tales of the Big Bad Wolf and Little Red Riding Hood and a hundred denigrating phrases on wolf viciousness and cruelty. And if not entirely false, these tales and stories were incomplete. For example:

- *If you live among wolves, you must act like a wolf.*
  Nikita Khrushchev
- *Careless shepherd makes excellent dinner for a wolf.*
  Earl Derr Biggers
- *The wolf on the hill is not as hungry as the wolf still climbing the hill.*
  Anonymous

THE GOLDEN RULE

Were there eyes on the hillside, quiet and attentive to the theater below? The wolf pups, however, were anything but; they jumped, tumbled, and ran continuously. This field in the valley below my home was their schoolyard where they played and prepared, on the edge of adulthood, practicing those behaviors life would need. To correct Descartes, "they play therefore they are!" At the crest of the valley, you could just hear their playful yelps and squeals. Otherwise, everything was quiet; time seemed imperceptible as the sunny field jumped with life. To paraphrase Dylan Thomas, these bouncy red balls ran their heedless ways in the sun born over and over. By producing pups, the alphas had fulfilled their genetic obligations, and their genes are still running through these and foreign fields.

The reader has seen a dozen or so documentaries on young animals playing. Inevitably, the commentator will point out that these young players are building muscle and stamina. He might also say that these pups are forming a dominance hierarchy among themselves, but he will never tell the following:

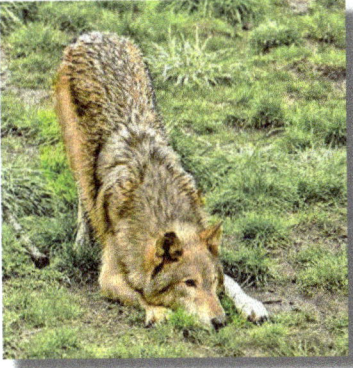

Wolf Play Bow
Courtesy of Dee Otter

The prelude to playing is the invitation to play (*see* photograph). Both dog and wolf recognize the downward-facing pose as "let's play." And there are rules in this game as Marc Bekoff and Jessica Pierce point out in their ground-breaking book, *Wild Justice: The Moral Lives of Animals.* Consider the following quote from page 116:

When animals play, they must agree to play. They must cooperate and behave fairly. Further, when fairness breaks down, play not only stops, it becomes impossible. Unfair play is an oxymoron, and this is why play is such a clear window into the moral lives of animals. [2]

Consider the playing between Little Red Ears and Paws when they were pups. Because of Paws larger size, their relative positions on the hierarchy ladder formed early, probably before they first left the den. Paws will play at her level of strength and vitality—that is, he will pull his punches. He knows what she can take and still be able to respond. In plain language, he is doing onto her what he wants done onto him. This is reciprocity at work, also called the Golden Rule. Big Red, who is stronger still than Paws, similarly treats his brother by pulling his punches.

If any infraction of the fair play rules occurs, say play biting too hard, the offender must ask for forgiveness or all play ceases. All the other players will shun a habitual offender to the point where no one will play with him. Often, these repeat offenders disperse early from their natal pack.

WHY ADULT WOLVES PLAY

What I wrote in Chapter-5 deserves repeating and expansion here. The prevailing paradigm for wolf behavior comes from Tennyson's *In Memoriam*, which calls nature's final law "red in tooth and claw." But if this were true of wolves, the pack would quickly disintegrate from animosity, injury, and death. If you risk your life every day, you will soon lose it. Of all wolf-pack interactions, at least 90 percent are prosocial rather than antisocial. That is not to say that wolves, like our military or our entire social order, do not have a strict hierarchy, which accounts for the remaining 10 percent.

In social groups with a hierarchical structure, a method is needed to release the tensions caused by restrictions on freedom. Ancient Rome developed the yearly feast of Saturnalia when masters served slaves. To be sure, the slaves prepared the food earlier. Wolves have a similar game in which the dominant individuals "handicap" themselves in role reversals with lower-ranking wolves by showing submission and allowing them to play bite. If a wolf bites too hard, it will "play bow" to ask forgiveness, and play resumes. This is a clear demonstration of fairness, so pack tensions diminish, and bonds strengthen.

Unlike the Romans who indulged in Saturnalia just once a year, wolves play fight regularly throughout the year. Bonding is tight and compassionate, especially around any newborn pups, to whom every wolf is a parent of sorts—older siblings from earlier litters, aunts, and uncles. If the alpha female happens to die giving birth or otherwise, various aunts will care for the young, and these females will even lactate. Wolf family values are legendary.

Marc Bekoff, Professor Emeritus of Ecology and Evolutionary Biology at the University of Colorado, claims that without a moral code governing their actions animals could not show these kinds of behaviors.

PROSOCIAL OR ANTISOCIAL

Wolves are rare, and hence rarely seen. Most people, even if they share territory with wolves, will never see one. In my area, wolf pack size—determined by the weight and the availability of prey—is five. And these few creatures hunt over a vast expanse of 80 mi.^{2} (210 km^2). To make the challenge of seeing them more difficult, most of their hunting occurs at night. So, your chances of seeing one are close to zero, and your opportunity to see wolf behavior is zero.

Photographers get their movie footage on wolf interactions exclusively from enclosures, compounds, or zoos. For an animal *born free,* these are unnatural conditions, and wolves react in unnatural ways: they are more aggressive and violent. Filmmakers like this because violence sells and makes money. This scenario fits Tennyson's "red in tooth and claw."

I have trail cameras that take photographs when activated by heat and motion in my absence. I have placed trail cameras in the forests of the farm for over two decades. Every path, burrow, pond, beaver damn, deer kill, and food cache has been memorialized. Initially, I used a film camera, but I quickly graduated to digital varieties when these became available. Instead of 24 shots on a roll of film, I have had as many as 16,000 on an SD card. To not startle the animal with a flashbulb, the newer cameras use infrared photography at night. Rarely does a bird or mammal realize it is being photographed, so all its behavior is natural. It seems clear that this unique and useful way to see wolf interactions is as normal as possible. Downloading the SD card onto my computer is like Christmas when you were a child: you never know who or what you are going to get.

My conclusion from viewing hundreds of short videos and thousands of photographs of wolves is simple: wolves rarely fight, scrap, or even snarl. Their behavior is almost entirely prosocial. We have been deceived by animal documentaries on the viciousness of wolves. Yet, this is not the full story.

WOLF BOY

There is a second way to enter the wild world of wolves, a way so bizarre that we readily dismiss it as outlandish: children "adopted" and raised by animals—usually wolves. Consider the following example taken from Wikipedia after *Googling* "feral children":

> Marcos Rodríguez Pantoja (born 7 June 1946, in Añora, Spain) is a noted feral child. He was reportedly sold to a hermitic goatherder at seven and after the goatherder's death, he lived alone with the wolves in the Sierra Morena. At 19, he was returned to civilization, but had difficulty adjusting. Gabriel Janer Manila went on to write a Ph.D. thesis concerning him, which was titled *He jugado con lobos* (English title *I Have Played with Wolves*).
>
> He later became the subject of the film *Entrelobos* (English title *Among Wolves*), in which he appears briefly.
>
> In March 2018 he gave an interview in which he said **he was disappointed in human nature and wished he could return to the mountains and leave society** [emphasis added].

At the time of writing, Marcos is still living at the age of 72. He is the most studied feral child ever. To this day, he dislikes cities with their pollution and noise, preferring the company of animals in the country. Remarkably, he often says wolves treated him better than humans!

Yet there is a need for caution here. Some of Marcos's later tales strain credulity and hence cast a shadow on his more important story. For example, he claims to have been "friends" with a snake and fed it milk from the goats and even more preposterous stories. Interested readers should *Google* "feral children" and follow the voluminous literature on him and view his many interviews on YouTube.

Legend declares that a she-wolf raised and suckled the twin founders of Rome, Romulus and Remus. Stories like this come from the time of myths and legends—at least we once thought so. A famous bronze statue called *The Capitoline Wolf* (*see* photograph) immortalizes these twins. Such tales have a kernel or more of truth, and we should not dismiss them out of hand. Of all the many stories of feral children abandoned by humans,

The Capitoline Wolf

wolves adopted most, perhaps because of their strong family values. Many of these children have profound difficulty integrating into human society, the language hurdle is the most problematic.

YAWNING

People do it; so do chimpanzees and bonobos, fish, cats, and dogs. Even human babies do it in the womb. But for our purposes, wolves do it. The biological use of yawning need not concern us. We are after other prey. Everyone knows it is contagious. Communal yawning is frequent among our closest relatives: chimpanzees and bonobos. Both have steadfast social natures. Intriguingly, it is *most contagious among social animals who know each other well*. Accordingly, we have the most potent yawning response to our family, our friends, acquaintances, and so on in that order. Why is this?

If you know someone well, you have a greater ability to understand and feel their emotions and are therefore more likely to yawn when they do. We call this ability to identify with others *empathy*, and wolves have it. At least they do for their friends and relatives (*see* photograph). And morality rests on empathy.

Yawning cultivates social bonds among wolves. Any individual not in sync with the group risks being left behind. This situation is analogous to the wolf who will not play fairly. Communal yawning does not definitely prove wolves have empathy, yet it is compelling evidence that wolves feel for their fellow lupines.

Let's all Yawn Together

A WOLF CALLED TRIPOD

Without their being able to speak, we have, nonetheless, gathered convincing evidence that wolves—at least for those within their pack—have a compelling moral code. Despite Hollywood and its love of violence, I see only prosocial behavior in thousands of my trail camera pictures. And the care they give to feral human children is startling and needs more investigation. Thirdly, communal yawning "speaks" clearly of deep empathy and an ethos that says we all stand or fall together. Lastly, we will recount the enduring story of a brave wolf called Tripod with the fierce green fire in her eyes.

In the time before memory, wolves ran freely across the Americas. They lived lives of great passion and immense bravery. As Charles Darwin said, "There is no fundamental difference between man and animals in their ability to feel pleasure and pain, happiness, and misery." But we have no records of these animals, so to us and to history, they never existed.

As I wrote previously, all that changed forever on January 12, 1995, when a long white truck rolled into Yellowstone Park through the Roosevelt Arch carrying its precious cargo of eight gray wolves from Jasper National Park in Alberta, Canada. Since then, the *Yellowstone Wolf Family Tree* records the birth, life, and death of every wolf in the Park. Find out more about the indomitable wolves of Yellowstone Park by becoming a guest of the Wolf Family Tree.

Visit www.wolfgenes.info, select the Ancestry tab, and follow the yellow brick road to become a guest of the Tree.

It is here that we can read the remarkable story of the small wolf with a fierce green fire in her eyes. Born April 2004 into the Cougar Creek Pack to an extraordinary mother from the illustrious bloodline of 7Fg and 2Mb, the founding alphas of the first-ever naturally formed family in Yellowstone Park—the Leopolds.

On January 24, 2008, Park officials radio-collared her as 632Fg.* Incredibly, she was missing a hind leg below the hock (*see* the photograph and note the human hand showing the missing leg). Undoubtedly, a snare inflicted this amputation when she wandered outside the Park's boundary.

A Wolf Called Tripod

Of all the fiendish devices man has constructed, snares are the cruelest. If it encircles your neck, death is inexorable, painful, and prolonged. You decapitate yourself—or amputate as in Tripod's case—by your struggling. She survived, and although she often fell behind during a hunt, she always caught up. Officially labeled 632Fg, visitors affectionately called her Tripod.

---

* The number identifies the radio collar, the uppercase F or M is for the gender, and the lowercase g or b stands for the coat color, gray or black.

During the winter of 2009, she left her family to join two dispersing brothers from Gibbon Meadows and founded a new pack in the territory north of her natal area. Nature will find a way and incredibly this wolf with the fierce green eyes—this runt amputee—became the alpha female and gave birth to two surviving pups. Life threw her to the wolves, so she returned as their leader.

It is my nature to be kind, gentle, and loving . . . but know this: when it comes to matters of protecting my friend, my family, and my heart, do not trifle with me, for I am also the most powerful and relentless creature you will ever know.

The Morality of Wolves

The largest killer of wolves is other wolves, just as the largest killer of humans is other humans. On November 5, 2009, after a heroic defense of her homeland, a rival pack of wolves killed Tripod. Upon death, her radio collar automatically went into mortality mode, alerting park officials who quickly arrived at the death scene. The question now was what would happen to her pups?

In an outstanding example of wolf family values, Tripod's mate, 647Mg, and an uncollared female raised these motherless pups to maturity. She had no genes in the game, nonetheless, she raised the pups as her own. Tripod, with her fierce green fire in her eyes, defied all the odds, so her genes still run all over Yellowstone Park.

Sometime before dawn, Spitfire gently disentangled herself from Big Red's sleepy embrace. She stood up and glanced back at her still sleeping lover and disappeared into the dark green forest.

Not long afterward, Big Red awoke in a panic. She was gone! Was this Vireo Lake all over again when Phantom went for a drink only to be killed? Or more likely had she just rejected him and moved on in search of a more suitable mate? He quickly found her departing scent, but he knew he should not follow her. She had made her decision and rejected him. The incredible pain of losing another mate and the impending loneliness was a dagger to his heart. In merciless grief, he stood transfixed oblivious to all the beauty and life around him.

Moments later, Spitfire strolled out of the forest with a freshly killed snowshoe hare in her mouth for breakfast. Big Red's mood instantly swung all the way from grief to joy as he licked and rubbed his body against hers while both their tails wagged wildly.

After enjoying a light breakfast of rabbit, all the world opened up to our wolf. The forest sang with the songs of the returning warblers, those jewel-like birds of the high canopy: Blackburnians, Nashvilles, and Yellow-rumps (*see* photographs). Our wolf had been foolish in his despair, his mate was just preparing breakfast.

Blackburnian   Yellow-rumped   Chestnut-sided

With the rabbit eaten, they trotted off in unison. Spitfire was aware Big Red had a destination in mind, and she also knew she would follow him anywhere. Each had found their mate till death do them part. They headed west.

Chapter—13

MOTHER COURAGE

*Every animal has his or her story, his or her thoughts,
daydreams, and interests. All feel joy and love, pain,
and fear, as we now know beyond any shadow of a doubt.*
Ingrid Newkirk, the co-founder of PETA

Together they trotted up through the evergreens toward a hardwood forest of maple, beech, and oak. At the top of the hill, these trees spill out carpeting a plateau. Midway through their journey, Big Red and Spitfire came to a spring bubbling out of the hillside and cascading down some smooth rocks to form small pools beloved by all the forest animals. They paused to lap the fresh, cold water into their thirsty mouths. Chipmunks, birds, and mice had been there earlier, and whirligig beetles skated on the pool's perfect surface.

All the trees were hardwoods now and our wolves noticed red squirrels biting on the lower side of sugar maple twigs to let the sap drip. Returning later to lap a sugary drink or lick a sweet icicle after a frosty night, these squirrels knew about tapping trees long before man. In unison, the wolves saw another animal in the distance eating wild leeks (aka ramps). It was a black bear trying to get his bowels moving by consuming these tasty wild onions. He ate them dirt, leaf, bulb, and all.

Farther up the expansive field of leeks was a smaller bear. Indeed, these bruins knew of each other's presence, yet there were more than enough wild onions for all.

Just Relaxing

Dabbled sunshine painted the forest floor since the trees were just beginning to leaf out. The songs of warblers, the screeching of red-shouldered hawks, and the croaking of ravens supplied a background of sound. Life was everywhere.

Since the wolves were downwind, the bears could not smell them. Anyhow, with their nostrils saturated with the pungent aroma of leeks, the bears could smell little else. Unless the previous fall had been a time of starvation, every sow has cubs in the springtime. Boars, other than impregnation, have no role in the life of their progeny. The first leek muncher was an old male who had eaten these delicacies every spring for many years. After his meal, he sat on what appeared to be a human-made pile of stones, his paw drooped, and time filled this moment with peace and calm (*see* photograph). Because Big Red and Spitfire wanted to dine on neither leeks nor bears, they quietly faded into the hardwood forest. This was bear country!

Any wolf of Spitfire or Big Red's age has had a good deal of experience with black bears. Given a chance, both bear and wolf will eat the other's young, yet this is a risky meal and best avoided. Our wolves were both alert to the opportunity and the challenge. Because of the acorns and beechnuts, this was indeed bear country. And these nuts make for big, fat bears.

Where's Mum?

Later that afternoon, the lovers came upon two small bear cubs (*see* photograph) who swiftly scaled a nearby tree to get out of danger. Like human children, bear cubs have much to learn. Lesson number one—taught by mum before they leave the safety of the den site—climb a tree if danger is present. When the threat is gone, the sow, with a few meaningful grunts, summons her cubs to scramble down, and then they vanish into the engulfing forest. A lesson taught, learned, and used!

Big Red and Spitfire were alert to the presence of the mother bear who was momentarily hidden by some boulders. Hearing the whimpering of her cubs, she rushed around the rocks like a T-Rex on a hunt (*see* photograph). An ancient scene unfolded, bear vs. wolves—where the outcome is never inevitable. Big Red knew from experience that of all the creatures he might meet in the forest, a mother bear guarding her young was the most formidable. Together the two wolves made their decision: leave now.

Mum aka *Ursus americanus*

In Big Red's mind, he never loses a fight, he just gains experience. He recalled the horrific encounter his family had during a starvation winter with a hibernating bear, who permanently injured his father. In a rite of passage, he and his brother, Paws, killed the bear and saved their family. That was a necessary battle; the present situation was a fool's challenge since food was abundant, and our wolves were not hungry.

In a gesture of bravado to show they were not afraid, just un-interested, both wolves walked away at a *leisurely pace*. The bear took note and waited until the wolves were gone before she called her cubs down from the tree. Then the entire family ambled off in the opposite direction.

Every action the sow took was to guarantee the safety of her cubs. Her fierceness was their shield. Her attention was that of a child worker. Her care was that of a human mother saying, "Do not mess with my children." The lessons she taught, the nursing she gave, the protection she provided, all serve as moral behaviors ensuring the survival of her progeny. Ethics and survival are inti-mately linked. Herbert Spencer's famous phrase,* "Survival of the fittest" is incomplete without moral values. Consider a salmon who lays thousands of eggs or a composite flower that releases hundreds of seeds. Neither has any morality, but both depend solely on their fecundity and luck to pass on their genes. Bears, wolves, and humans do not do that. They have few children and provide the precious few with incredible attention. That care is morally driven: protecting, grooming, teaching, and loving.

Mother & Child

---

* *Fittest is not strength*, but how the animal fits—as a hand in a glove—with the environment. If you are a bear or a wolf, a major part of that fitness is your moral behavior. Nature measures this fitness by the rate of survival of your selfish genes.

Trotting through the open forest under the hardwoods, Big Red and Spitfire made good time. During the day, the first blackflies of spring appeared, that scourge of the north woods. These pests wiggled into the wolves' fur and bit them until they bled. Favorite places are the nose, behind the ears, and the genital region. To escape these hordes, our wolves created a marital bed in a shallow rock cave since these annoyances like the light and fear the darkness. This cave could have been an old den. That night Big Red dreamt of bears and battles, and Spitfire felt his restlessness, so she drew closer.

A decade or so ago, I came upon a considerable mystery. It was a fall afternoon and, while walking down the road toward my home, I could not help but notice enormous undulations on the dusty road. A snake perhaps? Now I knew no part of Ontario, or indeed any place on earth, held a snake that huge, at least I hoped not. The S-shaped pattern was 30 inches (76 cm) wide, but its length was uncertain. I thought this thing must swallow deer for breakfast and dine on moose for lunch. My imagination was racing. Adding to the mystery were the occasional patches of dark blood—the remains of prey perhaps?

As the days passed and grew shorter, I often thought about this mystery. What if I ran into this creature on my daily rambles? Eventually, the first snow fell overnight, and that very morning, while checking for animal tracks, I came upon this fantastic winding trail for a second time—and it was close by my home! Once again there were dark bloodstains, this time on pristine snow. Should this alarm me? I thought not, because anything that large without legs could not move quickly.

On the other hand, if that were the case, how did this creature capture its prey? My mind was racing again. The mystery deepened when I saw fist-sized footprints in the snow on both sides of the undulations. If I had totally lost my mind, and I was not quite there yet, it is possible to imagine this as the serpent from the Garden of Eden. The creature God cursed and made legless to slither on its belly and eat the dust of the earth. In the real world, some snakes, particularly pythons, have vestigial legs. What was happening? How could I solve this enigma?

I have a few added delusions. In my imagination, I am a good wildlife photographer, but more interested in the subject than its quality. That is, I would prefer a poor picture of a moose, say, to an award-winning photograph of a landscape. As I mentioned previously, I have cameras that take photographs automatically by sensing both heat and motion. While these *trail cameras* take photos, I am usually at home drinking Glenmorangie single-malt scotch.

To photograph the extraordinary animal that made these tracks, I attached one of my unique cameras to a tree overlooking its trail. I activated it and left. Days passed, the snow melted, yet nothing happened: no photographs, no new tracks. I decided this camera trap needed some bait. Feed them, and they will come, or so I hoped. Nearby, I placed a large quantity of cracked corn on the off chance the creature was an herbivore and four lbs. (1.8 kg) of hamburger in case it was a carnivore—the more likely choice. The following morning, I could hardly wait to check the site. As I approached, I saw that all the food was gone, every bit of it and that there were tracks everywhere, including those of this undulating monster. More significantly, the display window on the camera revealed it had taken 186 photographs. Jackpot!

I replaced the memory chip and hurried home to boot up my computer to view these pictures. And what did I see? Bears, black bears, lots of them but no undulating monster. One large mother

Large Sow & her Two Small Female Cubs

bear or sow came early in the evening with her two small cubs—probably females (*see* picture). Four hours passed before a second mother bear arrived with her two large cubs—probably males. (The camera imprints the date and time on every photograph.) But still, I saw nothing to explain the strange undulations. What was I missing? I had pictures of the two different sows. Where was the monster?

Then I saw the problem. The solution to the mystery was apparent but so incredibly improbable. The mother bear in the next photograph had no use of her hind legs. She was a paraplegic! Note the worn-away fur and exposed flesh on her back legs plus their unnatural position. Unbelievably, *she was dragging her body everywhere*, and this was the source of the undulations.

Mother Courage & her Two Large Male Cubs

There was no serpent, just a mother bear of incredible endurance determined to feed her cubs and herself. I decided to call her Mother Courage. There never was a monster, just a delusion in my mind like the bells children sometimes hear in their heads.

I contacted the Ontario Ministry of Natural Resources (MNR) about what we should do to help this injured bear. "We" quickly became "me." But they did suggest that, if this sow made it to hibernation, about two weeks away, the cubs would have a better chance of surviving the winter—it can be 40° below zero where I live. Until then, I decided to feed Mother Courage and her cubs and to do it outside my back window so that I might see their behavior. After I began, they came *every night*; however, I never saw the other large sow and her two small cubs again. Two weeks passed, and then two more. Would Mother Courage ever hibernate? I telephoned the MNR to ask if my feeding was inhibiting them from going into hibernation—the officials said no! Another two weeks came and went; it was now the middle of December, and this family often arrived during a blizzard. The cubs were always first by several minutes until this heroic animal dragged her bleeding backside out of the deep forest only to collapse in exhaustion. On many occasions, she never ate—she just watched her cubs devour the cracked corn and dog food. Note the exhausted mother at the back right of the photograph "Mother Courage Collapsed in Exhaustion" and the concerned cub at the front left. This sow's mothering instincts could challenge those of Angelina Jolie and Sojourner Truth.

Mother Courage Collapsed in Exhaustion

I became curious about the location of their wintering den. Because of the broad blood-spotted trail she had imprinted on the snow, I surmised finding her lair would be easy. It must be close; how far can an animal drag itself? Yet it took me more than an hour of difficult scrambling to negotiate my way through an impenetrable tangle of fallen trees and branches. Finally, I reached an embankment sloping down to an ancient glacial lake and found her den. This daily journey—both ways—would have intimidated Marco Polo. Yet Mother Courage had done this daily trek for

Mother Courage & Her Children

weeks, maybe months. The magnitude of her endurance and the power of her instincts astonished me. Neither torn flesh, nor exhaustion, nor death itself I thought would prevent her daily rounds. Some will say I am anthropomorphizing; I would say it is pure empathy with a fellow mammal in great anguish—something the vivisectionist René Descartes (*see* page 53) never had.

It is almost impossible to assess an animal's weight accurately by sight alone, but by comparing my first photographs to the later ones, Mother Courage appeared to be losing body fat. So, on December 17, I decided *not to feed* her and her cubs anymore, hoping to force them into hibernation, lest she dies crawling. It was a melancholy evening for everyone. They came. They searched. They left. And they never came again. See above for the final photograph of that snowy evening.

Early in the New Year, I snowshoed to their den and was elated to find they were all safely asleep—or as asleep as hibernating bears ever genuinely get. The heat emanating from their bodies condensed to form ice crystals encrusting the den entrance. My flashlight revealed the back of a bear almost wholly blocking the access to retain this heat. I took this to be Mother Courage in her ultimate act of protection for her cubs. She, of course, knew little of this. Mother Courage was following those deep instincts that had preserved her genes through a million years of evolution.

Clearly, this mother bear's behavior must be described as *moral.* And just as clearly, this behavior was preserving her genes by enhancing the chance that her two male cubs would survive and reproduce. There was pressure for moral action, stemming from natural selection, because this behavior is adaptive for the preservation of genes, which are life itself.

A vast literature exists on these topics, not just anecdotal stories such as mine on Mother Courage. Scientists define this topic as follows:

> Sociobiologists believe that human behavior, as well as nonhuman animal behavior, can be partly explained as the outcome of natural selection. They contend that to fully understand behavior, it must be analyzed in terms of evolutionary considerations.

At my latitude, 45th parallel north, the average date for bears to come out of hibernation is April 10, so, about two weeks after that date, I revisited the den site. The Ministry of Natural Resources had assured me that this sow (Mother Courage) would not exit the den alive—I had to see for myself. With some difficulty—everything appears different without snow—I found the hole again. It was empty, completely empty (*see* photograph); the entire family had left. In the distance was a kettle of turkey vultures, and I wondered if they were recycling Mother Courage. I suspected as much, but I declined to investigate.

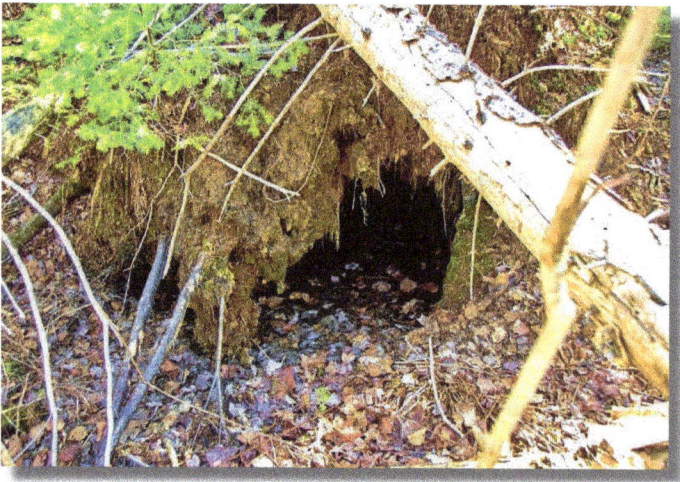

Empty Bear Den

Big Red slept with one ear open. And out of the darkness came the faint howls of a distant pack of wolves. Were they Spitfire's natal pack? He took the opportunity to pee high up a maple tree. Here in this heart of darkness, Spitfire slept quietly, beautifully, in the starlight. Our wolf realized his good fortune and returned to bed close by her side.

🐾

Male bear cubs leave their natal territory—following an instinctive taboo against incest. Because they leave their home area, they need a larger size, since trespassing on the lands of other male bears (boars) can be hazardous. On occasion, they will have to stand and deliver, so it is good to be near or in the same weight division. Genetics tells us that inbreeding is detrimental to the gene pool. And, again, natural selection is the source of our discomfort and bears' avoidance of this practice. Significantly, sows will share territory with their female cubs since this sharing presents no danger of incest.

Morality arises in a social context, but even hermits need it in their relationship with nature's wild creatures. All herd or pack animals have a significant moral repertoire: whales, elephants, and, as we have seen, wolves and bears.

Mother Courage—the Final Steps

Many readers may have wondered how Mother Courage came to be a paraplegic. Only two reasonable speculations are possible: she was either hit by a car or shot by a hunter. It was bear hunting season when I first noticed the undulations on my dusty road. Hunting or "harvesting," as the euphemism goes, is from September 1 until hibernation—almost three months. However, for bears, "harvesting" season on humans is always closed. Humans, however, have slaughtered hundreds of thousands of bears. We hunt bears, bears do not hunt us. All biology textbooks describe black bears as "shy woodland creatures," and they are rarely dangerous to humans. In this century, the number of people killed by a mother bear defending her cubs can be counted on the fingers of one hand. And most died as the result of a mauling. So, when it comes to protecting their young, we can say of mother bears that they maul, but they do not kill.

World black bear expert Lynn Rogers says the following on his website www.bear.org:

> Black bears have killed 61 people across North America since 1900. This no longer worries me. My chances of being killed by a domestic dog, bees, or lightning are vastly greater. My chances of being murdered are 60,000 times greater. One of the safest places a person can be is in the woods.

With our so-called God-given morality, we have driven hundreds if not thousands of species to extinction, and another universe must pass away before such creatures ever come again. Remember the Bible tells us God gave us dominion over all life and we have taken it furiously. I am not a vegetarian, but I would speak against the *senseless slaughter* of all those who cannot speak for themselves.

> *A dog starved at his Master's Gate*
> *Predicts the ruin of the State*
> William Blake, "Auguries of Innocence" (c. 1803) 1.9–10

Some moral behaviors exist outside and independent of humans. Even among those who did not hear Moses fresh back from Sinai where God gave him *another two tablets* and said call me in the morning! If, as a species, we had never existed or had gone extinct—and 99 percent of all species have—morality in terms we could recognize would still be flourishing on this planet.

The most fascinating behavior between animals—human or otherwise—is reciprocity. You scratch my back, and I will scratch yours. Or, unexpectedly, I will scratch yours even if I do not know you and will never see you again. Another name for reciprocity is the Golden Rule. Nonetheless, animals had it first, long before the Bible reiterated it, or Moses staggered down Mount Sinai in a rage.

To the shock of those who are stony-faced and stony-minded, the evidence that humans, apes and monkeys, whales, elephants, wolves, and even rats and mice inherit ethical behaviors honed by natural selection is profoundly disturbing. But should it be? We are a part *of*, not apart *from*, all life on earth. We are not descended from angels but ascended from a common ancestor to apes. Ours is a heroic past, at times so close to extinction that a wink might have made it so. Darwin would be pleased to witness the expansion of morality to non-human animals by natural selection.

POSTSCRIPT: I knew Mother Courage before she had that name. She was the little orphan with the porcupine quills in her face (*see* page 155) and a hunger in her belly. Her distinguishing mark was that she had none; her coat was a beautiful black sheen. Many bears have a white chevron on their chests of varying sizes and symmetry.

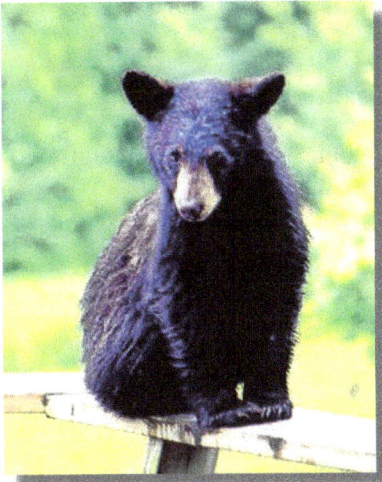

Stand & Deliver

A young male bear I knew had such a prominent and perfect mark that I nicknamed him "Chevy."

When she was a cub and a young mother, I would see Mother Courage every summer day. We were acquaintances, so neither of us feared the other although she ran from all strangers. This near friendship started shortly after she became an orphan. It was sealed the sunny afternoon she ventured onto my deck in search of seeds spilled from my bird feeders. When I first noticed her, she was sitting on the deck's railing looking directly at me as if to say, "Food, please." Instantly I grabbed my camera, and ever so slowly, I opened the door. The orphan seemed mesmerized yet held her position. Finally, I had the door opened far enough to get a few clear photos. The reader should note that, in her anxiety, the cub peed on the railing, but she stood her ground. *We are all afraid*, but some can control their fear, and this discipline became her defining feature. Even at an early age, she was a unique animal because most bears would have instantly disappeared into the forest. On this day, our relationship began; from here, it continued to its tragic end.

Young in a Beautiful Body

I knew her as a cub, teenager, young adult, mother, and finally as a paraplegic. My three favorite pictures of her are "Stand & Deliver," "Young in a Beautiful Body," and "Old in a Twisted Body." In the above photo, she is resting in my sunny orchard waiting for me to serve dinner.

In this last photograph (below) taken on a bleak November night, she is just hanging on to life. But to me, Mother Courage will always be the bravest and most enduring creature I have ever known.

Old in a Twisted Body

Big Red had traveled far since last winter when he determined to return home to his natal pack. He had been absent for two years, a long time in the life of a wolf who on average lives about six or seven years. Would his family recognize him? Would his fragile father still be alive? And his mother? What of his aunt and his sister, Little Red Ears? With Spitfire as his mate, Big Red intended to take control of his natal area founding a new pack to continue his bloodline. He would be Adam to her Eve.

Just before sunrise and against a background of a thousand frogs completing their nightly oratorios, a strange call abruptly awakened the two wolves. From a nearby pond, the booming call of the American bittern echoes from the cattails, saying this land is his land. The whip-poor-wills have already put away their mysterious, hypnotic melody and gone to roost. The night shift is over; the day shift is in progress. And just as our star peaks over the eastern horizon to reveal many fog-covered lakes, the triumphant call of the wild turkeycock erupts. All up and down this green valley and across the plateau his gobble, gobble, gobble resonates, and it sings of life. Its voice had been absent for more than a century.

With their incredible hearing, both wolves also heard some faint noises just north of them. Going to investigate, they discovered 11 large objects roosting high up in a sugar maple tree. Big Red wondered if the calling from the valley and these birds were related.

Turkey Roost

Once upon a time, there were genuine wild turkeys in Ontario, but by the early 1900s, they were extirpated (eaten). A wild turkey should not be confused with a feral bird which is just a domesticate that has escaped the barn. In 1984, the Ministry of Natural Resources (MNR) embarked on an ambitious program to reintroduce wild turkeys into Ontario. The MNR traded otters, fishers, and moose to various US states for wild turkeys, which the ministry released throughout the southern and central regions of the province. This reintroduction went spectacularly well; the wild turkeys lived, they thrived, they bred, and they greatly expanded their range.

Rumors of this success were everywhere: in the newspapers, on the radio, and on the TV. Then, one day in late April with the woods still clogged with snow and just a few brown patches appearing in my fields, I saw them. Like Alexander's Ragtime Band, a group of hen turkeys marched up through my orchard—for the first time in a century . . . maybe for the first time ever. I would not have been more impressed had they been playing "When the Saints Go Marching In." Male turkeys heard the hens' parade and quickly followed.

Our wolves would meet them again, but neither wolf gave these turkeys further thought. The morning was chilly, so the blackflies were not yet active, an appropriate time to travel. Spitfire followed Big Red's lead as they continued their trek west by southwest—back to the farm and his natal area.

And then to awake, and the farm, like a wanderer white
With the dew, come back, the cock on his shoulder: it was all
Shining, it was Adam and maiden,
The sky gathered again
And the sun grew round that very day.
Dylan Thomas, "Fern Hill"

Big Red & Spitfire: Adam & Eve

Chapter—14

THE CANIDAE

The fox knows many things,
but the hedgehog knows one big thing.
Isaiah Berlin, *The Hedgehog and the Fox*

Big Red and Spitfire were well matched, yet complemented each other in the ways they were different. She watched the ground as they flowed through the forest; he looked straight ahead. For three days, our wolves stopped only to drink and rest; it was now time for a substantial meal, and that usually means venison. Deer, however, do not like the deep forest since there is no grazing and little grass. Open fields, old farms, and the grassy borders of roads are their favorite haunts.

Big Red saw it first—an enormous open field going back to nature in the midst of the forest. What had it been in the past? Perhaps a farm, a logging camp, or some natural phenomenon. More significantly in the field was a flock of grazing wild turkeys, but no deer. These birds are omnivores eating insects, snakes, birds, mice, earthworms, and all varieties of vegetable matter. Their marvelous systems convert all this detritus into drumsticks and turkey breasts.

Foraging Wild Turkeys

Our wolves knew little of this; they could just see vulnerable turkeys *on the ground*. Since these hefty birds were novel prey for our wolves, they lacked experience hunting them. Doing the worst thing possible, they rushed these birds in the open field. Some turkeys sprinted across the ground into the bushes while others flew into the forest to the highest tree they could find. Big Red and Spitfire stood in the field hungry and dismayed with their failure. It would take practice and different tactics to catch one of these resourceful birds.

Plate VI: Hen and Poults

John James Audubon's
The Birds of America

Plate I: Turkey Cock

In North America, turkeys have an undeserved reputation for being "mentally challenged" and are actively maligned. It was not always so. I suspect that because of this reputation, the citizens of the country named Turkey call them the American bird. Benjamin Franklin, we know, admired these birds so much that he recommended they be the national symbol of the USA rather than the bald eagle. At Thanksgiving, someone always trots out this story to entertain us. But Franklin was right. Naturalist and painter John James Audubon thought so highly of them that he drew the gobbler (cock) on the first color plate of the first volume in his monumental *The Birds of America*; the hen was the sixth of 435 plates (*see* photographs). Audubon had a "wild" turkey as a pet that spent its nights on the roof of the naturalist's home. For its safety during the daytime, Audubon's wife tied a scarf around the bird's neck. Nevertheless, it was shot.

Turkeys have excellent vision and hearing, and they can outrun a man, but not a wolf. If a predator gets too close, however, these birds fly away. On this day, there were others watching this field of grazing turkeys, watchers who were experienced hunters of these wary birds. A dog fox (male) hid behind some bushes and let these birds, pecking their way methodically down the field, come to him. When our wolves charged the turkeys, one of the hens almost ran into the mouth of the waiting fox.

In the distance, Big Red and Spitfire saw the takedown. The dog fox had six kits to feed and a 10-lbs. turkey was a good menu choice. The fox was an experienced hunter of these birds, unlike *his cousins* the wolves. This canid wisely avoided adult male turkeys with their razor-sharp fighting spurs (*see photograph*), which could eviscerate him.

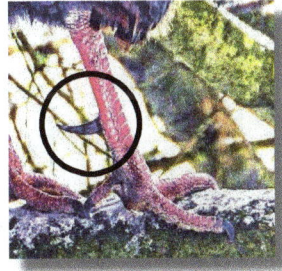

A Fighting Spur

Predators are smarter than their prey; they must be. Our wolves learned the fox's tactic at once, and they determined to try it. To double their chances, each wolf hid behind a different wisteria bush some distance apart on the edge of the field. They waited for turkeys or deer to stroll out of the forest. Turkeys have the dangerous habit of returning to the scene of an attack.

For the wolves, it felt good to rest when hungry. And within an hour, several turkeys drifted out of the forest into the field. Soon they arrived from all directions to form a sizable flock. All the while, they uttered clucking sounds as a signal to gather. The wolves waited as these plump birds continued their grazing down the field to their waiting jaws.

The blackflies were horrid, and Big Red tried to scratch them once too often. When these alert birds saw his movement, they scattered again into the forest. One bolted near enough to Spitfire for her to kill it instantly. She then shared it with her mate in the semi-darkness of a thicket of wisteria bushes.

Meanwhile, the dog fox had long since returned to his den to share the kill with the vixen and her six kits. These were nursing mostly, but still enjoyed the taste of fresh turkey breast.

After their turkey dinner, the dark shadows of evening crept across the open field; the air thickened and dew settled gently over the land. Nighthawks and whip-poor-wills roused themselves from sleep to do their evening shifts. Frogs croaked, and unknown voices spoke quietly in the darkness. The wolves would spend the night here on the off chance of a deer in the morning.

Spitfire & Big Red

The Canidae (aka canids) are members of the dog family (wolves, domestic dogs, coyotes, foxes, jackals, dholes, dingoes, and many other extant and extinct dog-like mammals). The red fox is the world's most widespread canid, and the reader is undoubtedly near one at this moment.

The Canidae comprise a vast family (*see* photograph), both those living and those dead. They went forth and multiplied in all the continents except Antarctica, occupying every possible ecological niche. You will find them in the jungles of Brazil, the wilds of Tierra del Fuego, and the sandy plains of the Falkland Islands. High up in the Andes, they hunt. And they once dominated throughout Mesoamerica and across the western prairies and the eastern forests in their quest for prey. In the frozen Arctic Islands, the tundra, and the mountains of Alaska, you will find these creatures hunting caribou and muskox. They range all around the world in the boreal forest of Canada to the taiga of Russia.

Some of the Existing Canidae
courtesy of Wikipedia

All over Asia, you can find them from the Gobi Desert south to India and China and on into the Malay Archipelago, and from there, south to Australia. Long ago they conquered Europe from its mountains to the snows of Scandinavia. The British Isles were a playground. Finally, they went to Africa, the home of the cats—lion, cheetah, leopard, and seven smaller felines—and the canids carved out homes there as well. In the mountains of Abyssinia, in the dark jungles of the Congo to the plains of the Serengeti down to the Cape, they roam freely. Occasionally, they took men with them as pets. Ultimately when Roald Amundsen went to Antarctica, his dog team led him to the south pole while Robert Falcon Scott's ponies led him and his comrades to a punishing death. And a Russian street dog conquered the final frontier—outer space—where no man had gone before, so a mongrel named Laika showed the way. Humans need to have respect in the presence of the Canidae—their superiors in so many ways.

Foxes are mostly nocturnal and extremely skittish, more so than wolves. It is not a stretch to imagine that those not so wary have been selected out of the population, that they have been shot, trapped, or poisoned. Yes, we humans have been responsible for some aspects of wolf and fox evolution. The discharge of a rifle will send many species, including my dog, scattering for safety.

On occasion in winter, I collect road-kill deer and put these in my fields for recycling. A carcass attracts a whole spectrum of birds and mammals for me to view and photograph. Feed them, and they will come! There is nothing ignoble in a significant predator scavenging—be it eagle, bear, wolf, fisher, or fox. Indeed, early man did the same. Life dances precariously on the edge between maximizing resources and death, and early humans heard that drum beat and knew that hunger. But since the agricultural revolution brought humans a great abundance of food, many have forgotten our hunter-gatherer-scavenger roots. Foxes are frequent visitors to my roadkill offerings. The incredible contrast of the fox's coat with the snow could not be more extreme. His bright colors and the fact that the snow shields his eyes (*see* photograph) makes him a target for eagles—which are now abundant and come to my free feast. With plenty of natural food, the eagle at the deer carcass wisely decides not to attack the scrappy fox and the fox. . . well, the fox knows many things.

Red Fox Chows Down

Humans adapt *by culture and construction*; non-humans adapt *mostly by bodily changes*. This ability to affect the environment is our advantage: it allows us to live on every continent, in space, and on the moon. Yet for all other species, an environment that changes too quickly for their bodies to adapt is a death sentence.

Jacob Bronowski expresses this view of humans eloquently in the first paragraph of his magnificent book and TV series *The Ascent of Man*:

> Man is a singular creature. He has a set of gifts which make him unique among the animals: so that, unlike them, he is not a figure in the landscape—he is a shaper of the landscape. In body and in mind he is the explorer of nature, the ubiquitous animal, who did not find but has made his home in every continent.[1]

Now, in no way do I wish to deny how remarkable humans are. But if you change just three things (in red), the Bronowski quotation applies equally well to the fox.

> The fox is a singular creature. He has a set of gifts which make him unique among the animals: so that, unlike them, he is not a figure in the landscape—he is a master of the landscape. In body and in mind he is the explorer of nature, the ubiquitous animal, who did not find but has made his home in every continent, except Antarctica.

Fox: The Master of the Landscape

The red fox is the world's most widely distributed carnivore. You can find them over most of North America, all of Europe, Russia, down into India, the north coast of Africa, parts of Saudi Arabia, as well as across China, and Japan. Australian settlers brought them Down Under, and they now rule most of that continent, including the vast and remote Outback.

I repeat, if you wander the forests and fields of any land, you will soon find death. It comes in the form of the rigid bodies of those who have left us. In recent years, I have discovered moose and deer carcasses from wolf kills, wings of hawks, headless snakes, dead kangaroo mice, weasels, raccoons, and porcupines. The dead litter this land. You cannot lie down anywhere in the forests or the fields without resting on the graves of the fallen (*see* page 5).

The engine of evolution is death. If we were immortals, evolution would not exist. Only by the passing of the less well-adapted, which leaves food for others, can the next generation test its genes.

One of my remote cameras photographed a fox on a road-killed deer that I had placed in the forest. A close examination revealed he had lost his symmetry and, with it, much of his health and vigor: I noted his "crunched face" and awkward left hind leg. One of life's contingencies had befallen him, perhaps an injury in a scrap over a vixen resulting in systemic infection.

The next day when I returned to check my camera, this fox was dead on my snowshoe trail where the walking was easiest. He had collapsed on his left side, but his right legs were still in stride. He died walking not after 10,000 steps, but 100,000 paces that morning. In unavoidable sympathy, I marveled at his endurance and hoped I would do as well.

It took some effort, but as a gesture of respect, I buried him where he fell. So that the next summer he might become a wildflower, then a rabbit, and finally a fox. Although he is mortal, he will have life everlasting and forever run on through the evergreen forests and the wisteria fields in his eternal pursuit of food.

The Red Fox—All but One of His Fires Out

All creatures great and small of the living world must practice an economy, whose purpose is to stay alive and pass on their genes. We have seen this in Reynard's double printing, the bumblebee's dedication to the work ethic, and the reflective layer on the retinas of nocturnal mammals (*see* pages 116-17). At a deeper level, chemistry and physics create the rules life dances to. If your niche is the water's skin, like the whirligig bug, you dare not gain too much weight, lose too many legs, or sharpen your nails. Charles Darwin authored the book on the innumerable minor rules of survival and the one supreme principle, *natural selection.*

It is later now; the sun is up, but light snow is beginning to fall while Reynard hunts on. As one of his many survival strategies, he caches food. Earlier, he had retrieved a previously hidden red squirrel; it made a sweet snack and has fueled his body. Like the lemmings that his arctic cousins devour in substantial numbers, the meadow voles in this field of wisteria go through high and low cycles, and this is a low year. Nevertheless, Reynard hears a vole seven body lengths away. He creeps closer, but not so close as to alert the ever-vigilant prey. The fox and the vole have been playing their evolutionary arms race for eons. Each has helped to shape what the other has become, and they are still engaged in this evolutionary contest, a tournament worthy of the mettle of both.

Here is the dilemma for Reynard. He must eat voles to live, yet he cannot approach them too closely because the least sound— the snap of a twig, the crackle of a leaf, or the crunch of compressed snow—sends the creature scurrying away into its network of tunnels. The solution: do a standing long jump from as far away as possible. He must launch himself like a rocket, bullet, or football; the physics is the same, discovered by Galileo and explained in his famous *Dialogue on the Great World Systems.* Just five factors determine the range (distance) of any projectile whatsoever, and on this planet, we have no control over one of these—gravity. So, the remaining four determine how far foxes can jump, and within these, evolution molded Reynard by natural selection to practice perfect science.

- The weight—foxes are the lightest of the canids.
- The length of time this force is applied—foxes have the longest hind legs of the canids.
- The muscular force exerted on the ground before the flight.
- The angle—the fox must find the one that maximizes his range.

At any given time, however, he is unable to significantly alter the first three of these factors: his weight and the *power* of the exerted force—the latter is determined by the length and strength of his hind legs. So these four conditions reduce to one, the angle of launch. This was a classic problem of early ballistics. The angle required for the furthest range is the same for all projectiles be they living or dead, pigskin or rock, frog or fox. It is 45°—*see the diagram.* For Reynard, every day is another Olympic event; jumps must be swift, high, and strong.

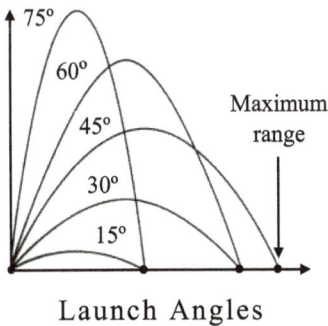

Launch Angles

Observation of foxes shows they use an angle close to 45°. If the snow cover is firm, however, and a greater downward force is required to trap the vole, then the angle is higher, lower if the snow is soft. Through practice, Reynard knows the geometry of range and impact, that the sum of these angles always adds up to 90 degrees.

The Fox Knows Many Things

Why does Reynard lunge? To catch voles of course. He is the ultimate mousetrap, but there is more to it than that. Scientists have been in a long retreat from earlier denials of all human feelings to other creatures, ascribing every animal behavior to instinct. I believe Reynard also lunges for the thrill of it! His ember-colored body soars in a graceful parabola to land precisely on his supper. The fox knows many things; the hedgehog knows only one.

🐾

Big Red jumped up abruptly! Even with his tail over his nose and his legs drawn up, bloodthirsty mosquitoes had found their way to tender areas. Together with a constant load of fleas and ticks, life is tough on wild animals. By now, Spitfire was also up and rubbing against her mate—unwittingly they were sharing fleas and ticks.

Both wolves watched the field for deer; the wise deer never came. Soon the bloodsuckers drove them to action, and they sprinted into the forest to escape this menace. Within minutes, they came to another large open field with tall grass growing. In the distance, the wolves noted an unusual red pole upright in the field. The post moved ever so slightly revealing it to be a fox standing on its hind legs to better see—and to be seen—over the grasses.

Fox Kit under the remains of an Old Building

To best chase the fox, Big Red and Spitfire fanned out. Wolves and foxes eat different items and so are not in competition, turkeys excepted. After a few strides, Big Red veered hard left, and Spitfire followed his lead. His instinct told him this highly visible fox was decoying them away from something. What was it?

Emerging from the grasses, the wolves found an area padded down by the constant playing of six fox kits. These red balls instantly disappeared under the scant remains of some old building. The wolves waited. Within a few minutes, the bravest, or most foolish, poked his head out to look directly at them (*see* photograph). Soon, his more cautious littermates followed. Trotting off toward new adventures, our wolves left the kits to their playtime and familial affairs. Just as bears do not eat raccoons, wolves do not eat foxes, but they will chase them from kill sites.

The fox was decoying the wolves from her kits, unsuccessfully as it turned out. But long ago, Big Red's father lured a black bear away from his natal den. Returning to his guard position in the mottled sunshine on the rock, his father thought little of risking his life. Such is the banality of heroism in wild nature.

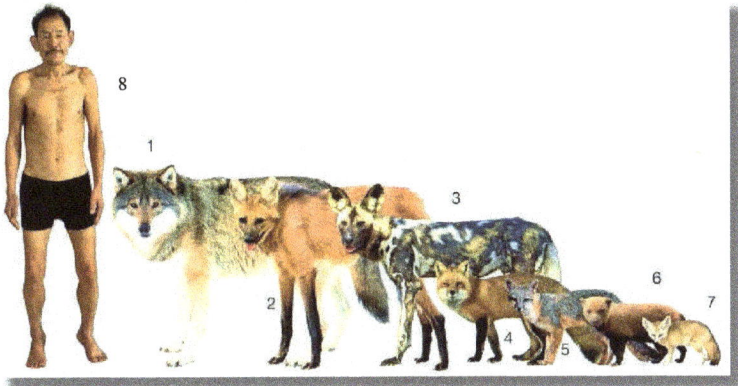

RELATIVE SIZE OF CANIDS: (1) Gray Wolf; (2) Maned Wolf; (3) African Wild Dog; (4) Red Fox; (5) Gray Fox; (6) Bush Dog; (7) Fennec Fox; (8) adult human.
© Copyright, Princeton University Press

All species of fox are small compared to other canids (*see* picture), and they have many cat-like features. Evolution has honed them to be the perfect mousetrap. On a starlit night in winter, life reduces to its fundamentals as the heartless stars shine overhead. On such nights, I have followed the meandering tracks of foxes over the snow to discover holes where they have plunged headfirst to catch a meadow vole wandering in its sub-nivean world.* Later, with Orion riding high in the sky, a fox often curls up in a ball on the top of the windswept snow. Wrapping his ample tail over his nose and saying some thoughts to the cold and perfect wilderness, he dreamt perchance of a plump partridge in its snow cave.

How does the fox know where the meadow vole is? I speculate, he *hears it chattering* its teeth under the snow. And unexpectedly, this chattering is not because of the cold—the temperature in the subnivean zone is just above freezing and far warmer than on the surface. Would not evolution soon select these "chatterboxes" out of the breeding population leaving less loquacious voles? That would appear evident, but after millennia of natural selection, it has not happened. Therefore, I speculate that chattering must be essential to the voles' survival: it is a form of echo-location in their black tunnels beneath the snow. They "see" with sound as their cousins the bats do.

Meadow Vole Tunnels

When the snow melts in the springtime, you can clearly see the circuitous tubes of these busy voles (*see* photograph). Any swift transit down a tunnel requires a roadmap of sorts; in the case of the voles, one formed by echolocation through chattering. By detecting this constant chattering, the fox found a way to find food in his winter world in the wilderness. As I said, the fox knows many things, as do all the Canidae.

The wolves ran on through the hardwood forests in their eternal pursuit of deer and a new home. Unknowingly, they were approaching the unmarked boundary of Algonquin Park. Once outside the Park, it would be open season on wolves with steel-tooth

---

* Beneath the thick snow exists an active, shadowy world called the sub-nivean, meaning "under the snow." This area exists as an air space above the ground's surface but below the snowpack.

leg traps, deadly snares, terrifying guns, and lethal poisons. Big Red's natal pack was beyond the Park but in an area of abandoned farms going back to nature.

They were small creatures, Big Red and Spitfire, wandering in an immense wilderness without compass or technology of any kind. Even on sunny days, they were often unable to see the sky through the dense growth of hardwood trees. How could they find their way? "The Canopy of Algonquin Park" (*see* below) is what the land looked like in pre-Columbian times—one contiguous forest all across eastern North America. Yet today, man has startlingly altered the land outside the Park with open fields, fences, roads, and danger.

The Canopy of Algonquin Park
courtesy of Wikipedia

Yet, at no time was Big Red disoriented. His internal compass carried him safely through a puzzle, a maze of Brobdingnagian proportions, with never a misstep. Our wolves were tiny creatures in a primeval forest, but they were never lost. One of them knew exactly where he was going; we call it home.

Chapter—15

THE ANCESTORS

They move finished and complete, gifted with extensions of the senses we have lost or never attained, living by voices we shall never hear. They are not brethren, they are not underlings; they are other nations, caught with ourselves in the net of time, fellow prisoners of the splendor and travail of the earth.
Henry Beston, *The Outermost House*

A black dot shimmers in what little sunshine still reaches the forest floor as it continues up through a hardwood grove of maple and beech trees. Vernal flowers decorate the open forest floor catching a few rays before the green canopy of spring shades them in darkness. Trout lilies carpet vast areas while white trilliums linger in the sunnier spots. Single red trilliums, pollinated by flies attracted by their scent of rotting meat, grow in scattered regions. Closer now, the single black dot transforms into two dots, both walking up through the forest at a leisurely pace. It is impossible to figure out what they are, but they are getting larger. Delicate spring beauties

Red Trillium

bloom in a few places, and the rare dutchman's breeches grow amidst other plants. The open forest afforded a clear view of the

Dutchman's Breeches

approaching black forms weaving a path around trees like water around rocks but treading firmly on the carpet of flowers. Coming closer, they morph into two large wolves, the ones we know, Big Red and Spitfire. Sauntering like the lords of creation, nonetheless, they are subject to the slings and arrows of outrageous fortune like the rest of us.

Parasites riddle their bodies both inside and out. But thousands of years of evolution has prepared them to carry this burden with pride and a strut that all can notice. So close now that you can see their blood-stained muzzles. Earlier that morning, they had killed a buck whose antlers were just beginning to bud. Their tactics were classic. Spitfire gave chase while Big Red waited in ambush. The takedown was quick and clean for they were already an accomplished team. With swollen bellies and satiated appetites, they moved slowly for wolves. All the remaining venison, they gave to the ravens, fishers, and other wolves.

Up ahead was a vernal pond nestled in the Precambrian Shield with its shallow bottom decorated with last fall's maple and beech leaves. The wolves approached, eager to drink from its perfect surface. The pond presented the illusion of lifelessness, yet life lay between the leaves, under the fallen logs, and in the water itself but invisible by virtue of its microscopic size. The surface had three flotillas of something shaped like flat ovals moving with a delicate motion. Although the footfalls of the two wolves were light, nonetheless, they produced slight vibrations causing the "ovals" to break up and scatter under the water. These were the larvae of blood-sucking mosquitoes that bedeviled the life of all forest mammals. Liberally lapping freshwater into their mouths, the wolves then licked each other's muzzles clean. It was past noon, and the bird song marking the rite of spring had ceased, and

Napping Wolves

the woods were quiet, peaceful. With the full bellies and the warm temperatures, our wolves grew sleepy and finding some leafy bushes by the edge of the pond, they curled up for a long afternoon nap. They slept, but the woods awakened.

After a few minutes, a groundhog (aka woodchuck) ambled noisily over the leaves to take a drink at the pond's edge. Previously unseen, ovenbirds and hermit thrushes flittered about catching insects and drinking while a broad-wing hawk circled in the green canopy. From under a half-submerged log, a rare yellow-spotted turtle stirred and rose to the surface to gulp some air before falling back and disappearing again. Giant water beetles coursed through the tea-colored water searching for prey near the napping wolves. Two red squirrels and a chipmunk had a drink and suddenly scurried away when a red fox approached. The wolves were dreamily aware of this activity. Life was good—they had full bellies and each other. And life was everywhere. In the antepenultimate sentence of *Walden*, Thoreau wrote, "Only that day dawns to which we are awake."

By now blackflies and mosquitoes had found the snoozing wolves. They roused from their spring idyll, had another drink and

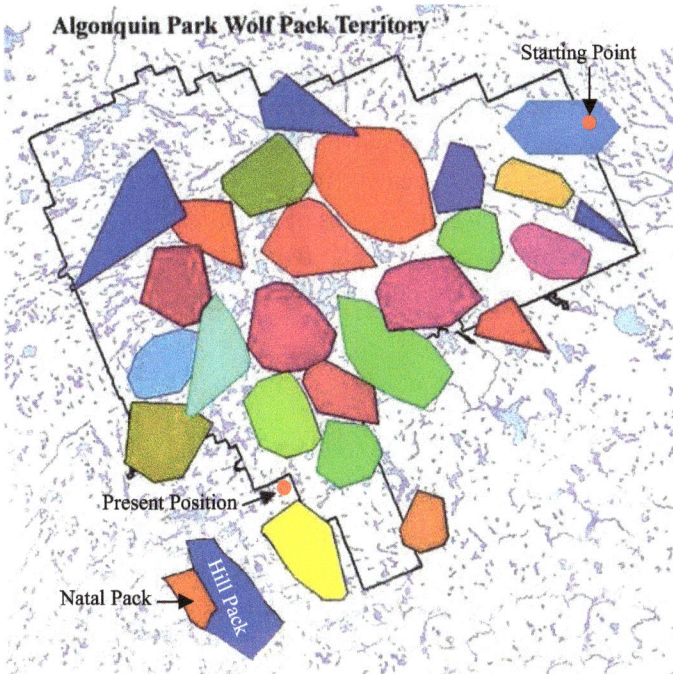

Algonquin Park Wolf Pack Territory

trotted away. It was late afternoon when they approached the invisible fence—the western boundary of Algonquin Park. Had it been marked with feces or urine, our wolves would have been aware of its existence. But wolves have no knowledge or understanding of imaginary fences that were mere lines on maps. Big Red had no maps except for his internal geography that had accurately directed him across a wild landscape which would have daunted Dr. Livingstone.

To no fanfare or notice, they stepped out of Algonquin Park! Our wolf continued with uncanny accuracy toward his home, his Natal Pack (*see* map). Just before sunset, Big Red caught the scent of a human, and all his systems went on high alert. It was the same odor he detected just before stepping in the leg-hold trap and losing one of his toes outside the eastern boundary of the Park.

Meanwhile, on a limestone embankment of a river, Spitfire discovered a sizeable cave. While Big Red was thinking of their safety, Spitfire was exploring the high limestone ridge of a small stream searching for a place to spend the night. Discovering a hole too small to enter, she quickly enlarged it with vigor and her claws. Both wolves entered to find a vaulted chamber with pools of clear water. Sticks hung from the ceiling and grew up from the floor. With their night vision and a sliver of light from the entrance, they could just make out this unique labyrinth. For a fleeting moment, Big Red wondered what enormous animals had used this lair in the past. Safe from blackflies and mosquitoes, our wolves huddled inside the cave. Big Red knew they would have to advance with care and awareness of potential traps, snares, and humans. After much agitation and twitching, he fell asleep that night. He had already lost one mate and determined never to lose another.

Nulla dies umquam memori vos eximet aevo.
—No day shall erase you from the memory of time. —
Virgil, *The Aeneid*

Virgil was mistaken! There will come a time when all this will be forgotten. You will be forgotten; I will be forgotten. No one will remember Leonardo, Shakespeare, or Einstein. This will be a time when we are all dead. All of us! Everything that humans have created, written, or built will disappear. Of the Seven Wonders of the Ancient World, just one remains, and it is in significant decay. There was a time before you were born, and there will be a time after you die, and you will have no memory of either. In the distant future, most of the stars will disappear from the night sky. Before this, our sun will become a red giant and envelop the Earth in a blazing death. Even if we should escape this, there will come a time when the universe itself dies a heat death. Virgil was mistaken!

Before this, long before this, we will have forgotten other life forms on Earth. This has already happened. Who remembers the ancestors of wolves? I mean the wolves of deep time, millions of years ago. They have no listing in Ancestry.com. Early man, *Homo habilis* and so on, have been justly celebrated in books and papers. But for a few paleontologists, we would not know that ancient wolves ever existed. The ancient Canidae were a large family of forms most beautiful and most wonderful. They and we will be forgotten someday, *but that day is not today*. We will hold to memories of them. Life is valuable precisely because it is not everlasting. Time is valuable just because it is not eternal. Do not be concerned about oblivion; it is a good thing. It makes life worthwhile!

As I wrote previously, death litters this land with the bodies of the fallen. You cannot place your hand on the ground without touching the heart of some deceased animal. And as you move down

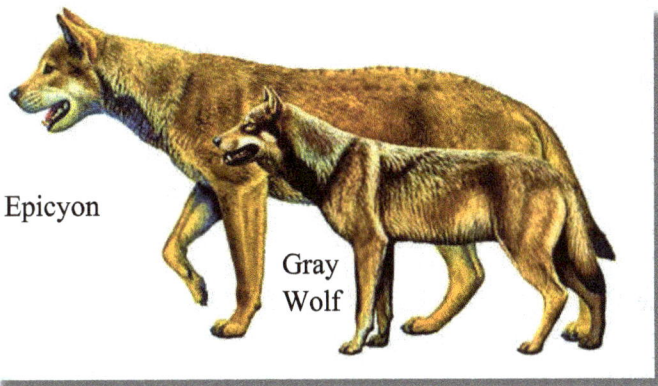

Epicyon

Gray
Wolf

Epicyon compared to the Gray Wolf
courtesy of *Google Images*

through the earth, the bodies of the fallen change over time in incredible variety and size. These are the shadows of forgotten ancestors, and although they may have survived for 10 million years, they are all gone now—erased from history.

Once upon a time, 40 million years ago, there were three dogs or dog-like animals. We will call them Small Dog, Big Dog, and Biggest Dog. Over time, Biggest Dog evolved to gigantic proportions specializing in hunting megafauna and crushing bones.

The largest of these was *Epicyon* weighing in at an incredible 320 lbs. (145 kg) or the size of three gray wolves (*see* picture). Larger than a jaguar, the size of an African lion, Epicyon was indeed an intimidating beast. The smaller dire wolf was intermediate in size between this creature and the gray wolf. Epicyon's massive head, foreshortened muzzle, and large teeth give evidence that it was reaping the rich reward of marrow from the megafauna bones. He did not nibble and chew, he crushed and swallowed.

Specializing is a gamble. In the case of Biggest Dog, his size and relative slowness prevented him from catching all smaller animals. This would be a winning strategy if the megafauna remained abundant. Consider the tiger; it does not live on mice and even if it could catch them, they are too small to sustain him. Epicyon, because of his specialization as a bone crusher and his size, out-competed Big Dog driving him to extinction. His vector for increasing size became so overpowering that Biggest Dog could *only* kill megafauna. He had rushed past the "sweet point" of the generalist to the far end of the specialist scale.

Then cats arrived in the Americas ruining life for the dogs. During one of the ice ages, cats crossed through Beringia to the Great Plains of America and all its abundance. Whether in a pride or solo, as we see in Africa today, cats are superb hunters of large herbivores. By giving direct competition to Biggest Dog, they helped drive him to extinction. And you wonder why dogs hate cats.

Wolves found the sweet spot long ago and stayed there. As Farley Mowat points out in his classic book, *Never Cry Wolf,* during times of starvation these canids can survive on mice alone. Or during times of plenty when hunting in packs, they take down caribou, muskox, and bison. Any creature with a menu this broad will ride the sweet spot to be the last dog standing in the

Dawn Dog — *Cynodictis*
courtesy of Wikipedia

whirlwind of life. So, of the original three dog-like canids, just one remained, and this creature became the mother of all dogs and dog-like animals. Most paleontologists think *Cynodictis* was that animal (*see* drawing).

🐾

Sometime during the night, Big Red jumped up fully awake wondering where he was. What was this place? Spitfire comforted him until he remembered. This was his birth den, and he was with his mother, Paws, Little Red Ears, and his dead sisters and brother. Still, his mate comforted him in his agitation in this chamber of memories. Determined to leave, he followed his scent trail around the pools of water and the dripping walls. She stayed close. Something touched his leg, and he recoiled before realizing it was an ancient pile of shattered bones. Up ahead was the faintest glow of light from the entrance. They exited this cavern of horrors and laid down under the stars, sleeping till dawn.

🐾

Your life is determined by your size. If a mosquito moves from the sun into the shade, it cools in seconds and the reverse. But a wolf can curl up in an arctic storm at 40 degrees below zero, put its tail over its nose, and sleep comfortably all through the night. Some people who only see coyotes believe all wolves are creatures of modest size. In fact, wolves are among the largest of all animals on earth; more than 99 percent of all species are smaller. And we know from Bergmann's rule (*see* pages 42-43) that as you move farther north, the canids grow larger going from coyote to Algonquin wolf to gray wolf.

Your life is determined by your size, and your size is defined by your genes. And these genes are so minute they could fit inside your eye without discomfort. Some say all these genes (genotype) use the body (phenotype) to reproduce themselves be you man or canid. The genotype for being dog-like conquered the world long before man scampered out of the trees onto the savannas of Africa. Over vast periods, these unique genes morphed the canids' bodies by using slight variations in the genes (alleles). These various phenotypes filled the valleys of the Amazon and the mountains of the Andes, the western prairies of America, the eastern forests, the boreal forests, the tundra, north to the arctic islands. Asia is their original home from the taiga to the jungles of Sumatra and on down into Australia. Asia is still their stronghold nation. Throughout Europe, wolves were the stuff of terrifying legends and stories, but today they have retreated to distant mountain ranges and a few backwater regions of that continent.

Africa was man's first home, yet it was the canid's last. Africa is the land of the cats—those annoying cats. Although we can find canids there in wide varieties, their numbers are relatively small. These canids adapted by genetic variation to different environments. And they were masters at it. *I never ascribed anything to the canids that they did not already have.*

Although canids dig burrows, beavers build dams, and birds construct nests, such activity is miniscule compared to man's terraforming. We have paved over vast areas of land pouring three tons of concrete each year for every human. The canids adapted their bodies to the environment; man adapts the environment to his body. Therein lies the gore and the glory. With rare exceptions, our alterations are in direct conflict with all other life on earth. And humans might just get away with all this incredible terraforming, if and only if they leave enough space for other species in the form of parks, green spaces, and wilderness areas.

Wolves and humans live in different worlds. You might say that is obvious, but I mean this in a unique sense. Nature "wants" half your children to die before they mature. Nature also "wants" you to die before you are 40. Anything beyond this is a gift from science and technology. Recall Big Red's parents had six pups yet three perished before they grew up, and wolves in the wild live an average of six or seven years—half their life expectancy in a zoo. This is why wolves live in life's whirlwind while humans, by comparison, dwell in air-conditioned palaces and will never give up this luxury.

The principal question of our time is, will we devastate the environment and all other species with our selfish materialism? If history is the only true philosophy, then the future is bleak. By continuing to breed, pollute the air, contaminate the water, rupture the earth for its natural resources, we are destroying ourselves and deservingly so. And fools will stand in circles and wonder why and how this happened. Right now, life is challenging us: can we share this earth with other creatures, or will we destroy nature by creating a world of manufactured landscapes. The answer is coming!

The Wolf Nation

A breeze touched their sleeping forms, while a diminished dawn chorus of bird song still echoed through the forest. During the night a light dew descended covering their bodies and binding their guard hairs into pointed forms. They appeared ragged. Spitfire rose first and began to explore the nearby area when Big Red joined her to "discourage" this activity. With the scent of a man still present, there was danger here. Both returned to their bed in an open meadow. Our wolf thought it his responsibility to protect his exuberant mate.

Up ahead was the ancestral territory of the Hill Pack wolves, a vast land bordering on the Natal Pack area (*see* map page 211). For some time, Big Red had not seen, smelt, or heard other wolves, but he was sure this was about to change. His father had been in a continuing struggle against the intrusions of the Hill wolves. Did this pack now control his natal area? Would any family members still be alive to greet him? His father? His mother? His aunt? Would they welcome him and his mate?

But our wet wolves have miles to go before they reached the Natal Pack area. To keep his mate safe from traps and snares, Big Red "convinced" Spitfire to follow him rather than trot at his side. This cut their chances in half of encountering either fiendish device.

The woods are lovely, dark and deep,
But I have promises to keep,
And miles to go before I sleep,
And miles to go before I sleep.
Robert Frost, "Stopping by Woods on a Snowy Evening"

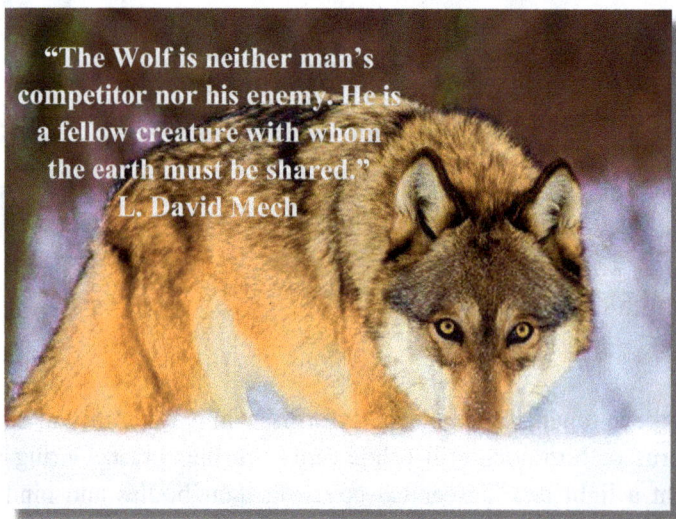

"The Wolf is neither man's competitor nor his enemy. He is a fellow creature with whom the earth must be shared."
L. David Mech

This Land is My Land

Chapter—16

PAINTED WOLVES

*Every creature is better alive than dead, men
and moose and pine trees, and he who understands
it aright will rather preserve its life than destroy it.*
Henry David Thoreau, *The Maine Woods*

For 10 miles (16 km), they trotted single file before stopping to rest. Big Red chose a knoll overlooking a series of connected fields, treed on both sides but clear in the valley. During their trot, they met neither snare nor trap because our wolf kept to open areas devoid of the scent of man. Outside Algonquin Park, they were traveling through abandoned farmland now used for grazing cattle and sheep. Lying in the shadows cast by an ancient sugar maple tree, our wolves rested—expecting nothing, but ready for everything.

Their bodies were in prime condition with that combination of health and fitness known only to youth and early middle age. The air was still and redolent with the scent of spring lulling our wolves to stretch out and nap. Not long after getting comfortable on a thick carpet of fallen leaves, they drifted off to pleasant dreams.

CRACK! A loud report of a rifle bolted them awake. The sound was so incredibly intense and high pitched—beyond anything humans can hear—transfixing Big Red and Spitfire. They drew closer to each other and crouched by a huge fallen branch that had long since split from this ancient maple. Immediately after the crack of the rifle, some animal shrieked in agony. The wolves may not have known the sound of a gun, but they were familiar with the cries of pain and death. Keeping low, they crawled into some bushes beyond the drip line of the maple and decided to stay there until nightfall.

The sun progressed across heaven's blue vault, punctuated by lone rifle shots throughout the afternoon. Buried deep in the genes of wolves and dogs is a profound fear of sharp, loud noises like rifle reports and lightning strikes. Our wolves counted the number of shots; there were six at half-hour intervals. Each bullet took the life of an eastern coyote accompanied by a pandemonium of screams and cries—all else was silence.

Eastern Coyote Resting

The majestic maple registered no disdain for this fanfare and death. Over two centuries, it had seen everything. The coyotes from the next valley often slept peacefully on its carpet of soft leaves (*see* photograph). On one of its lower branches, industrious robins had built a nest of mud and grass with a hole allowing rainwater to drain. Five voracious nestlings with extended necks and open red mouths begged for food. In its highest branches, a noisy red-eyed vireo has just finished its nest of grasses interwoven with pieces of a wasp nest.

In years past, every variety of animal of central Ontario had either roosted or rested in or under this magnificent tree. Pileated woodpeckers evacuated oblong holes in the tree's trunk to retrieve an abundant harvest of black carpenter ants. And years later they used one of these holes as a nest. For several winters three male raccoons spent the snow season safe and warm huddled in one such cavity. In its own steadfast way, this maple was a giver of life. Mice grew fat on its abundant maple keys and these, in turn, fed foxes and owls. On winter evenings, a great-horned owl, always sitting on the same high branch, would survey the valley for snowshoe hares. Admittedly, this was a tree of life!

Earlier that morning in the adjacent valley, a Toyota Tundra trunk drove over old roads and trails to a predetermined spot. When it stopped on a ridge hidden by trees and shrubs, two men and a sleepy boy tumbled out. Rapidly they set up for the day's hunt. First, they deployed a "bird topper," an electronic device waving feathers (looks like a woodpecker) and emitting painful squeals. Out came a "game caller" of recorded voices and sounds guaranteed to attract varmints*—in today's case, eastern coyotes (*see* photograph). Next, the rifles with small-caliber bullets, hot and fast, for long-range shooting equipped with a bipod rest and a high-powered crosshair scope. If they do not kill, they will at least cripple the coyote.

First Varmint

Both Nimrods and the still sleepy boy had full-body camouflage coveralls with head covering—all the better not to see you with. Taking their seated position on folding chairs, with decoy deployed, coyote call at hand, rifles at the ready, they opened a thermos of hot coffee. It was near noon before the boy was fully awake. Big Red and Spitfire knew nothing of this. Their first indication was the initial rifle crack followed by the pitiful death squeals and screams.

---

* According to Wikipedia, *varmints* are "predators which can kill farm animals: badger, bald eagle, barred owl, bobcat, cooper's hawk, cougar, coyote, feral dogs, foxes, golden eagle, goshawk, great-horned owl, lynx, mink, osprey, raccoons, screech owl, snapping turtles, snowy owl, sparrow hawk, weasel, wolverine, and wolves."

When the bullet passed through his soft body, the coyote spun in tight circles, rolled over, and then struggled to his feet only to fall dead on his side. The "brave" killers strolled down the hill to examine the limp, lifeless carcass. It was a large male weighing in at 40 lbs. (18 kg), his body enclosed in a beautiful coat of multi-colored fur. The bullet entered his right shoulder and escaped through his left lung.

After dragging the cadaver back to their picnic area, the victors returned to their coffee. Lunch was roast beef sandwiches on rye with dill pickles and mustard, washed down with four cans of Budweiser beer. The boy had a peanut butter and jam sandwich with a Coke. Lathered in bug repellant, they dozed contentedly in their comfortable chairs—God rest you, merry gentlemen, let nothing you dismay, nor worry about the pain and death you brought this sunny day. And the flies, well, they sucked the bodily fluids oozing out of the coyote's carcass.

Well rested after their nap, they reactivated the bird topper, readied their rifles, and resumed their "sport." Within minutes, a coyote appeared on the far side of the valley, partially hidden by new spring foliage. As a further incentive to come closer and into the open field, the "sportsmen" played some coyotes calls. It worked, and shortly a second varmint whirled in circles crying pitilessly—the bullet passed right through his nose just below the eyes. He was still alive when the Nimrods arrived, and the larger man delivered the *coup de grace* by crushing the coyote's head with a steel-toed boot sending him to eternity. The boy, not fully tutored in the ways of manhood, recoiled at the cracking of the small dog's skull and the gushing of the brains from its eye sockets and mouth. The second man steadied the boy's shoulders. Then the heroes dragged the mangled corpse back to their picnic area and tossed it on the growing pile.

At intervals, this banality of killing continued throughout the afternoon. At its conclusion, these "sportsmen" had five dead and decaying coyotes in a pile close by their comfortable chairs. Sat-isfied, they began to break camp to drive home. At that moment, the larger man noticed some movement on the far side of the val-ley. Another varmint! It was a long shot, at least 300 yards (275 m), but just possible. The smaller man cautioned, the other not to shoot at that extreme distance, but he did, and the varmint fell to the ground at once. "Too far to walk," they said, so they left it to the vultures and ravens. After tossing the five corpses in the back of their Toyota Tundra, the heroes drove off with their prizes. The larger Nimrod said to the smaller that the boy was becoming a man, and before long, he could join them in the "hunt."

The Prize—Five Dead Varmints

Well after midnight, our wolves left the protection of the ancient sugar maple tree and descended into the valley. Big Red and Spitfire could see clearly by the light of a half-moon and the stars. Trotting quickly, they soon entered the valley of death; their sensitive noses instantly gave evidence to what had happened here. Crossing the valley without incident, they passed through the wire fence and started up the far hill. It was here that the last varmint had disappeared after being shot. Each wolf could smell the trail of blood it had left, and they instinctively followed that scent.

As they progressed, the wolves saw that the soil was disturbed as if by some movement, as if the varmint were now crawling. Near the crest of the hill, close by a den, our wolves discovered her still limp body. The bullet had entered her bowels that now spilled out as she relentlessly dragged her corpse up the steep hill. What remained of her belly revealed six teats. And unbelievably, she was doing the only thing she knew—going home to feed her babies.

Less than a body length distant was the entrance to her den with her still-living puppies. Alone now for some hours, they were hungry and afraid. Where was mum?

We have no way of knowing if our wolves had any empathy for the victims in this tragic scene. But clearly, they had more than the two "hunters," who today had killed 12 coyotes, not 6. Wolves will kill or run off coyotes since they compete for the same food, just as coyotes will kill or run off foxes for the same reasons. But neither eats the other, wears their fur, collects a bounty, or kills for "sport. That is a human hobby.

There is a sickness all over this land, a sickness that finds power in pain, joy in killing, and good in nothing; a disrespect for all living creatures, including ourselves. On this day, these two Nimrods killed coyotes for "sport." To show what little morality they have, they will say they did it to protect the farmer's sheep. Although they saw no sheep, there were fences . . . for something.

Coyote on a Stick

Those who love coyotes call them the *song dogs of America* (*see* photograph). Their eerie arias fill the night air with ancient energy, and they speak of a life we have long forgotten and will never know again.

Those who hate them call them varmints and every year kill 500,000 in a wide variety of ways. I cannot discover how many exist, but it must be millions even though they are the most persecuted animal in North America. They ride on through the bullets, poisons, traps, snares, snowmobiles, helicopters, and cars, passing through this whirlwind of death to come out alive. Coyotes are a native American species initially confined to the deserts of the southwest. From there they expanded into the eastern farmlands created by humans, and then north into Canada and over the ice to Newfoundland, nor did they forget about Mexico and Central America.

In later years, these song dogs have invaded our cities running through ravines, parks, and backyards, enjoying new territory and a whole new food menu. By natural selection and interbreeding with Algonquin wolves and dogs, they produced coywolves and coydogs, both capable of bringing down deer and even moose. The Vireo lake wolf that Big Red drowned mated with a coyote, but they were unsuccessful in rearing their puppies. It takes a pack to raise a litter.

Two Song Dogs of America

It seems reasonable that with a death rate of 500,000 per year—executed by humans—that coyotes are dancing on the edge of eternity. Why have they not gone extinct the way the gray wolf did in the lower 48? They flourish in every state except Hawaii. Incredibly, these song dogs patrol Central Park in NYC every night and the other parks in the surrounding boroughs. The Nation of the Song Dog is robust. The answer to their ubiquity is a lesson in adaptation. They are shapeshifters, a truly Protean animal.

Since they are half the size of Algonquin wolves, they need less food, plus they will devour anything, including feral cats and small dogs. And moreover, their diaspora is so vast, they cannot all be found. Hunting by stealth rather than a direct attack, coyotes are smart or wily as their enemies would say. Humans, even with an array of technical devices and rifles, have not exterminated them.

Much the opposite, coyotes have followed us to our farms and into our cities—they have adapted. The question is, can we adapt to this unique canid now living in our parks and ravines? Incredibly, humans would have to kill more than 40 percent of all coyotes to reduce their overall number, and 500,000 is far below that quantity. Recall that the rangers in Algonquin Park—those pledged to protect its animals—killed upward to 50 wolves per year by bullets, poison baits, snares, and traps. This left more food for the remaining wolves, especially for next spring's pups, so the total number of animals in the Park remained constant. Even after the rangers stopped this slaughter, the number of wolves the following spring was the same, 150. *A fixed prey base equals a fixed number of predators.* Everything else is noise!

Traveling all through the night, Big Red and Spitfire left the valley of death far behind them. They met no wolves, just their noisy cousins, the song dogs. This was coyote country. Between our wolves and their destination, lay only the Hill Pack, the ancestral enemies of his Natal Pack.

It was near sunrise when they sought out a place to rest until evening. Because of the smell of humans, Big Red reversed his travel plans: move at night, sleep during the day. This was also lake country, and when the scent of freshwater reached their noses, they went down to the shore to drink. Wading chest deep, the wolves noticed a small island close by the beach. Walking half the way, they swam the rest. Big Red realized the water was much warmer than the night he dog-paddled across a frigid lake with an injured leg to escape a pursuing pack of wolves. By the time they reached the island, the crimson brushes of morning had painted the eastern horizon.

Two Raccoons

It had no human habitation, just a few trees, pine and maple, and some bushes. Two raccoons (*see* photograph), scouring the shoreline for food, scampered up a sugar maple tree lest they become a meal. On the side opposite the shore, our wolves made a bed together. The isolation of the island and the breeze off the lake reduced the blackflies and mosquitoes to tolerable levels. And then they slept.

Algonquin wolves are extremely rare, and even though they are a species at risk, the Ontario government does not provide anything close to full protection. Estimates vary, but less than 400 exist with fewer than 60 breeding pairs. Big Red and Spitfire, two wolves in their prime, were crucial to the survival of their species. Something of the future of their kind rested on them.

On another continent far, far away, a cousin of the Algonquin wolf races down a narrow path to extinction. This is the savanna country of South Africa: a few trees scattered over a harsh landscape with the air punctuated by the voices of bird, beast, and insect. In the heat, cicadas sang so exquisitely and long, that they mesmerized the animals. It was the dry season.

In the expanse of the plane, a small cloud of dust appeared, and it grew bigger as it approached—perhaps a dust devil agitated to life by a wayward breeze. When time halved the distance, a Thompson's gazelle appeared in the center of the dust cloud with a pack of painted wolves (aka African wild dogs) close on its hooves. Both prey and predator were exquisite creatures. Each painted wolf had a unique coat of many colors enough to make the biblical Joseph envious. And they moved with such grace and swiftness that fleet-footed Mercury might well fall behind. Their long legs barely touched the ground, and often they were entirely airborne. Incredibly, 85 percent of their pursuits are successful; their prey might feel that "Resistance is futile." Coming over a small rise in this otherwise flat land, the wolves were almost upon the hapless gazelle, and every other animal crouched low less they become an appetizer. In the next instant, they were on the animal, swiftly devouring it lest they lose it to lions or hyenas. Afterward, they returned to their den to regurgitate part of their meal for ten ravenous puppies.

Painted Wolves

Like the tide withdrawing from the land, the Nation of the Painted Wolf has been in a long retreat. In the past, they ruled all sub-Saharan Africa, except the Congo Basin. They were everywhere and in vast numbers. Their gene pool was immense and interconnected to defend against exotic diseases and prevent inbreeding. All that is gone now! Their huge gene pool like the tide has withdrawn to isolated puddles where inbreeding is common. (*See* map, note the few red areas.)

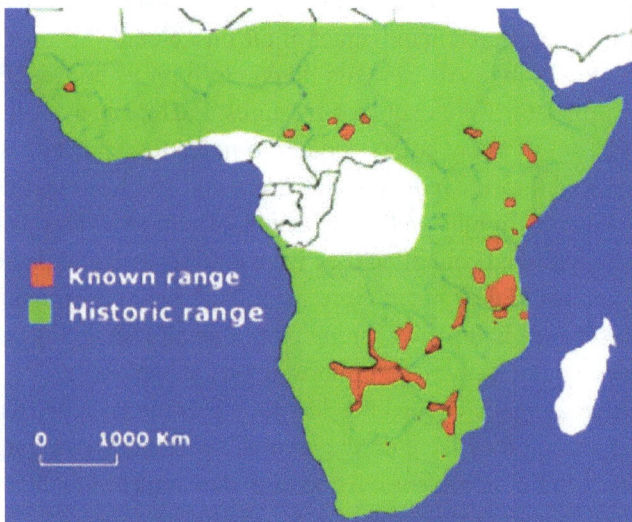

Historic and Present Ranges of the Painted Wolf

During the chase for the Thompson's gazelle, one of the young female wolves fractured her right front leg by stepping on the *edge* of a dried elephant's footprint. With any other animal, a broken leg would be a death sentence, but painted wolves are not ordinary animals, not even close. Surrounded and protected by her parents, siblings, and cousins, she limped the long distance back to the den site. Here the others will feed her (regurgitated meat), and she will rest while the leg heals, until she can again run with the wolves. This is a form of health care, one without cost or clauses.

Life at the den site revolves around the puppies—feeding, teaching, and protecting. They are never left alone; a guardian is always present and considers it an honor to puppy sit. Sometimes to their detriment, adults will do without food to be sure the pups are well-nourished. Whether at home or on the hunt, wild dogs express affection for each other; they are a unit, and this is their strength.

In Africa, man and painted wolf have lived side by side for tens of thousands of years, and during all that time, humans never domesticated a single one. None went to the other side, the way a few Asiatic wolves did 35,000 years ago. For African wild dogs, their first and only loyalty is to their family pack and no other living creature. They stand together, live together, fight together, and when the time comes, die together. Their wild nature is deep, too deep to be tamed. "Live free or die" is their unspoken motto.

Natural Selection   Artificial Selection

For wolves, going over to the other side offers exceptional rewards: more food, less danger, longer life, and comfy chester-fields. Yet it brings boundless peril when man artificially selects for personal and perverse reasons (*see* photograph on selections). Man also "modifies" all creatures great and small for his own convenience. Neutering or spaying is such a permanent condition. Not only is the sexual drive weakened or absent, but also the genetic line is virtually extinguished. You may end up on a leash wearing a collar. By these means and selective breeding, we subdue the wild element in animals and make them placid and pliable to our wishes. Beyond even this, we dehorn, debud, and declaw. We use gelding, spaying, castrating, sterilizing, neutering, fixing, emasculating, or any other action, surgical, chemical, or otherwise, to subdue. We will be masters of the beasts! Man will have dominion over the other animals! Few creatures exist that cannot be tamed. Among the canids, painted wolves stand alone.

Whether man or wolf, whether conscious or not, we make decisions for our life. For a few Asiatic wolves, they welcomed the warmth of the hunters' campfire, the tidbits of food, and the companionship of a man. And man, by the power of artificial selection, has created some beautiful dogs: Labradors, Shepherds, and Bearded Collies (*see* next chapter). But in perversity, we have stewed up some monsters. And be aware, although much is given much is denied. It is a Faustian bargain.

In the wild, wolves live the greatest adventure of all time—the struggle for existence and reproduction against a cruel and uncaring universe. Their life may be short, but it is incredibly intense. A day in the wild is worth a year on the couch. To those few who do the dance, find a mate, and successfully reproduce belongs the power and the glory to laugh at the universe with all its tragedies. You cannot ask for more!

After a lifetime of bringing us the wonders of nature, David Attenborough arrives with his most powerful series ever: *Dynasties: The Greatest of Their Kind.* All life is about leaving children to continue your bloodline, your dynasty. Miss one generation and you erase yourself from history! Those that do leave descendants are the greatest of

Attenborough

their kind, going through battles beyond any written in the *Iliad* or *War and Peace*.

Tait's Pack courtesy of Nicholas Dyer

The producers of this new series describe this astonishing tale of nature's power struggles:

> *The renowned Sir David Attenborough narrates this extraordinary journey inside the world of dynastic power struggles and family treachery that is more dramatic than any work of fiction. Follow the lives of five animals [chimps, lions, emperor penguins, tigers, and painted wolves] and their families as they unfold, day-by-day, hour-by-hour, where the tiniest incident may end up having huge consequences on their future. Their chances of success depend on their own strength, their alliances, and the power of their families. This series shows for the first time what an animal must do to create and maintain a dynasty and leave the most important legacy in nature.[1]*

Dynasties was four years in the making. David Attenborough recounts the saga of Tait, a painted wolf living along the Zambezi river. She was the alpha female of a pack fallen on hard times and reduced to 15 wolves, half their usual number. Painted wolves need enormous areas to find enough food to live. Yet, she is hemmed in on all sides by hyenas, lions, humans, and by Blacktip, her aggressive daughter. Taking advantage of her mother's weakened pack, Blacktip and her horde of thirty drive Tait from her territory, deep into lion country. With her broad experience and skill, however, Tait manages to protect her pack for eight months surrounded by lions who often steal their kills and threaten their existence.

Typically, mother and daughter would not fight, but both were under pressure from the dry season and a shrinking home territory due to human encroachment. After eight months, Blacktip again pushed deeper into Tait's land—lion country—trying to drive her mother even farther away. But events go badly for the invader when hyenas eat two of her pups, and one of the adults is snatched and devoured by a Zambezi crocodile. Blacktip, recognizing her mistake, and mourning her losses, turns tail and runs all the way back home to her original territory. As Attenborough narrates, "They run and run, mile after mile all through the day, all through the night, all the way back home."

Tait's smaller pack, recognizing what is happening, gives chase in this marathon to reclaim their original land. But after seven and a half years as alpha female, Tait—at the limit of painted wolf longevity—is too old and worn out to follow. She lingers, staying behind to walk home at a leisurely pace over several days. Her alpha mate, Ox, will not abandon her, and he stays back as well. And as fortune would have it, they met lions. While standing side by side against these beasts, they died together somewhere on the vast savanna, somewhere near the Zambezi River, somewhere. And those who were seen weeping were thought to be insane by those who could not feel the pain.

Ox and the Legendary Tait courtesy of Nicholas Dyer

As David Attenborough recounts near the end of the episode on painted wolves, Tait's life had been an outstanding success. She was indeed the greatest of her kind. She left 280 descendants and counting, a significant contribution to only 6,600 painted wolves left scattered across Africa in isolated pockets.

Finally, the rains came and with them, an abundance of life and rebirth. Tait's old pack was now without a leader, but not for long. The concept of an alpha male and female is misguided, although I have often used it. The pack is a cooperative, where members "elect" leaders to their positions, not a warring hierarchy. Tait's pack, in a bizarre ritual, never seen or recorded before, elect a new leader with a series of haunting calls.

Three months later, Tait's youngest daughter Tammy gave birth to seven puppies. With this addition, the pack size increased to a healthy twenty-three members. Tait's legacy is secure, and her dynasty lives on—at least for now. Yet, there may come a time when painted wolves will be forgotten, but this is not that day.

The sun had long set before Big Red and Spitfire rose to continue their night journeys. During the day they neither heard nor saw wolves, but several song dogs added their voice to the late spring orchestra. Going to the nearby beach, they drank and bathed as if at a spa.

Big Red thought his mate beautiful (*see* photograph), and his size and virility enchanted her. They would claim his natal territory from his father who had sired no new pups since the winter when their family attacked a hibernating bear that swatted him into unconsciousness. With fewer than 400 Algonquin wolves in existence, their future is far more precarious than that of painted wolves. Our wolves knew little of this, but they did intend to have a family and eventually establish a dynasty and so delay the day when Algonquin wolves will be forgotten.

Unlike humans, female wolves are receptive to copulate just once a year in February. This is so the puppies will be born in the spring, mature over the summer, and be strong enough to endure the brutal winter. Winter is always coming! On average, just half the litter survives. Recall, our wolf's mother had six pups, but only three lived to maturity: Paws, Little Red Ears, and Big Red.

Spitfire

The chilly water felt good on their warm bellies as the wolves stood shoulder-deep in the lake. The mosquitoes and the coagulated blood left from their bites had washed away. The surface of the lake was black and flat, not the least wavelet disturbed its flawless calm. The remains of a once full moon rose from the depths of the lake to shine upon its perfect surface.

A distant movement caught the eye of both wolves, a movement close by the shore and coming directly at them. Our wolves did not move but appeared mesmerized by the creature's progress. A sharp V on the lake's black surface came closer. As this "thing" approached, its velocity increased, and the V narrowed. Again, the wolves did not move. At the tip of the V, a menacing object the size of a human fist appeared above the water's face. Our wolves did not move.

Now within two body lengths, the undulating creature swam directly for Big Red's head. And as only a wolf can do, he opened his jaws to an incredibly large angle as this "thing" lunged to bite his tongue. With a single snap of his jaws, Big Red decapitated a huge northern water snake (*see* photograph). At that same moment, Spitfire sunk her fangs into its writhing body and carried it to shore. For several minutes, the headless form wiggled as if still alive. When all squirming ceased, our wolves ate it as a light breakfast. These snakes, although not venomous, are exceedingly aggressive—this time to its detriment.

Northern Water Snake

Both wolves were familiar with these serpents. Big Red recalled chasing, catching, and eating them as a puppy at the den site. Often, they were smooth green snakes with the color of emeralds (*see* photograph). Other times they were larger, but none were venomous.

Smooth Green Snake

Several hours earlier, the two raccoons hanging around in the maple tree came down headfirst and swam the short distance to the mainland. Given the opportunity, wolves, unlike bears, will eat raccoons as a side dish. After their light breakfast, Big Red and Spitfire walked to the other side of the island, waded, and swam to shore and continued their journey.

They ran on through the hardwood and evergreen forests deep into the night. Spitfire trusted her mate's instincts and was fully engaged in his quest. Wolves bond "until death do us part." Shortly before sunrise, Big Red picks up a familiar scent, but one he had not encountered in a long time. The nose never forgets. It was a marker for the western boundary of the Hill Pack, his father's ancient enemies. There was danger here, so both wolves had to be alert. The Hill Pack had traditionally been large for Algonquin wolves, seven or eight members, due to the abundant wildlife on their vast territory. Our wolves trotted for another hour, and the sun was fully round before they made their bed at the foot of an ancient hemlock tree. A confrontation with the Hill Pack was inevitable, but they were two—young and vigorous. Yet, the outcome was uncertain!

A dark wood fell before them, and all the paths were overgrown—but this did not matter for they were wolves.

We are wolves!
We will go around, over,
or under an obstacle.
And if that fails,
we will go through it.
We have attitude.
We are wolves!

We are Wolves

Chapter—17

MAN'S FIRST FRIEND

When the Man waked up he said, "What is Wild Dog doing here?" And the Woman said, "His name is not Wild Dog anymore, but the First Friend, because he will be our friend for always and always and always."
Rudyard Kipling, *The Jungle Book*

Wolves speak without words. In the last few days, Spitfire realized that Big Red was behaving strangely. Their runs were longer and more intense. She thought their destination must be close. As a plow horse on his final furrow of the day, our wolf was heading back to the barn at a gallop.

With tail wagging, raised hair on the nape, tooth displays, snarls, whines, and a hundred other signs, canids have a rich vocabulary in a wolfen language. And then there is scent reading and marking. Canids are forever smelling each other's butt as if reading an encyclopedia. All their senses gather knowledge. And who is to say their howls, sniffs, whimpers, and growls, and so on are not words simply because they lack an alphabet? Experts say 93 percent of all information gathered by humans is non-verbal; can wolves be far behind? Anonymous declared, "A picture is worth a thousand words."

Spitfire Nibbles Big Red's Ear

However she did it, Spitfire convinced her mate that they needed to eat and rest. Now just a mouthful and a memory, her belly had forgotten the snake breakfast. Without snow, deer and moose are much harder to catch, so the next item on their menu was beaver.

Wolves hunt by two different methods: they either run prey down, or they ambush them. The first method works for deer and the second for beaver. It is astonishing to people unfamiliar with this rodent just how large they can grow. As adults, they can weigh anywhere from 40 – 60 lbs. (18 – 27 kg), a good chunk of meat. As previously noted, this was lake country with abundant marshes and streams where the beavers are active after sunset. To double their chances, our wolves each hid behind some bushes by a different rivulet that drained into a pond with a beaver lodge. To get at the tasty aspen trees and other delicacies, the beavers swim or wade up these feeder streams, cut the trees down, float or drag them back to their lodge.

Our wolves could smell the beavers . . . it is not difficult. It was well after midnight when they assumed their different hiding positions behind low bushes near feeder streams. One, two, three hours passed before Spitfire heard some splashing near her. An enormous wet beaver glistening in the slowly setting moon waddled upstream near her. Beavers are not defenseless; they often escape a wolf attack as healed teeth marks on their tails show, and they can inflict frightening wounds. Yet Spitfire, with astonishing quickness, killed the rodent striking and breaking its ample neck as a trap would a mouse.

With a distinctly low howl, Spitfire summoned her mate for supper. Dining contentedly, they got that strength and vigor needed for their inevitable encounter with the Hill Pack. Land is food, and those wolves will not be happy with interlopers eating "their" beavers. Because of their leisurely dining, the sun was now up.

It was then they first heard them. Somewhere in a remote valley, a faint cacophony of voices echoed through the forest. A tintinnabulation of three voices. What were they? Who were they? What did it mean? Spitfire had never heard such sounds, but Big Red knew them well from the time he lived outside Algonquin Park's east side.

Dogs, at least three of them! These canines are wolves' closest relative, but they are not always on friendly terms. Big Red surmised by their frenzied barking that they were chasing some animal. Coming in the general direction of our wolves, their voices grew louder and more crazed. Big Red and Spitfire bedded down on a hillside overlooking a mixed valley of hardwood and evergreen trees and waited for the dogs' arrival. Until they have met a wolf, all dogs think they are alphas, so dogs pose no problems for wolves.

Some minutes passed when suddenly a black bear burst from the forest with two cubs in tow. The sow could run forever, but her cubs were clearly exhausted, so she climbed up an old white pine tree. The mother sat on one of the tree's lower branches, but the cubs disappeared into the canopy, as she waited and watched for her tormentors to arrive.

The Worried Look of a Mother Bear

Within minutes, a Plott Hound on a leash dragged a stumbling hunter out of the forest, quickly followed by two more hounds and hunters in the same condition. Once the hunters saw that the dogs had treed the bear, they let them off their tethers. The hounds circled the base of the tree in a pandemonium of barks and yelps while the bear crouched behind a limb. All three hunters had a rifle in a sheath on their back: two Winchesters and one Marlin. And as if synchronized, they shot the bear together. This magnificent animal plummeted to the ground as a lifeless sack of flesh; instantly, the dogs were on her in a frenzy of biting and ripping. All the while, her two cubs hid in the pine tree's high canopy.

Plott Hound aka Bear Hound Dog

Hidden on the hillside, our wolves saw all this, both the hunters and the dogs. Inconceivably, this slaughter is legal, part of the Ontario Spring Bear Hunt. To record their heroism and prowess, the hunters took each other's photograph with their smartphones, and then they left. The ill-fated sow was neither skinned nor eaten— simply abandoned as a crumpled, bloody jumble of flesh and fur at the base of the tree. Swaggering away like the lords of anarchy, these three matricidal killers were unaware of the two cubs and fortunately so. The Plott Hounds, however, did not go so easily. Again, the men tethered and dragged them away, protesting into the forest. All that remained were two terrified and trembling cubs in the tree's crown.

> *A bear's days are warmed by the same sun,*
> *his dwellings are overdomed by the same blue sky,*
> *and his life turns and ebbs with heart-pulsings*
> *like ours and was poured from the same First Fountain.*
> John Muir, naturalist, "Finding a Dead Yosemite Bear," October 1871.

Big Red and Spitfire would spend the day on the hillside camouflaged by white and pink wisteria bushes. The hounds, with their noses saturated with the scent of bear, had no room left for another animal. In a rite of spring, two exquisite indigo buntings began to construct their grassy nest in the wisteria bushes managing to annoy our wolves until sunset.

Where's Mum?

The cubs did not know what to do. It was late afternoon before the bravest, or less obedient cub, came partway down the pine tree, far enough to see his mother's ripped and torn lifeless form. Calling to his brother still in the canopy, they descended the final few feet together. They pushed, poked, and nudged their mother, hoping she was napping. One cub tried to suckle from an empty, cold teat while the other snuggled close to her mangled form.

It was four hours until sunset when five turkey vultures glided in for dinner. With awkward struts, they advanced toward the carcass before the cubs drove them back into the sky. But these birds were late. Flies had already arrived and found the open wounds from the rifle bullets, and the chunks of flesh ripped away by the frenzied hounds. In these cavities, they laid their maggoty eggs and left. The deep orange and black carrion beetles, the undertakers of the insect world, would soon come. Given the power of speech, the cubs might have expressed the pain in their hearts in terms we could understand. The two orphans, one on each side like guards, snuggled close to their lifeless mother all through the day, all through that night. Bears may be beasts, but man can be a monster.

There is life after death, it just does not include you. The diligent indigo buntings continued to build their nest. Stuffed with beaver steaks, our sleepy wolves had no desire to eat them. Big Red and Spitfire slept and dreamt through the remains of the day from their hillside lookout dimly aware of the appalling drama in the valley below.

🐾

Think back to your earliest memory. Now think further back, not to something your parents told you, but something you recall with all its sights, sounds, and smells. My earliest memory, even before that beautiful morning my mother pointed out the doe and her fawn drinking from the lake, was of puppies.

It was a rare occasion because my father was doing something with me! On an early summer evening, he suggested I go to the horse barn with him. We were in the kitchen at the lumber mill where my mother was busy preparing for tomorrow's breakfast. Three kerosene lanterns hung from crossbeams, casting a pale light.

My father took one of those lanterns, and we stepped out the screen door into the enveloping darkness where a coterie of moths soon fluttered near the light. In the distance, I could hear the secretive whip-poor-wills calling their name while a chorus of bullfrogs from the lake sang "rum, rum, jug-O-rum, rum, rum, rum." It was a short walk to the barn, and as my dad opened the solid plank door, a pungent odor filled my nostrils. This was a magical place! The placid four-legged giants in their open stanchions were contentedly munching on oats and hay. The faintly lit interior was alive with the power of life: the horses feeding, the barn cat watching mice running across the manger boards, and the moths tickling our faces.

One double stall was empty and we went up to the manger. While holding the lamp high in his left hand, my father picked me up and held me over the manger that I might see. In the bottom of this crib was a bed of straw with our dog Queenie and her 16 newborn puppies, blind and squirming. To the eyes of a four-year-old, a manger full of puppies is a transcendent experience. Queenie was a gentle and loving animal, and she trusted me when I picked up a puppy and held it to my chest, and ever after in my memory. In a few minutes, my dad put the puppy back, and it quickly found a teat and happily nursed. After that perfect moment, I can recall nothing more—as if that memory were so strong, there was room for nothing more.

Everything from that time has vanished: the mill, the cookhouse, the lumber piles, the barns. All the men who worked as machines are gone; my mother and dad are gone. The horses, cats, mice, dogs, and whip-poor-wills are gone. Unless they left progeny, they are meaningless to the genetic history of life on earth. No photographs of these animals, people, or places exist. All this has been forgotten! I have only a sacred memory of a gentle dog in a manger with her puppies, and perhaps if I write about this remembrance, it may yet live a little longer.

As I wrote previously, dogs are just friendly wolves . . . mostly. Wolves and dogs share 99 percent of their DNA, but by artificial selection, man has "created" 300 different breeds, large and small, beautiful and ugly, friendly and vicious.

Jared Diamond in his ground-breaking book *Guns, Germs, and Steel: The Fates of Human Societies* [1] points out that man has domesticated just 14 animals: sheep, goats, horses, and so on. Strikingly, he does not list the dog/wolf among them—for good reasons. Initially, man *did not domesticate* wolves, but a few, a very few, were *tamed*. A lone wolf, probably a female, not wanted elsewhere, found the meat scraps around campsites attractive. One night, as she crawled closer to the campfire, a hand stroked her back. And when she had puppies, some of these proved too wild and returned to the forest, while others grew closer to humans and these took a micro-step toward domestication. This early version of natural/artificial selection played itself out over thousands of years until the family dog, *Canis familiaris*, was born.

Man & Wolf: Invincible Pair

It is clear how the wolf benefits by being "tamed," but how does this profit a man? A single night living in the wilderness with a dog will give you the answer. They hear and smell trouble long before you do, and they never seem to sleep. And they will be the first to attack beasts: bear, hyena, or lion. In the world before history, groups of humans and packs of wolves roamed the same landscape in search of the same prey, but wolves were superior at it. Their success rate was double or triple that of a man who spent much of his time scavenging. And together, wolf and man would feed each other and conquer the world.

As a child, I instinctively knew the value of dogs. The next summer we had just one dog from Queenie's considerable litter of puppies—I dare not reflect on what happened to the others. We called him "Jeff." During those idyllic summer days, Jeff, Queenie, and I were inseparable. The dogs were my lone friends since I was the only child and my mother the only woman at the lumber mill. We particularly loved the beach where I searched for minnows, frogs, crayfish, and clams while they joyously splashed about in the shallow water and then slept on the warm sand. For reasons unknown, we three friends decided to explore one of the many old logging roads leading to the mill.

I would walk in the middle, often with an arm about each dog. Expecting to find new adventures around every turn and over every hill of this rugged path, we walked all morning. This road was not for cars or even trucks but was just the result of horses skidding logs out of the forest to the lake in winter. We walked farther. At one point, some partridges boomed out of the under-growth, but the dogs restrained their natural instincts to stand by me. We walked farther. When the men from the mill found us, they said we were lost—although I have no recollection that we were. When I did not show up for lunch, Mother had the entire mill shut down, and all the workers dispersed to search for me.

When you are with a dog in the forest, you fear no evil; he will be your first line of defense. And what if you have two dogs? These were mongrels, these were hounds, but these were my friends. Until you have loved an animal, a part of your spirit still sleeps.

Whenever and wherever there was danger, man brought dogs for protection and comfort. When the Paleo-Eskimo people 4,500 years ago came out of Siberia, they did so with sled dogs. The Thule people later replaced them 1,000 years ago bringing their own version of the Canadian Eskimo Dog. Their vast travels and heroics are just legends and whispers now of a forgotten people in a land beyond harsh in an age before memory. These dogs were superbly suited to wintry weather, curling up in a ball and sleeping through the fiercest Arctic blizzard. Alerting the Inuit to both danger and food as well as supplying transportation, they proved themselves indispensable. Without dogs, there would be no Inuit.

During the modern era of exploration, heroes came in two types: those who could learn from the Inuit and those who could not. The former lived, the latter perished in horrible conditions. The latter included men like Robert Falcon Scott and Sir John Franklin. The former went on to glory, men like Roald Amundsen and Sir Ernest Shackleton. Most Europeans would not learn from the "filthy savages" they met during their explorations, and they paid a price for such arrogance.

In his early years, Amundsen lived in the Arctic and learned much from the indigenous people concerning clothing, dogs, and sleds, which he put to meaningful use and success in the Antarctic. Scott used ponies! Amundsen led a team of five men and 52 dogs on a race to the South Pole (*see* photograph) beating Scott by five weeks. Although Scott reached the Pole, he and his men all perished on the return journey from starvation and hypothermia. On the other hand, Amundsen's team all returned safely, and astonishingly they had put on weight. Closer inspection reveals why—he started with 52 dogs and returned with only 11. You do the math. They ate the difference! Without a doubt, Amundsen was a heroic explorer, but to me, the eating of his dogs puts a

Amundsen & his Dogs at South Pole, December 14, 1911

bloody stain on his legacy. But a little voice says, "He would never have reached the pole and returned alive, otherwise." To which I reply, "Choose life over imaginary dots on maps."

Of those 11 surviving dogs, only the one called *Colonel* returned safely to Norway although his real home was Greenland. The others died of disease or were sold. I would say we owe the same loyalty to dogs as they give to us. If a dog could speak, he would bark, "Stand by me, as I have stood by you."

🐾

Spitfire and Big Red were warm as they slept under the wisteria bushes in the mottled sunlight. The industrious indigo buntings flew back and forth carrying construction material for their nest.

Male Indigo Bunting

It was an idyllic scene. The female bunting, wishing a soft, warm lining for her eggs, flew to Big Red's backside and pulled out a mouthful of his shedding fur. She continued this for some time until the male joined her in this shopping spree on Spitfire's butt. After much coming and going, the agitated wolves awakened, and the birds flew off.

Both wolves took this opportunity to pee and see the theater below. It was almost dusk, and the vultures had won the rights to the great bruin's carcass, forcing the bear cubs to withdraw to the lower limbs of the pine. They stayed there until the satiated vultures finally left. In the darkness of a moonless night, they descended the tree one last time, glanced at the remains of their mother, and disappeared together into the enveloping forest.

The wolves slept.

🐾

Of all the explorers in the modern heroic age, Sir Ernest Shackleton is the most remarkable. Yet, he never reached either pole or discovered anything new geographically. His most famous ship, the *Endurance,* sank in the Weddell Sea, crushed by enormous blocks of ice. Moreover, he died at the early age of 48 on South Georgia Island. Despite all these misfortunes, he did what few other polar explorers did: *he never lost a man.**

Shackleton was a learner. From his own experience and that of Scott, he avoided the use of ponies. They sank into the snow, fell into crevasses, and all their food had to come from Europe. So, they killed and ate them! Instead of ponies, he brought 70 dogs and one cat. Even of greater importance, Shackleton hired an Australian photographer, one Frank Hurley, to record a visual record of their entire transpolar expedition of 1914-17. Hurley matched Shackleton in bravery and ability.

After the *Endurance* sank, this expedition became a survival quest, one that belongs in the annals of heroic treks. The crew of 28 were to pull three lifeboats over the frozen Weddell Sea until they reached open water, and then row to the Antarctic Peninsula. Shackleton declared, "We're traveling light today." And by throwing his money on the snow along with the Bible, he proved

The *Endurance* about to Sink

his intent. Others were to follow his example. Hurley refused and ultimately convinced Shackleton this was a mistake, at least in his case. Without a photographic record of their exploits, this trek would go down in history as just a group of fools who died wandering in the Antarctic wilderness. The problem was the legendary motion-picture films, and the glass-plate images were *weighty*. Worst yet, they were still on the *Endurance* in the ship's lower section and *under* the Antarctic waters.

Hurley, intent on retrieving these films and photographs on glass-plates, decided to do the impossible, the ridiculous. He would enter the ship, strip off most of his clothing, dive into the freezing water, and bring them to the surface. Two shipmates went

---

* On this voyage.

with him for assistance, but they would not enter the water. After each dive, these companions had to slap him into consciousness. He continued to dive until he had retrieved many of the glass plates and most of the films. Physically unable to do more, Hurley and his shipmates carried these to one of the lifeboats and dragged them back to civilization.

Imagine a time machine, and by dialing it up, you could go back and see any historical event you wished. Where would you go? Who do you want to see? The choice is endless, but the past is all gone, gone, gone, forever. Or is it? Let us look at a near miracle.

Recently, the National Film and Television Archive (NFTVA) of Australia restored Frank Hurley's films—those he retrieved from under the Weddell Sea. By applying tinting and toning, they matched the originals and recreated a transcendent moment in the history of exploration. Extra features including Shackleton's funeral and *Southward on the Quest*. The film, titled *South*,[2] is a tribute to Hurley's genius and bravery, as he records Shackleton's ill-starred attempt to cross Antarctica by dogsled. This is a unique historical record and a poem of praise to the unconquerable spirit of 28 men and 70 dogs. It is a time machine where you are on the deck of the *Endurance* with the dogs and the men. You can meet Samson and Sally and see their puppies. You can even meet Mrs. Chippy, the carpenter's cat. You can meet the men. And, yes, you will see the ship and the Antarctic wilderness!

What follows is part of an exuberant online review of *South* by a young woman who uses the moniker "Yours Truly," posted September 1, 2016. It is clear, right from the beginning of the film, that Hurley has as much if not more interest in animals, particularly dogs, as he has in the crew. Tom Crean, pictured here holding the puppies (*see* photograph), was the head dog-handler, but all the men loved these dogs, as the dogs loved them:

> *The footage is AMAZING. Hurley was an artist! You can tell that he was interested in filmmaking for its own sake, not just for documentary evidence. There are some truly exceptional shots. There are shots taken head-on and right up close, of the Endurance breaking through pack ice, and it's hard to imagine how the shot was achieved.*

Turns out, Hurley was obsessed with the dogs, and with animals in general! By far the longest uncut shot in the film is of the dogs in their onboard kennel. He intercuts titles telling their names (Hercules, Sue) and commenting on details of their behavior and care. There was so much dog footage that I briefly forgot this was a documentary of the Endurance. Dogs getting fed! Dogs pulling sleds! A litter of pups born on the boat, held in the burly arms of a ship's mate who grins into the camera as he jostles them! Close-ups of the brand-new baby pups' faces. A hilarious shot of the ship's smallest crewmember [see photograph] wrasslin' with the ship's largest dog. I think it's clear that those damn dogs are the only reason everyone on board did not go instantly insane. The psychological uplift of watching a goofy dog rolling around in the snow or of fondling a precious newborn pup must have been huge.

Tom Crean with Sally & Samson's Puppies

Also, it is poignant to watch 100-year-old footage of people playing with dogs. It's like, some things never change; you can imagine the exact same scene 200, 500, 1,000 years ago. The dogs all act the same way, and the people act the same way. Everybody knows you scratch a dog behind his ear just so; everybody has that urge to ruffle up a dog's neck feather; every dog does that soft-mouthed joyous biting thing on your arm to tell he loves you. God bless all the dogs.

Dr. Leonard Hussey with Sally & Samson

Smuts & Soldier: Two Brave Crew Members

The men took all the dogs still alive* off the *Endurance* and billeted them in wooden huts on the sea ice. In retrospect, they did not retrieve enough food from the ship—perhaps because of Shackleton's edict to "Travel light." Besides, they and the dogs were to eat penguins and seals as they found them.

Sometime, somewhere, in this place at the ends of the earth, they shot all the dogs. "Not enough food," declared Shackleton. They even killed Sally and Samson's four puppies. "Not enough food," declared Shackleton. *So, they ate some of the dogs*—they piled others like the bodies at Auschwitz-Birkenau and covered them with snow. Shackleton personally shot McNeish's cat, Mrs. Chippy. The carpenter never forgave him! Shackleton threatened to shoot the rebellious McNeish as well who declared the cat could eat half his food.

Sometime, somewhere, somehow, the human crew slaughtered 70 grand dogs, four beautiful puppies, and one impish cat on the Weddell Sea. And when the ice thawed these lifeless forms plunged 300 fathoms to the ice-water mansions on the seafloor joining the *Endurance*. For years their bones and bodies wandered looking for the crew that "loved" them, looking for their "friends."

---

* A few dogs had died of worms because the expedition's negligence in forgetting to bring deworming powder.

I choose not to record all the names of the human crew. The reader can easily find these online, but here are five:

Ernest Shackleton – expedition leader, called BOSS

Frank Worsley – captain of the *Endurance* and the *James Cairn* on the trip to South Georgia Island

Henry McNeish – carpenter & shipwright and the owner and caregiver of the cat, Mrs. Chippy

Percy Blackborow – stowaway who had all the toes on his left foot amputated on Elephant Island

Frank Hurley – legendary expedition photographer.

I choose to record all the names of the dogs on the *Endurance*—at least the ones we know. Their names are colorful and descriptive, showing a conscious creature with joys, fears, loves like all of us. Again, as Darwin wrote in *The Descent of Man*, "There is no fundamental difference between man and animals in their ability to feel pleasure and pain, happiness, and misery."

THE 74 DOG CREW ON THE ENDURANCE

Rugby	Upton	Skip	Hercules
Bristol	Millhill	Hackenschmidt	Samson
Songster	Sandy	Skipper	Caruso
Tim	Mercury	Sub	Sammy
Wolf	Ulysses	Spotty	Bosun
Slobbers	Sadie	Sue	Sally
Jasper	Tim	Sweep	Martin
Satan	Luke	Saint	Chips
Stumps	Snapper	Painful	Owd Bob
Splitlip	Snowball	Jerry	Judge
Sooty	Rufus	Sidelights	Simeon
Swanker	Chirgwin	Steamer	Peter
Fluffy	Steward	Slippery Neck	Elliot
Roy	Noel	Shakespeare	Jamie
Bummer	Smuts	Luipold	Spider
Sailor	Wallaby	Mooch	Soldier

Unknown Dog 1	Unknown Dog 2	Unknown Dog 3
Unknown Dog 4	Unknown Dog 5	Unknown Dog 6

Sally and Samson's Puppies

Nell	Toby	Roger	Nelson

When they reached the open ocean, they launched the three lifeboats rowing to Elephant Island in the Southern Shetlands. This was like no other place on earth—desolate, black, rocky, but with some penguins and seals. Such was this place that no human had ever set foot on it before or wished to.

Shackleton and Worsley proposed an audacious rescue plan—they would make an open-boat journey to South Georgia Island. Of the three lifeboats, only the one called the *James Cairn* was seaworthy for such a mission. McNeish, with his shipwright and carpenter skills, reinforced the boat and covered the top with wood and canvas to make it capable of surviving the stormy Southern Ocean. With captain Worsley navigating by the stars, they safely sailed 800 miles (1,300 km) reaching South Georgia Island after 16 days. But they were on the wrong side! Three of the six men were unable to travel farther, so Shackleton, Crean, and Worsley resolved to cross the central mountain range on foot to reach the whaling station on the far side.

History often depends on small events, events, so small "experts" often overlook them. On the day of the Battle of Waterloo, Napoleon could not ride his horse and direct the troops with his usual genius—he had a bad case of hemorrhoids. Now Henry McNeish was a curious and resourceful person, and before the *Endurance* sank, he removed a handful of screws from her boards. These he now screwed into the soles of the boots of Shackleton, Crean, and Worsley so they might have some chance of scaling these icy, treacherous mountains. All history knows they made the trek and returned to pick up McNeish and the other two.

After three futile attempts to reach Elephant Island, Shackleton finally arrived after a three-month absence. As he approached the shore in a rowboat, he yelled, "Is everyone alive?" To which Percy Blackborow, the only crew member on the beach responded, "Yes, Boss."

This was one of the supreme survival stories of all time. "I have done it," writes Shackleton, in a message to his wife, Emily. "Not a life lost, and we have been through Hell!" They undoubtedly had. But a tiny voice says that from the beginning Shackleton caused this hardship by arrogance and a quest for fame. And in an act of outrageous meanness of spirit, Shackleton denied McNeish his Polar Medal though the carpenter had twice saved everyone's life.

Yet, more important than their medals, honors, and fame, and something we must never forget, they slaughtered 75 of their friends, ate some, and tossed the others on the Weddell Sea ice.

There will never come a morning when your dog wakes up and no longer loves you. Never! No human can say as much. There are two types of people: those that love dogs and those who do not. Nothing can be done for the latter group, theirs is a grim existence.

To paraphrase the iconic opening sentence of Tolstoy's novel *Anna Karenina*, "All happy families with a dog are alike; each unhappy family with a dog is unhappy in its own way." What is a dog to do when his family no longer loves him? He cannot return to the wild the way a tame wolf might because he is domesticated, meaning he has lost the skills necessary to live in the forest. This confines him to a twilight world between the wild and the civilized. Where are such places? The bleak streets of Moscow have an estimated 35,000 feral dogs. This is a stable number causally related to handouts and garbage. This stability is comparable to the stability of wolves in Algonquin Park, causally related to their prey base of deer and beaver.

Of these 35,000 feral dogs, there exists a minute subset of just 20 or so who have a made an astonishing adaptation. Let me explain. But it is cold on these dull, gray streets. Come, walk with me in the Mendeleyevskaya Station (*see* photograph) part of the vast Moscow Metro beneath the city. Winter has come!

Mendeleev & the Periodic Table in Moscow Metro

After the frigid streets, this was a paradise—warm, bright, and decorated with inspirational sculpture and art. Each of the over 200 stations has a central theme. This one is dedicated to the famous Russian chemist who discovered the periodic table of the elements and created a pattern out of chaos.

As we walk down its ornate halls, a train arrives, and a flood of passengers pours out the open doors. Near the front of the train, a dog steps off, taking his time, moving at the pace of the crowd, not barking, not running. Walking toward us, I notice he looks well-fed, medium size, shepherd strain, dark-brown spotless coat, but without that aura of joy that surrounds a happy dog. He walks with his ears straight up, but his tail never wags. This is a Moscow Metro dog, one of 20 or so super-intelligent dogs who has mastered this complex subway system to travel around the city. Several hundred others live in Metro stations, yet do not use the trains. Intelligence gives dominance among these canines, not physical power. They are more Odysseus than Achilles.

As this dog swam effortlessly through the crowd, he read the faces of the passengers. He knew those who might give him a treat or a pat rather than a kick. Middle-aged women with shopping bags were a good target and most generous. His "home" was outside Moscow, and he daily took the Metro to the inner city to find food and affection. Many commuters knew him, most loved him, and some regularly gave him scraps. Later that day on his way home in the evening, he would fall asleep on the soft seats (*see* photograph), but he never missed his station.

Riding the Moscow Metro

But right now, he walked toward the escalators in lockstep with the flow of passengers for we were deep underground. On the escalator, he stayed on the right so impatient people might run past him. Arriving at the top, close to the exit, there was another animal, but it was a bronze figure of a dog scratching his ear. The Metro Dog we were following just glanced at the statue and pushed his body against an exit door opening it onto Moscow's snowy streets. We stayed behind to read the inscription on the statue's base. It said, "Compassion."

This was Malchik (*see* photograph) who made this station his home for three years before an insane Moscow "top" model stabbed him to death. She was wearing a hat of black velvet, a blue fur-trimmed coat, a short skirt, and tall black leather boots. The police arrested her, and she underwent a year of psychiatric care— her outward beauty concealed inner darkness. Muscovites were outraged at her cruelty. A group of artists, well-known Russian actors, and public figures decided to put up a monument to this street dog—thousands contributed from Russia and abroad.

In life as in death, Malchik was a well-liked dog. While living, commuters brought him treats; in death, they bring him flowers, and old ladies with shopping bags bend down to kiss his nose. The leader of the group to erect the monument declared this statue to a slain feral dog would have a huge ethical significance. She said, "The question of respect for the world of animals is the first stage of morality, which one cannot skip to proceed to all further stages." And someone else said, "Dogs are not our whole life, but they make our lives whole."

Malchik (Little Boy)

Big Red was already on his feet when he first heard it, an ungodly screech long and lonely covering the whole valley and the surrounding hills. It came from the direction of the bear carcass. Spitfire was also up and close by her mate; she looked at him as if to ask what creature could emit such an infernal sound. Our wolf knew it was a fisher (aka fisher cat), a four-foot-long weasel. This animal was claiming ownership of the remains of the bear. This beast screamed again, but Big Red lost interest. Neither wolf was hungry, and fishers are quick to climb a tree to avoid danger.

Despite the blackness, the wilderness, and the shrieking of the fisher, Big Red had a joy in his heart for he knew this would be the final day in his long journey. Some internal geography mapped on his brain told him he was close to home, a day's journey close. To share his joy in this unlikely place, he invited Spitfire to play, and she accepted for she was a wild free spirit. And so, two wolves danced in the darkness and defied life's pain in this place, on this small planet, for an hour. After this, they trotted off in the blackness of a sliver of a new moon that you can fit your left hand into. Our wolf was determined to run until they reached his natal territory and see who of his family was still living and who was not. The fisher has ceased his noise, but other sounds adorned their journey: barred and saw-whet owls sang, bullfrogs and green frogs called until sunrise.

Big Red in the Night

On the high ground of the Hill Pack, the forest was open, dotted with a mixture of hardwood trees: maple, beech, ash, basswood, and oak. The trees were large and ancient. This was a climax forest where no tree knew a chainsaw or an ax—a land no man had touched. It was too remote, too rugged, strewn with rocks and boulders, and set amid ancient trees. Big Red's fear of traps and snares gave way to other concerns. Sometime before sunrise, he heard them: wolves calling from three directions all around them. Wolves are good at arithmetic, and Big Red and Spitfire counted seven different voices. One pack of four sounded closest—the Hill Pack had detected the intruders. Nonetheless, our wolves kept to their path toward home.

Even though the sun was now full-circle, Big Red had no intention of resting or sleeping because this was *the day of homecoming*. The sun was at their backs when they trotted into a large meadow. Halfway across, four wolves slipped out of the surrounding forest to confront them: three of last year's pups and their mother, the alpha female of the Hill Pack! Big Red and Spitfire had been expecting them. What Big Red could not know was that this old she-wolf was his maternal grandmother.

When Big Red saw them, he laughed internally and smiled at his mate. These four wolves were no match or threat to two wolves in their prime. *Is this the best you can do*? thought our wolf.

Spitfire & Big Red Dancing

And in a bizarre act of defiance, he again invited Spitfire to play. She caught the spirit of the moment and recognized what he was doing. So, our two wolves danced in the meadow before an astonished audience of four. Their message was clear: we are too strong for you. Pass on by, try another time. As a further display of his disdain, Big Red laid down and watched his mate dance. She moved as if on air; her paws barely touched the ground as she spun and twirled—a vision of physical fitness no human knows. After this, she nudged his nose (*see* photograph) with an invitation to the dance. The old she-wolf correctly understood their ballet. Last year's pups, however, were eager to attack. With difficulty, the old wolf grabbed the most excited juvenile by the scruff of the neck and dragged him off. With this, the Hill Pack slunk away.

And those who were seen dancing
were thought to be insane
by those who could not hear the music. *

---

* Usually attributed to Friedrich Nietzsche.

Chapter—18

THE HOMECOMING

There is no place like home.
L. Frank Baum, *The Wonderful Wizard of Oz*

Something watched the dancers in the meadow below, something sitting black against the sky in a dead beech tree at the edge of the forest. Nothing escaped his eyes, not the least movement. Without warning, he vaulted into the air and for an instant, gravity won, and he descended the length of his body. But then his mighty wings, like pistons in a steam engine, starting slowly yet with incredible power, pumped the air, and he did rise. He had a family to feed, two eaglets and their mother. A plump woodchuck would be nice or even a feathery partridge, but this bird was an opportunistic hunter, taking whatever came along.

The meadow held nothing for him, just two wolves making bizarre movements with four more watching. For a few seconds, one of the spectators howled for some reason. Gaining altitude, the eagle's keen vision caught the motion of three more wolves, two coming from the north and one from the west. Before he disappeared into heaven's high vault, the four wolves in the

Something Black Against the Sky

meadow slipped into the hardwood forest. These animals may be wolves of the woods, but the golden eagle knew he was the wolf of the skies.

Big Red detested these birds! One of his earliest memories is of a golden eagle snatching and eating one of his little sisters. It could easily have been him or Paws had they not seen the bird coming and hidden under a wire bush. Memory chiseled this death on his brain and given, the opportunity, he would quickly kill an eagle. Wolves are all about family.

The meadow was deathly quiet now; the Hill Pack had slinked away, and the eagle flew off. Our wolves resumed their mission and trotted toward home. Big Red thought he should soon smell his father's urine markings of the western boundary of the Natal Pack. What our wolf could not know was his father had died the previous fall after the first heavy snowfall, died without producing any pups during the last two years of his life.

His father had known better days. His coat was patchy, his muzzle white, and what little fur he had clung to his body as if it were wet. He meandered with a faltering gait, a strange combination of stiffness and pain caused by his infirmities, his head held low as if he had not the strength to raise it. Those once beautiful amber eyes now had a dull cloudiness, and little caught their attention. Then, after stumbling a few body lengths, he tumbled to the earth one last time—his legs no longer responding to his commands. Lastly, with his great gray head resting on his paws, he closed his eyes and this remarkable animal, with his own concept of death, knew he was ready for his final journey, the long sleep.

When the pack—his mate, her sister, and Little Red Ears—found him later that day, he appeared to be heading toward the massive rock he often rested on in the dappled sunshine. The same rock where in earlier years, he protected his family in their nearby den. Unlike dead puppies, wolves do not bury adults, but they may kick some debris and earth over the body. They leave the dead where they lie, open to the elements. The forest creatures will recycle the body's parts in life everlasting.

Each of the three family members nudged him with their wet noses as if to awaken him from his long sleep. Then they sang, not as a pack but individually, each expressing their own grief.

His mate sang first (*see* photograph), a song so long and mournful that the very trees might cry. Her sister performed next and lastly his daughter, Little Red Ears. They lost their spirit and playfulness—depressed they wandered around with heads down, tails between legs, and ears pinned back.

Make no mistake, the bonds in the pack are adamantine, and they will grieve for weeks. More than that, they will often visit the body even after it is gone as if that site were sacred. They mourn, they howl, and then they move on. But they never forget!

Cry of the Wild

In the present moment, Spitfire sensed her mate's agitation. Big Red recognized the land they were passing through—it was the land where he was born. But why had his father not marked its boundary? Our wolf could not detect the faintest odor from his urine or feces. Was this no wolf's land? Could his family all be dead? At least, he thought his father must be dead. But right now, they had a more pressing situation: all seven Hill Pack wolves were almost upon them.

Within seconds a young wolf burst from the forest, fangs flashing, and his whole body aflame with fury. It was the same young animal the old she-wolf had to restrain in the meadow. Big Red was weary of his nonsense. Moreover, the Natal Pack's boundaries had to be reestablished. With a quickness and a ferocity the young wolf could never match, Big Red sank his fangs into the wolf's shoulder, picked him up, and shook him as if he were a woodchuck. Our wolf decided to let the yearling live—a harsh lesson would be best. Immediately after casting him aside, our wolves bolted toward home.

A mere 300 yards (270 m) behind them were the other six wolves of the Hill Pack, their ancient rivals. Big Red ran directly toward the Natal Pack's favorite rendezvous site in the same valley as their den but on the opposite side (*see* map). Those pack members still living would likely be there. This was a fortunate choice because, at that moment, his mother, aunt, and sister were all relaxing there in the ample sunshine. Upon hearing the howls and cries of the Hill Pack, they scrambled to their feet and intently surveyed the other valley wall. Within seconds, Big Red and Spitfire sprinted out of the forest and began their steep descent. At their distance, Big Red's family was unsure who they were. Before there was time to consider this, six more wolves in furious pursuit ran onto the valley wall. Immediate identification became a pressing problem.

For a fleeting moment, Big Red's mother thought she recognized her son, but she was uncertain. Little Red Ears knew him first, and she ran joyously to greet her brother. The long-lost son had returned and brought a bride with him. His mother and aunt were close behind. They jumped, kissed, licked, and rubbed their bodies together in a joy unrestrained and unreserved. As I wrote previously, wolves never forget.

At some unknown signal, they all turned and stood shoulder to shoulder against the attacking Hill Pack. Spitfire was at Big Red's right side and his mother, at his left. His aunt and Little Red Ears were on the flanks. It was six on five, a fair fight. The pursuers stopped abruptly just a few body lengths away, to size up this new pack. The old she-wolf and her equally aged mate were careful. She gazed intently at Big Red's mother and aunt and knew they were her daughters from many years ago. The she-wolf had to decide, odds and outcomes predicted, costs and rewards calculated, past and present considered. She was conflicted and trespassing, and so she turned away. And with that, it was over. The Hill Pack walked off, and Big Red let them. They would not be back. On their return to their territory, the she-wolf encouraged her injured son to limp home.

The celebrations for the return of the native continued deep into the night. Big Red's Natal Pack accepted Spitfire as if she were a sister. And when they finally rested, it was in a loose, comfortable pile. There was a profound need to touch each other, a need unsatisfied for too long.

When they awoke, the scent of the red pine trees near the valley wall gave freshness and vigor to the morning. This was the first day of a new beginning, and a recognizable joy flowed through this pack of five wolves. Their movements were light, their energy boundless. Yet, Big Red's mother had a miserable mission to do. She led her son and Spitfire to the site of his father's death. Every part of his body was gone, the forest animals and insects had been busy, yet his mother uncovered a single rib, the final remnant of a once-formidable animal. Big Red knew this site without monuments, this song without words, and he continued to honor it for rest his life.

Spitfire Comforts Big Red

When the dominant male dies, more than his body is gone. Without writing, without books, he was the repository of a lifetime of knowledge on how to survive in this harsh land. Most importantly, he knew and marked the boundaries of their pack territory. By good fortune or planning, Big Red's father regularly took him and his brother Paws on long marking expeditions around the Natal Pack's boundary.

His mother, aunt, and sister just assumed Big Red and Spitfire would be the dominant pair, the alphas if you wish. His first task had to be marking his domain. This boundary expedition was no task for old wolves like his mother and aunt. But they would not be separated from their son and nephew, so the entire pack set off. They would catch their dinner along the way and sleep under the stars—so things were as usual.

The original Natal Pack area was 80 mi.^{2} (210 km^2) of forest, beaver ponds, marshes, lakes, bogs, fields, rivers, and lakes, trees, and more trees. The author's property was the heart of their homeland, the place of their den, and where they spent most of their time at rendezvous sites. The rest of the land included abandoned farms and crown land, making up an enormous hunting range.

By noon, Spitfire had killed another beaver she found foraging for aspen trees, and Little Red Ears captured a plump turkey. These formed an excellent lunch for five wolves. The pack passed through 20 or more abandoned farms, places of memories and misery.

As I wrote previously in the last two centuries, there has been a new creature on the land who by labor and passion thought to mold this rugged wilderness closer to the heart's desire. Like Sisyphus, they would roll the rocks into piles and fences, cut the trees into houses and barns, and scratch the fields with shovels and plows to grow a few vegetables. Since time is the overlord of all ventures, these hardy, brave, and foolish pioneers are all gone now as are their houses and fields. They were the author's people.

Bush land scrub land –

. . . .

where a man might have some opinion of what beauty
is and none deny him for miles –
Yet this is the country of defeat
where Sisyphus rolls a big stone
year after year up the ancient hills
picknicking glaciers have left strewn
with centuries' rubble backbreaking days in the sun and rain
when realization seeps slow in the mind
without grandeur or self-deception in noble struggle
of being a fool –
Al Purdy, "Country North of Belleville"

Carefully constructed cairns of fieldstone marked the boundaries between farms. These now became markers between wolf packs after the indignity of Big Red christening them with a shower of urine. Fields, not totally gone back to nature, proved excellent places to catch woodchucks, rabbits, turkeys, and deer. Occasionally, they came upon a log building long since abandoned by its human hosts, now billeted by different creatures. Other times, they would discover piles of decaying logs, assembled for no apparent purpose.

Logs Gathered for some Ghost Purpose

They were joyful! They were together! They were strong! Their leader was a huge, handsome Algonquin wolf with a mate to match. Happiness was evident in their playfulness, kindness in their interactions. Other than this territory they were reclaiming, they had no possessions—they travel light every day. As a pack, teamwork, respect, curiosity, and compassion were their code.

> *For the strength of the pack is the wolf,*
> *and the strength of the wolf is the pack.*
> Rudyard Kipling, "The Law for the Wolves"

None of the beauty of this stern land escaped their eyes and ears. The freshness of the morning with mist on the ponds and lakes. The first chorus of birdsong and the evening choir of amphibians. The mysterious night songs of owls, foxes, migrating birds, cuckoos, and of course, their own evensong. Since wolves' sense of smell is incredibly more sensitive than humans, they experience an unseen world we are oblivious to, a world we will never know.

Man has been in a long dreary retreat about the abilities of animals—from automaton to sentient being. Let me count the ways:

They are just animals, automata, not conscious creatures. Hence, they cannot feel pain. Recall the horror of live vivisections like those done by the French philosopher René Descartes on dogs (*see* pages 53-54), believing these canines were not conscious beings. The dog often licked the hand that nailed his paw to the table before the scalpels came out. If they feel no pain, then they must experience no joy, Descartes concluded, but Darwin laughed at such foolishness. Are we to believe the frantic reception a dog gives to a long-absent owner is an act?

They are just animals; they have no morals. Remember the bear called Mother Courage and her heroic struggle to care for her cubs although she was a paraplegic (*see* Chapter-13). She crawled so that her babies might live.

They are just animals; they have no sense of beauty. Charles Darwin laughed at such outrageous speciesism* with his almost forgotten theory of sexual selection. By this Darwin meant that one gender, often a male among birds, increases his chances of acquiring a mate by being more "beautiful" than his competitors. The incredible tail of the peacock, the brilliant red of the cardinal, or the beautiful markings of the Blackburnian warbler spring to mind. Such extravagant displays of color and song result in higher predation rates on males, a price they willingly pay to pass on their progeny. Discussing birds with elaborate plumage in *The Descent of Man* [1] Darwin wrote, "it is impossible to doubt that she admires the beauty of her male partner. . . The sweet strains poured forth by many male birds during the season of love, are certainly admired by the females."

Wolf Cub Smells Flower

I will counter this human prejudice with the photograph of a wolf cub enjoying the sight and scents of a flower. The nose of a wolf is a hundred times as sensitive as a human's; therefore, any sniffing of a flower must be a deep and memorable experience.

---

* Speciesism: a belief that all other species of animals are inferior and may be used for human benefit without regard to the suffering inflicted.

This pack of five wolves—fully conscious, experiencing pleasure, pain, and beauty—freely roams the land as the penniless lords of creation. Tied together by blood bonds and a morality rivaling that of humans, their only equals were the human hunter-gatherers of prehistory. They traveled through the primeval forest without the least fear of any man or beast for this was true wilderness. On the third day, the pack killed a large buck and ate everything even crushing the femurs for the fatty bone marrow. Sometime toward morning on the last night of their marking expedition, they passed by the author's home (*see* house lights in the photograph) but without dread. Later in that fall, they would return to eat windfall apples, pears, and plums in his orchard before the deer, bears, and raccoons devoured them (*see* photograph).

Spitfire Eating Windfall Apples in My Orchard

Big Red had "known" the author since he was a pup. And because his father and mother had no fear of him, neither did our wolf. On the other hand, the author had known at least seven generations of wolves in this valley: Big Red's grandparents, great grandparents, and so on back in time. Although the author and the wolves may not be friends, neither were they enemies, just acquaintances. The author glimpsed them in the moonlight, listened to their transfixing oratories roll over the hills and down the valleys. He had long ago left the childhood stories of the Big, Bad Wolf behind him and come to love his companions in this immense land. A forest without wolves is just landscape.

Man and wolf stand on the peaks of different evolutionary mountains. Nevertheless, they share many abilities, yet a few are exclusively their own. Wolves adapt by evolving their bodies to fit the forest, the field, and their prey. Man adapts by terraforming the earth nearer to his heart's desire. The first is sustainable, the second is not. One lives within the incredible matrix of life, the other destroys life from without and shuffles the pieces into cars, houses, and trinkets.

There will come a time when all this *will be forgotten*. There will come a time when all *this will be gone*. Count on it! The creature who would have dominion over all of nature will be gone. Before that, all the wolves will be gone. Count on that too! But that day is not today in this happy valley of five wolves and one fortunate man:

> *Nothing I cared, in the lamb white days, that time would take me*
> *Up to the swallow thronged loft by the shadow of my hand,*
> *In the moon that is always rising,*
> *Nor that riding to sleep*
> *I should hear him fly with the high fields*
> *And wake to the farm forever fled from the childless land.*
> *Oh as I was young and easy in the mercy of his means,*
> *Time held me green and dying*
> *Though I sang in my chains like the sea.*
> Dylan Thomas, "Fern Hill"

That summer was an idyll for both wolf and man. When wolves are happy, which is most of the time, they play, they play a lot. The author would often see one or more trotting across his fields with a rabbit or a woodchuck in their mouth. During the summer months, they hunted smaller, easier to catch prey while the deer fattened up for the fall rut and the winter endurance. They "wasted" a good deal of their time playing at the rendezvous site at the base of the hill close to the author's home and directly across from Big Red's birth den. Wolves believe "wasted" days are added to their lives not subtracted.

That fall and winter went well for the wolves since Big Red was a superb hunter, and with the help of Spitfire and Little Red Ears, they were overpowering. By mid-January, the snow was so deep the pack walked single file, stepping in each other's pawprints to conserve energy as they traveled between deer yards. At this time, Big Red became unusually solicitous of Spitfire's welfare for this was a once a year event—mating season. During a ferocious winter storm, on the Ides of February, they copulated for an hour. Nine weeks later, Spitfire gave birth to seven large, healthy puppies: four males and three females. And the birthing chamber was a place Big Red knew well, a place where he and many of his ancestors first took a breath.

Euphoric, Big Red crawled into the den to be near his mate and their babies. Our wolf might not have been able to squeeze in, but for Spitfire renovating and enlarging this ancient den. The entire pack was overjoyed, everyone helped. Big Red's mother would be wet nurse, his aunt and Little Red Ears would puppy sit, and his duties involved bringing home the food to keep the pack healthy. On a few days, Big Red went to the rock to protect and remember. In the speckled sunshine, he put his great head on his paws, closed his eyes, letting his memory wander to past times.

Big Red on the Rock

So long ago, so many memories. The day he lost a toe to a brutal leg trap, and afterward determined to go home all the way across Algonquin Park. No one wanted him—he was too large, too intimidating. As Robert Frost said, "Home is the place where, when you have to go there, they have to take you in." He Recalled the morning when he spotted a pack of wolves patrolling a frozen lake in a blizzard, and he faded into the forest. Soon after, he killed the doe who almost beat him to the logging road. And then the battle at Grand Lake where he would have died had his brother Paws not intervened. Followed by his audacity in confronting the six wolves resting on the lake ice even though he was wounded. . . . On the eighth day, Big Red left his hospital bed under a white pine tree. His lameness prevented him from catching deer, but with that good luck which favors only fools and children, he discovered a moose who died from hypothermia caused by winter tick. His dream drifted to Shadow, one of the young female wolves in the standoff at Grand Lake, who followed him perchance to mate. Tragically the Vireo Lake wolf killed her, and in a berserk rage Big Red drowned him in his namesake lake. Our wolf shivered to recall the night he swam across an icy lake to escape a pack of wolves. Then with a smile, his first meeting with Spitfire floated through his dreams and the killing of the wild boar for the wedding feast. . . .. Crossing the invisible western boundary of Algonquin Park, they rushed away from the coyote killing fields. Nearing home, our wolves confronted the Hill Pack's old she-wolf and three of last year's pups. This was just a rehearsal

Present & Past

to their "battle" on the back-barn flat and its resolution. . . . Back even further in time, it was black, and Big Red struggled to raise his head until he bumped it hard against the den's wall.

🐾

With this, he awoke and knew had been dreaming. But dreams of past deeds and dangers could never match the happiness of having his own family, Spitfire, and their puppies. His existence had meaning! In that great chain of life linking past and future, Big Red—just as his father had—held his place. He had won the day!

Animals Who Have Found Places in My Heart

Early in the morning, just at sunrise, I left my home and turned toward the east to watch our star ascend. On the far horizon, I could see a *myriad of black specks* dancing in the light. At first, I thought they were flocks of migrating geese. The rising heat causes the small dark dots to shimmer in the sunlight and wobble from side to side. Occasionally they dip below the horizon and disappear.

I wait. They resurface but are fewer in number. The fluctuations continue with maddening frequency for what seems an eternity, and every time the small black dots reemerge ever larger but fewer. I wait! My anticipation increases with the size of the dots. They shimmer, wobble, dip, and resurface like immortals. Again, I wait! Ultimately, I discern some shape. One appears to be a wolf with an ape-like creature running at his side, and the other dots have the vague silhouettes of animals.

As they approach, the shapes morph more than the distance should allow. The bravery of the wolf excites my admiration as he repeatedly tries to avoid the hominid. I shout encouragement! He does not hear me. Again, the Ryder in the whirlwind appears to transform. Once again, he dips and disappears. And once more, I hold my breath and wait! I cheer as he and a few others miraculously break free of the horizon. Much closer now, so that this time he hears me shout. He is so close that I sense his determination and passion for life. The whirlwind of events pummels him ever harder; I despair, but he stays the course with the others at his side. Now I clearly see the wolf with his surviving companions. He howls words of recognition. The Ryder in the whirlwind is the wolf I know, and his companions are all the animals who have found places in my heart.

The wolves run on through the evergreen forests in their eternal pursuit of the deer. For their part, the deer lead the wolves on a deadly chase. Each hones the other to perfection by natural selection. It is not only the weak and the old who falter and fall, but the inefficient—the ones who stray too far from the edge. To those who do the dance, whether deer or wolf, belongs the day and the future. It is not a good day to die. It never is. So, the wolves run on through the evergreen forests.

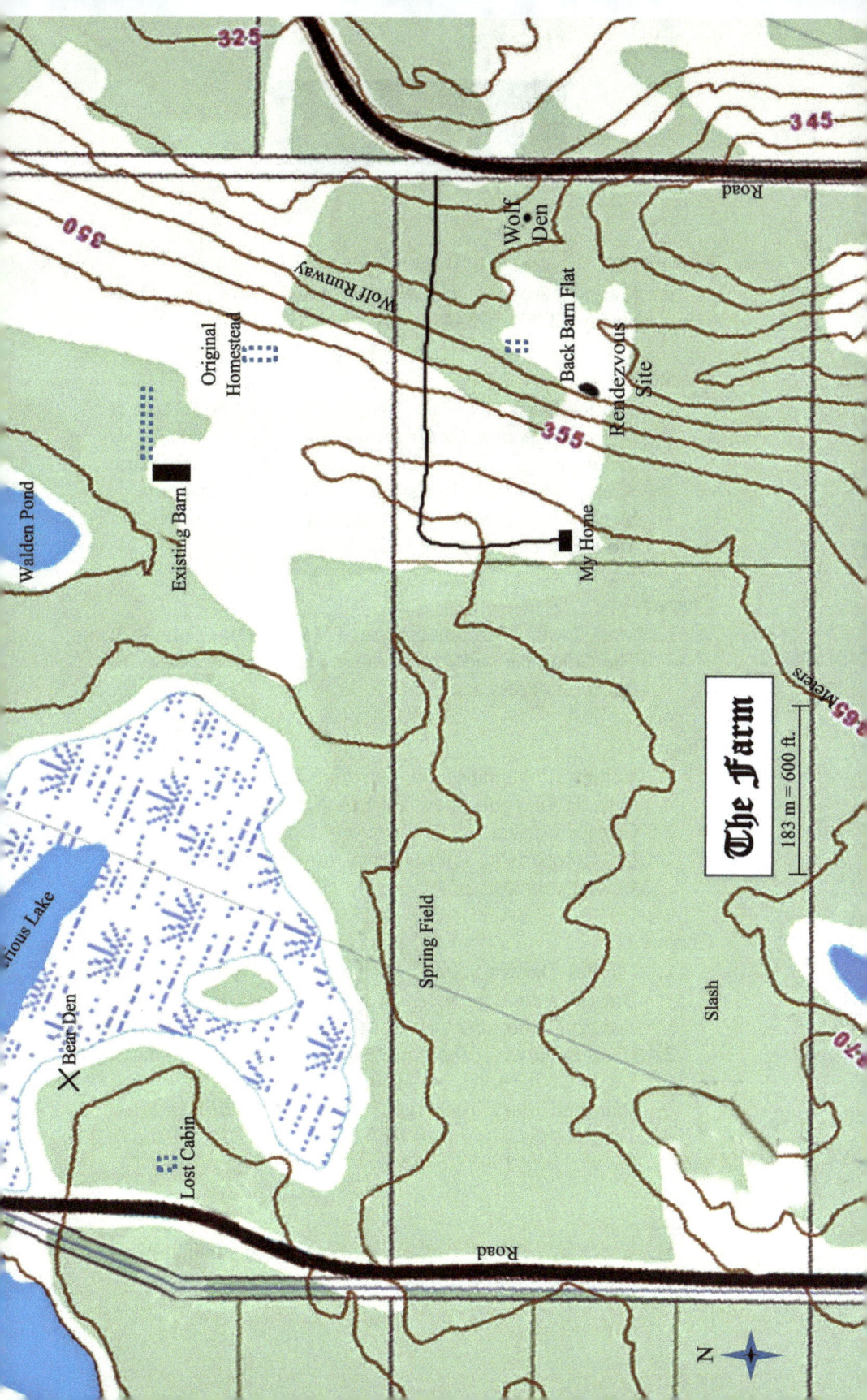

The Farm

183 m = 600 ft.

Walden Pond

350

325

345

Road

Wolf Den

Wolf Runway

Original Homestead

Back Barn Flat

Rendezvous Site

355

Existing Barn

My Home

365 Meters

...rious Lake

Bear Den ✕

Lost Cabin

Spring Field

Slash

370

Road

N

ENDNOTES

Front Matter

1. Margaret Atwood, *The Blind Assassin*, (New York, Doubleday, 2000), p. 344.

Chapter-2

1. Charles Darwin, *On the Origin of Species by Means of Natural Selection, Or the Preservation of Favoured Races in the Struggle for Life* (London, John Murray, Albemarle Street, 1861), The final sentence of the last paragraph.
2. Stephen Jay Gould, "A Biological Homage to Mickey Mouse," *Ecotone 4*, no. 1 (2008), pp. 333–340.

Chapter-4

1. Mark Twain, "Autobiography of Mark Twain, Volume 3: The Complete and Authoritative Edition," University of California Press, p.169.

Chapter-5

1. Voltaire, "Animals," in *The Philosophical Dictionary*, trans. H. I. Woolf (New York, A.A. Knopf, 1924), p. 22.
2. Charles Darwin, *The Descent of Man*, volume I, chapter II: "Comparison of the Mental Powers of Man and the Lower Animals," p. 40.

Chapter-6

1. Charles Darwin (2000). Richard Keynes (ed.). *Charles Darwin's zoology notes & specimen lists from H.M.S. Beagle*. Cambridge University Press.
2. Charles Darwin, (*The Voyage of the Beagle*), III. London, Henry Colburn, pp. 149–150.
3. John and Mary Theberge, *Wolf Country: Eleven Years Tracking the Algonquin Wolves* (Toronto, McClelland & Stewart Inc., 1998), p. 244.

Chapter-7

1. Grey Owl, *Pilgrims of the Wild*, ed. Michael Gnarowski (Toronto, Dundurn Press, 2010), pp. 52–53.

Chapter-9

1. Aldo Leopold, *A Sand County Almanac* (New York, Oxford University Press, 1949), pp. 129-132.

Chapter-10

1. Edith Hamilton, *Mythology: Timeless Tales of Gods and Heroes* (New York, Mentor Books, 1953), p. 216.
2. Boris Pasternak, *Dr. Zhivago* translated by John Bayley (Toronto, Random House Inc., 1958), p. 438.
3. Farley Mowat, *Never Cry Wolf* (Toronto, McClelland & Stewart Inc., 1963), pp. 70-72.
4. Katie Hunhoff "South Dakota's Killer Wolf" (Minnekahta Messenger, Jan. 5, 2018), p. 9, free online.

Chapter-12

1. John and Mary Theberge, *Wolf Country: Eleven Years Tracking the Algonquin Wolves* (Toronto, McClelland & Stewart Inc., 1998), p. 218.
2. Marc Bekoff & Jessica Pierce *Wild Justice: The Moral Lives of Animals* (University of Chicago, 2010), p. 116.

Chapter-14

1. Jacob Bronowski, *The Ascent of Man* (London, Random House, 2011), p. 19.

Chapter-16

1. Sir David Attenborough, *Dynasties: The Greatest of Their Kind* (2018 British nature documentary TV series).

Chapter-17

1. Jared Diamond, *Guns, Germs, and Steel: The Fates of Human Societies* (New York, W. W. Norton & Company, 1997), p. 159.
2. Frank Hurley, *South: Shackleton's Glorious Epic of the Antarctic,* a restoration of Frank Hurley's films by National Film and Television Archive (NFTVA) of Australia.

Chapter-18

1. Charles Darwin, *The Descent of Man* (London, John Murray, Albemarle Street, 1871), p. 92.

SAVE OUR WOLVES
BY JOINING ONE OF THESE GROUPS

Earthroots - Canada
www.earthroots.org

Defenders of Wildlife
www.defendersofwildlife.com

Sierra Club
www.sierraclub.org

PETA
www.peta.org

Yellowstone Wolf Project
www.yellowstone.org/wolf-project

International Wolf Center
https://wolf.org/wow/world/

Pacific Wolf Coalition
https://www.pacificwolves.org/about-us/

Wolf Watcher
https://wolfwatcher.org/links-to-other-organizations

Coyotes, Wolves and Cougars . . . forever
coyotes-wolves-cougars.blogspot.com/

World Wildlife Fund
https://www.worldwildlife.org/

The Painted Wolf Foundation
https://paintedwolf.org/

Animal Welfare Institute
https://awionline.org/cases/protection-red-wolves

www.ingramcontent.com/pod-product-compliance
Lightning Source LLC
Chambersburg PA
CBHW051713020426
42333CB00014B/967